Mobil
Travel Guide®

ANTIQUES & COLLECTIBLES

ACKNOWLEDGMENTS

We gratefully acknowledge the help of our inspectors for their inspections of the hotels, restaurants and spas listed, the establishments' proprietors for their cooperation in showing their facilities and providing information about them, and the many users of previous editions who have taken the time to share their experiences. Mobil Travel Guide is also grateful to the talented writers who contributed entries to this book.

TABLE OF CONTENTS

WRITTEN IN THE STARS

Because your time is precious and the travel world is ever-changing, having accurate travel information when you hit the road is essential. Mobil Travel Guide has provided the most trusted advice to travelers for more than 50 years.

The Mobil Corporation (known as Exxon Mobil Corporation since a 1999 merger) launched the Mobil Travel Guide books in 1958 following the introduction of the U.S. interstate highway system two years earlier. The first edition covered only five Southwestern states. Since then, our books have become the premier travel guides in North America, covering all 50 states and Canada. Recently, we've added international destinations, expanding the Mobil Travel Guide brand around the world.

Today, the concept of a "five star" experience is one that permeates the collective consciousness. In fact, it's a concept that originated with Mobil. Mobil Travel Guide created its star rating system to give travelers an easy to recognize quality scale for choosing where to stay and dine. Only Mobil's star ratings deliver a rigorously tested formula for determining if a hotel, restaurant or spa is as luxurious as its owners claim. Our rating system is the oldest and most respected in North America, and most hoteliers, restaurateurs and industry insiders understand the prestige and benefits that come with receiving a Mobil Star rating.

We inpsect hundreds of attributes at each property we visit, from cleanliness, to the condition of the rooms and public spaces, to employee attitude and courtesy. It's a system that rewards those properties that strive for and achieve excellence each year. And the very best properties raise the bar for those that wish to compete with them.

Only facilities that meet our standards earn the privilege of being listed in the guide. Properties are continuously updated, and deteriorating, poorly managed establishments are removed. We wouldn't recommend that you visit a hotel, restaurant or spa that we wouldn't want to visit ourselves.

If any aspect of your accommodation, dining, spa or sightseeing experience motivates you to comment, please contact us at Mobil Travel Guide, 200 W. Madison St., Suite 3950, Chicago, IL 60606, or send an email to info@mobiltravelguide.com. Happy travels.

STAR RATINGS

HOTELS

Whether you're looking for the ultimate in luxury or the best bang for your travel buck, we have a hotel recommendation for you. To help you pinpoint properties that meet your needs, Mobil Travel Guide classifies each lodging by type according to the following characteristics.

★★★★★The Mobil Five-Star hotel provides consistently superlative service in an exceptionally distinctive luxury environment. Attention to detail is evident throughout the hotel, resort or inn, from bed linens to staff uniforms.

★★★★The Mobil Four-Star hotel provides a luxury experience with expanded amenities in a distinctive environment. Services may include automatic turndown service, 24-hour room service and valet parking.

★★★The Mobil Three-Star hotel is well appointed, with a full-service restaurant and expanded amenities, such as a fitness center, golf course, tennis courts, 24-hour room service and optional turndown service.

★★The Mobil Two-Star hotel is considered a clean, comfortable and reliable establishment that has expanded amenities, such as a full-service restaurant.

★The Mobil One-Star lodging is a limited-service hotel, motel or inn that is considered a clean, comfortable and reliable establishment.

For every property, we also provide pricing information. The pricing categories break down as follows:

$ = Up to $150
$$ = $151-$250
$$$ = $251-$350
$$$$ = $351 and up

All prices quoted are accurate at the time of publication, however prices cannot be guaranteed.

STAR RATINGS

RESTAURANTS

All Mobil Star-rated dining establishments listed in this book have a full kitchen and most offer table service.

★★★★★The Mobil Five-Star restaurant offers one of few flawless dining experiences in the country. These establishments consistently provide their guests with exceptional food, superlative service, elegant décor and exquisite presentations of each detail surrounding a meal.

★★★★The Mobil Four-Star restaurant provides professional service, distinctive presentations and wonderful food.

★★★The Mobil Three-Star restaurant has good food, warm and skillful service and enjoyable décor.

★★The Mobil Two-Star restaurant serves fresh food in a clean setting with efficient service. Value is considered in this category, as is family friendliness.

★The Mobil One-Star restaurant provides a distinctive experience through culinary specialty, local flair or individual atmosphere.

Because menu prices can fluctuate, we list a pricing category rather than specific prices. The pricing categories are defined as follows, per diner, and assume that you order an appetizer or dessert, an entrée and one drink:

$ = $15 and under
$$ = $16-$35
$$$ = $36-$85
$$$$ = $86 and up

STAR RATINGS

SPAS

Mobil Travel Guide's spa ratings are based on objective evaluations of hundreds of attributes. About half of these criteria assess basic expectations, such as staff courtesy, the technical skill of the employees and whether the spa is maintained properly and hygienically. Several standards address issues that impact a guest's comfort and convenience, as well as the staff's ability to deliver a sense of personalized service. Additional criteria measure the spa's ability to create a completely calming ambience.

★★★★★The Mobil Five-Star spa provides superlative service in an exceptionally distinctive luxury environment with extensive amenities. The staff at a five-star spa provides extraordinary service beyond the traditional spa experience. A Mobil Five-Star spa offers an extensive array of treatments, often incorporating international themes and products. Attention to detail is evident throughout the spa, from arrival to departure.

★★★★The Mobil Four-Star spa provides a luxurious experience with expanded amenities in an elegant and serene environment. Throughout the spa facility, guests experience personalized service. Amenities might include, but are not limited to, single-sex relaxation rooms where guests wait for their treatments, plunge pools and whirlpools in both men's and women's locker rooms, and an array of treatments, including a selection of massages, body therapies, facials and a variety of salon services.

★★★The Mobil Three-Star spa is physically well appointed and has a full staff.

INTRODUCTION

Rummaging through an antique shop or attending an acres-large flea market buzzing with activity and filled with hundreds of tables brimming over with cast-offs and family heirlooms taps deep into the psyche, plumbing that passion for the hunt, the excitement for hidden treasure, the delight in digging through the clutter and unearthing that long-hidden gem.

At some point almost everyone has stopped into a roadside market or pulled into an antique shop looking for a bargain or an unexpected find. Maybe it's the search. Or maybe it's the idea of filling your home with pieces that don't all come from a department store. You can look around your living room and see items that tell a story, whether it's about the object's original owner, a place in time, or simply what you yourself went through to get your hands on it (like the time you found that great lamp in Palm Beach). Shopping for antiques is the highest form of retail therapy—there's the rush when you find that truly unique chair or vase, and the satisfaction of piecing together a collection. Then there are the interesting people you meet and the history you learn, and all those fun shows you get to attend. It's even environmentally friendly (there's no finer form of recycling than buying an item that will never find its way into the local landfill).

Once you've unearthed that longed-for trunk, or discovered the chair that reminds you of the one you sat upon as a child at Granny's, or an old mink coat or Star Wars figurine, you're hooked. Next thing you know you're spending weekends traveling distances to further fill those already cluttered shelves back home, watching "Antiques Roadshow" re-runs and perusing local papers for spontaneous flea markets and estate sales. Then you decide that you are tired of your Americana phase and want to clean out the lot of Federalist doo-dads you purchased on a whim. Or you set up your own booth at Renninger's in Mount Dora, Florida, or you're off to set up shop at the vast, twice-annual Brimfield show in Massachusetts. At this point, there's no turning back.

Whether you are a die-hard antique shopper or have just been bitten by the bug, this soup-to-nuts guide to the country's finest seasonal antique shows and top antique shops should engender numerous weekends of fun. So empty out the car, grab a few sturdy totes or a rolling cart, load up the iPod with road trip-worthy tunes, and hit the highway. There are antiques out there with your name written all over them. The search is on.

MID-ATLANTIC

PACKED WITH U.S. HISTORY, THE MID-ATLANTIC REGION, INCLUD-ing Pennsylvania, Maryland and Washington, D.C., beckons with its graceful architecture and equally sublime antiques stores brimming with collectibles and museum-quality finds. Finish off a morning of antique hunting in the District with a stop at the Smithsonian, or wander the wonderful and historic streets of Georgetown. Be sure to visit fun and funky Baltimore for a mix of retro finds in the indie-inspired Hampden neighborhood, as well as fine European imports in Fells Point—and beyond—which will turn up priceless touches for any home décor. Then there's the urban sophistication of Philadelphia—where tip-top hostelries and cutting-edge eateries provide the perfect foil to a long day spent browsing for Federal period chairs and highboys. Don't forget the areas outside of Philadelphia proper, where Amish finds meet important American objects in villages like charming Denver and Adamstown. Welcome to the mid-Atlantic!

MARYLAND

BALTIMORE

MIXING THE TRADITIONAL AND FUNKY WITH THE ELEGANT AND DOWN-home, Baltimore is the perfect city for a weekend of antique hunting. You'll find charming neighborhoods filled with cobblestone streets and plenty of waterfront dining choices for a relaxed dinner after a long day of digging.

WHERE TO SHOP

Anne Smith Antiques & Fine Arts
222 W. Read St., Baltimore,
410-728-0101;
www.antiqtoymuseum.com
Charming and knowledgeable Anne Smith stocks an enormous variety of items, ranging from furniture to toys in her antique shop set in the historic downtown Mount Washington neighborhood. Find everything from vintage fragrance bottles to colorful circus posters and be sure to wander through the stunning Antique Toy Museum, which houses endless cases filled with more than 40 antique doll houses, hat and cigar boxes, Victorian dolls, puzzles and more. You can spend hours just studying the miniature furniture filling each tiny dollhouse room. Thursday-Saturday, 11 a.m.-4 p.m; also "by chance" and by appointment.

Another Period in Time
1708 Fleet St., Baltimore,
410-675-4776;
www.anotherperiod.com
Located in the atmospheric waterfront Fells Point neighborhood with its charming eateries and cobblestone streets, Another Period in Time features merchandise from 15 dealers covering more than 8,000 square feet of space. Here you are sure to find lots of variety and the unexpected, from porcelain wares to vintage toys. Look no further for a selection of Roseville vases, a Lenox condiment server (in its long-ago discontinued pattern), groovy '50s red leather bar stools or an antique clown cast iron mechanical bank—this huge store has it all. Monday-Thursday, 9 a.m.-5 p.m.; Saturday, 10 a.m.-6 p.m.; Sunday, noon-5 p.m.

★
★
★
☆

Antique Row Stalls

809 N. Howard St., Baltimore,
410-728-6363;
www.antiquerowstalls.com

The 10,000-square-foot Antique Row Stalls houses more than 20 dealers who specialize in such items as European furniture, Tiffany lamps, china and rare books. Peruse Stalls' contents for terrific finds, including vintage prints, Wedgwood china, Carl Sasse furniture and 18th-century black lacquer designs. Wednesday-Monday 11 a.m.-5 p.m., closed Tuesday.

The Avenue in Hampden

W. 36th St., Baltimore,
www.hampdenmainstreet.org

Novelty shops, vintage clothing stores, casual restaurants and art galleries line Hampden's main drag with treasures both kitschy and sublime. The Hampden neighborhood has to be seen to be believed. This avenue is home of the city's big hair and famous "hons"—we suggest you set aside a few hours to do it right. Stop in at **Galvanize** (*901 W. 33rd St., Baltimore, 401-889-5237*) for the terrific selection of vintage men's clothing or **Fat Elvis** (*833 W. 36th St., Baltimore, 410-467-6030*) for a Jimmy Carter lamp. You just never know what you'll find.

French Accents

3600 Roland Ave., Baltimore,
410-467-8957, 866-467-8957;
www.faccents.com

The name of this shop is a little misleading, as the selection appeals to more than the token Francophile. Here, you'll find a wonderful assortment of 17th-, 18th- and 19th-century French, Italian and other Continental antiques, such as a glorious early 19th-century Dutch marquetry settee or an exquisite papier-mâché tilt-top table and chairs set painted with floral inlays made from shell. By appointment.

Rediscovered Furniture

1117 W. 36th St., Baltimore,
410-366-1530;
www.rediscoveredfurniture.com

Because this high-style resale shop culls its wares by relieving homes and offices of unwanted furnishings, the stock is constantly changing. This often yields a pleasant surprise: a pristine Heywood-Wakefield kneehole desk or one of those fabulous 1950's table lamps shaped like a dancing figure. What's more, owners Corbin Small and Jasper Fair like to keep the merchandise moving, so prices are discounted regularly on stock that doesn't sell within a couple of days. Wednesday-Saturday 11 a.m.-7 p.m., Sunday noon-5 p.m.; closed Monday-Tuesday.

Craig Flinner Gallery

505 N. Charles St., Baltimore,
410-727-1863;
www.flinnergallery.com

The Craig Flinner Gallery specializes in vintage posters, antique prints and maps, as well as furniture and home decorations. If you are looking for a museum-worthy selection of 19th-century botanical prints, this is the place. Also check out the gallery's retro travel posters, including a color-packed poster of England circa 1960 and a glamorous image of the Cunard Line's "Scythia." There are also some great old maps, both framed and unframed. Monday-Saturday, 10 a.m.-6 p.m.; Sunday, noon-4 p.m.

Crosskeys Antiques
801 N. Howard St., Baltimore, 410-728-0101, 877-228-9164; www.crosskeysantiques.com

For high-quality reproduction paintings check out Crosskeys Antiques. Preserved in ornate gilt frames, these colorful canvases reawaken the mastery of English, French and Italian portraiture. You may be further wooed by the impressive collection of 20th-century decorative European antiques, which include a William IV–style card table with a chocolate leather top (Texas hold'em will never be the same again) and a stunning set of mahogany candlesticks. Saturday, 10 a.m.-4 p.m.; Sunday, 11 a.m.-3 p.m.

Gaines McHale Antiques
700 S. Caroline St., Baltimore, 410-625-1900; www.gainesmchale.com

This shop's classy red brick exterior is a dead giveaway to the veritable treasure trove of vintage furnishings that awaits inside. The shop, which specializes in original antiques and replicas, carries a varied assortment of fine French and English cabinets, tables, chairs and sideboards. Whether you're looking to fully revamp your kitchen or find that perfect conversation piece to your sun-

room, Gaines McHale's attentive and knowledgeable staff can assist. Monday-Saturday 10 a.m.-6 p.m.; Sunday noon-5 p.m.

WHERE TO STAY

★★★Hyatt Regency Baltimore on the Inner Harbor
300 Light St., Baltimore, 410-528-1234, 800-233-1234; www.baltimore.hyatt.com

Located across the street from Baltimore's Inner Harbor, this hotel is linked by a skywalk to the convention center and shopping at Harborplace. It is also situated within minutes of the National Aquarium, Maryland Science Center and Oriole Park. Guest rooms are decorated with off-white wall coverings resembling white leather, white bedding with gold accents and marble bathrooms. In addition to a rooftop pool and a huge fitness center, amenities include a basketball half-court, putting green and jogging track along with 29,000 square feet of meeting space.
488 rooms. Wireless Internet access. Restaurant, bar. Fitness center. Tennis. Pool. Business center. $$$

★★★InterContinental Harbor Court Hotel
550 Light St., Baltimore, 410-234-0550, 877-424-6835; www.intercontinental.com

The InterContinental Harbor Court Hotel re-creates the spirit of a grand English manor home. Located across the street from the Inner Harbor, guest rooms offer

BALTIMORE

views of the water or the courtside garden. The professional staff attends to every need, even offering hot, buttery popcorn for guests enjoying in-room movies. A fitness center and yoga studio await guests itching to burn those post-film calories.

195 rooms. Wireless Internet access. Restaurant, bar. Fitness center. Pool. Spa. Business center. $$

WHERE TO EAT

★★★Black Olive
814 S. Bond St., Baltimore, 410-276-7141;
www.theblackolive.com

This Mediterranean restaurant (formerly Fells Point's General Store) has retained the building's original hardwood floors and brick archways, making the interior a salvager's dream. The restaurant also offers outdoor dining under a grape arbor. The food here is organic, and fresh fish is displayed in front of the open kitchen. Each fish entree is filleted tableside. The carrot cake is a perfect finale.

Mediterranean, seafood menu. Lunch, dinner. Bar. Children's menu. Business casual attire. Reservations recommended. Valet parking. Outdoor seating. $$$

★★★★Charleston
1000 Lancaster St., Baltimore, 410-332-7373;
www.charlestonrestaurant.com

Chef/owner Cindy Wolf's regional American/French restaurant serves up dishes such as sautéed Gulf shrimp with andouille sausage and Tasso ham with creamy, stone-milled grits. The restaurant also has an impressive wine list, which includes several dozen sparkling wines and a selection of about 600 well-chosen whites and reds from both the New World and the Old. Or, if a cold one is more your speed after a day of treasure troving, there are more than a dozen microbrews and imported beers.

American, French menu. Dinner. Closed Sunday. Bar. Business casual attire. Reservations recommended. Valet parking. Outdoor seating. $$$

★★★The Prime Rib
1101 N. Calvert St., Baltimore, 410-539-1804;
www.theprimerib.com

Whether it's the black and gold lacquered walls, the nightly pianist or the tuxedoed wait staff, this Baltimore mainstay epitomizes ageless elegance. Seafood, lamb and chicken fill out the menu, but it's the long-aged prime rib that has kept diners coming back to this classic steakhouse since 1965.

American, steak menu. Dinner. Bar. Jacket required. Reservations recommended. Valet parking. $$$

PENNSYLVANIA

PHILADELPHIA

ELEGANT PHILADELPHIA PAIRS A WONDERFULLY RICH HISTORY—THINK
the Liberty Bell and Betsy Ross—with glorious antiques shopping and
plenty of world-class eateries and hotels. Expect to find plenty of Federal and Colonial period antiques, from furnishings to paintings and
accessories.

WHERE TO SHOP

Antiquarian's Delight
615 S. Sixth St., Philadelphia,
215-592-0256
Locals frequently shop this Southside favorite, housed in a former
church, in search of what the
antiques trade terms *collectible*
or *vintage thrift*—items respected
more for their sentimental value
than their monetary importance.
Insider tip: Come for the bargains
and vintage clothing dealer Wilbur's first floor booth. Wednesday-Thursday noon-7 p.m.,
Friday-Saturday noon-8 p.m.,
Sunday noon-7 p.m.

Calderwood Gallery
1622 Spruce St., Philadelphia,
215-546-5357;
www.calderwoodgallery.com
Every time we walk through the
doors of this exquisite shop, we
feel as though we've been transported to a chic 1920s Paris apartment furnished by the likes of
Jacques Ruhlmann, Jules Leleu,
Jansen and their contempo-
raries. The stock, an eclectic mix
of upholstered seating, tables,
cabinets and the like designed by
some of the early 20th century's
top designers, has us under such a
spell that we just want to pack our
bags and move in. Perhaps that's
why the Gallery's owners ask that
you make an appointment to view
their stock. Open by appointment.

Classic Antiques
922 Pine St., Philadelphia,
215-629-0211, 800-450-2621;
www.classicant.com
Located in the antiques district
of Philadelphia, Classic Antiques
specializes in French and English
chests, mirrors, lamps, chandeliers, sconces and other furnishings. It also carries a smart selection of Art Deco pieces. Visitors
love to peruse the terrific selection of antique mirrors, including
a Vegas-worthy gilt frame with
cherubs dating from 1900 and a
floral design chandelier in metal
with brass grapes circa 1930.
Monday by appointment only,

Tuesday-Saturday 11 a.m.-5:30 p.m., Sunday 1-5 p.m.

Freeman's Auction

1808 Chestnut St., Philadelphia,
215-563-9275;
www.freemansauction.com

Freeman's, the oldest auction house in the United States, features a diverse line of European and American decorative furnishings, paintings, glassware and jewelry. Check the Web site for upcoming auction schedules: You'll find everything from sales devoted to European furniture and decorative arts to fine books, manuscripts and ephemera. There's something here for every taste and budget. And if you've never been to an auction before, this is a user-friendly place to learn the ropes before heading to the big-time bidding at Christie's or Sotheby's. Auction schedule varies.

Indigo Art & Antiques

151 N. Third St., Philadelphia,
215-922-4041, 888-463-5278;
www.indigoarts.com

This funky, colorful shop specializes in antiques from all over the world with an emphasis on African tribal and South American folk sculptures, jewelry and artwork. Check out the selection of masks, including a rather devilish looking creature fashioned by the Yoruba people of Nigeria and a charming lion's head crafted by Nigeria's Ibibio people. Monday-Saturday 11 a.m.-6:30 p.m., first Friday of every month to 9:30 p.m., Sunday by appointment only.

M. Finkel & Daughter Antiques

936 Pine St., Philadephia,
215-627-7797;
www.samplings.com

M. Finkel & Daughter covers two floors and is filled with antique furniture from the 18th and 19th centuries, as well as a large collection of internationally acclaimed needlework and silk embroideries from the 17th through the mid-19th centuries. If you thought you'd never be interested in antique embroidered samplers, this place may change your mind—one features a pair of birds and rings from Europe circa 1820 and another, a flower-bedecked sampler from Germany dating back to 1766. Monday-Friday 9:30 a.m.-5:30 p.m. (call ahead to confirm), Saturday-Sunday by appointment only.

Mode Moderne

159 N. Third St., Philadelphia,
215-627-0299; www.modemoderne.com

If you dream at night about such design luminaries as Charles and Ray Eames, Milo Baughman, Gilbert Rohde and T. H. Robsjohn-Gibbings, then you will definitely not want to miss this cozy little Philadelphia boutique, which stocks some of the best vintage home furnishings we've seen on the East Coast. Recent finds include a glam white lacquered lady's writing desk that can only be described as Hollywood chic. Wednesday-Saturday noon-6 p.m., Sunday 1-5 p.m.; closed Monday-Tuesday.

MID-ATLANTIC

Moderne Gallery

111 N. Third St., Philadelphia,
215-923-8536;
www.modernegallery.com

Located in a four-story, 16,000-square-foot warehouse, this mecca to modernity stocks a vast assortment of high-style, high-end furnishings from 1920s French Art Deco to the rustic, earth-sensitive pieces of celebrated 20th-century craftsman George Nakashima. Tuesday-Saturday 11 a.m.-6 p.m.; closed Sunday-Monday.

WHERE TO STAY

★★★★Four Seasons Hotel Philadelphia

1 Logan Square, Philadelphia,
215-963-1500, 866-516-1100;
www.fourseasons.com/
philadelphia

The eight-story Four Seasons located on historic Logan Square is a Philadelphia institution in itself, from its dramatic Swann Fountain to the highly rated Fountain Restaurant. The rooms and suites are a celebration of Federalist décor, and some accommodations incorporate deep soaking tubs. Rooms have city views of the Academy of Natural Science, Logan Square and the tree-lined Ben Franklin Parkway, while others offer views over the inner courtyard and gardens. The spa focuses on nourishing treatments, while the indoor pool resembles a tropical oasis with breezy palm trees and large skylights.

352 rooms. Wireless Internet access. Restaurant, bar. Airport transportation available. Fitness center. Pool, whirlpool. Spa. Business center. $$$

★★★The Rittenhouse Hotel and Condominium Residences

210 W. Rittenhouse Square,
Philadelphia,
215-546-9000, 800-635-1042;
www.rittenhousehotel.com

This intimate hotel occupies a particularly enviable address across from the leafy Rittenhouse Square and among the prestigious townhouses of this exclusive area. The accommodations, among the most spacious in the city, are decorated with a sophisticated flair. Guests at the Rittenhouse are treated to the highest levels of personalized service. From the mood-lifting décor of the gracious Cassatt Lounge and the striking contemporary style of Lacroix to the rowing memorabilia of Boathouse Row Bar and the traditional steakhouse feel of Smith & Wollensky, the Rittenhouse Hotel also provides memorable dining experiences to match every taste.

98 rooms. Wireless Internet access. Two restaurants, two bars. Fitness center. Pool. Business center. Pets accepted. $$$$

★★★The Ritz-Carlton, Philadelphia

10 Avenue of the Arts,
Philadelphia,
215-523-8000, 800-542-8680;
www.ritzcarlton.com

This one-time home to Girard and Mellon Banks was designed in the 1900s by the architectural firm

PHILADELPHIA

of McKim, Mead and White and was inspired by Rome's Pantheon. Marrying historic significance with trademark Ritz-Carlton style, this Philadelphia showpiece boasts handsome décor. Impressive marble columns dominate the lobby. The rooms and suites are luxurious; dedicated to exceeding visitors' expectations, the Ritz-Carlton even offers a pillow menu, a bath butler and other unique services. Dining options are plentiful, and the Sunday jazz brunch is a local favorite.

300 rooms. Wireless Internet access. Restaurant, bar. Fitness center. Spa. Pets accepted. $$$

★★★Sofitel Philadelphia

120 S. 17th St., Philadelphia, 215-569-8300, 800-763-4835; www.sofitel.com

Modern French style permeates the Sofitel Philadelphia. This elegant hotel sits on the former site of the Philadelphia Stock Exchange, and its downtown Center City location makes it ideal for both business and leisure travelers. Warm and inviting, the accommodations offer a variety of thoughtful touches, such as fresh flowers and plush towels. Comfortable chic defines the lobby bar, La Bourse, while the bistro fare and unique setting of Chéz Colette recall the romance of 1920s Paris.

306 rooms. Wireless Internet access. Restaurant, bar. Fitness center. Business center. Pets accepted. $$$

★★★Bistro Romano

120 Lombard St., Philadelphia, 215-925-8880; www.bistroromano.com

When you walk into this cozy Italian restaurant located in the Society Hill area, one of the first things you see is the majestic oak bar from the *City of Detroit III*, a 1912 side-wheel passenger steamer. A beautiful painting of a sea nymph from the ship hangs in the stairwell that leads downstairs to the romantic dining room. Besides the décor, Bistro Romano is well known for its tableside Caesar salad, homemade ravioli and award-winning tiramisu.

Italian menu. Dinner. Bar. Children's menu. Business casual attire. Reservations recommended. $$

★★★★Fountain Restaurant

1 Logan Square, Philadelphia, 215-963-1500; www.fourseasons.com/philadelphia

The Fountain is the stunning flagship restaurant of the Four Seasons Hotel Philadelphia. The wine list, which spans the globe, is just one of the highlights of dining here. The kitchen often uses ingredients from local producers and includes the farms' names on the menu. As you'll see here, the best ingredients really do make a difference. Vegetarian items are available on request, and the kitchen offers several selections that are marked as healthy fare.

American, French menu. Breakfast, lunch, dinner, Sunday brunch. Bar.

Children's menu. Jacket required. Reservations recommended. Valet parking. $$$

★★★Jake's Restaurant
4365 Main St., Philadelphia,
215-483-0444;
www.jakesrestaurant.com
Located in Manayunk, Philadelphia's funky, high-energy, artsy neighborhood, Jake's Restaurant is a lively spot to meet friends for drinks and stay for dinner. Chef/owner Bruce Cooper's chic regulars make a habit of staying all night, savoring his unique brand of stylish, regional American food. At the bar, go for one of Jake's wild house cocktails or take a chance on a unique microbrew. The kitchen is in sync with its customers' desire for both fun and flavor in their food. For instance, on a recent visit, the prix fixe menu was titled Jake's Clam Bake and featured a popular four-course, clam bake–style shellfish menu paired with wine.
American menu. Lunch, dinner, Sunday brunch. Bar. Business casual attire. Reservations recommended. Valet parking. Outdoor seating. $$$

★★★★Lacroix at the Rittenhouse
210 W. Rittenhouse Square, Philadelphia,
215-546-9000;
www.lacroixrestaurant.com
Set in the stately Rittenhouse Hotel, Lacroix is a restaurant of understated elegance. The kitchen plays up fresh local ingredients with influences from around the world, while guests dine in posh, sophisticated luxury and enjoy views of the charming Rittenhouse Square. While acclaimed Chef Jean-Marie Lacroix has retired, the kitchen is still in able hands under the direction of Chef Matthew Levin. The flexible tasting menu is the best option here, where diners can choose three, four or five courses, and desserts are a gift from the chef.
International menu. Breakfast, lunch, dinner, Sunday brunch. Bar. Children's menu. Jacket required. Reservations recommended. Valet parking. $$$

★★★Moshulu Restaurant
401 S. Columbus Blvd., Philadelphia,
215-923-2500;
www.moshulu.com
Moshulu is a stunning South Seas–inspired restaurant housed in a 100-year-old, 394-foot, four-masted sailing ship. Its several dining rooms are elegantly decorated with rattan chairs, cane furniture, dark mahogany and Polynesian artwork. The kitchen, headed by executive chef Ralph Fernandez, churns out creative, delicious dishes that will keep you coming back for more.
American menu. Lunch, dinner, Sunday brunch. Bar. Business casual attire. Reservations recommended. Valet parking. Outdoor seating. $$$

★★★The Saloon
750 S. Seventh St., Philadelphia,
215-627-1811;
www.saloonrestaurant.net

Richard Santore has been operating this venerable establishment in Philadelphia's Bellavista neighborhood (bordering Center City and South Philly) for nearly 40 years. The food is classic Italian fare, served for lunch and dinner. Appetizers include poached pear and gorgonzola salad with roasted walnuts, baby greens and red onion with pear vinaigrette. Fettuccini lobster Amatriciana is a toss of house-made fettuccini with lobster, bacon, onion, fresh tomato and pecorino cheese in tomato sauce. Daily dinner specials range from beef carpaccio drizzled with truffle essence and served with fava beans to a double veal chop marinated in white wine, pan seared and served with Yukon gold potatoes.

Italian menu. Lunch (Tuesday-Friday), dinner. Closed Sunday; also one week in early July. Bar. Business casual attire. Valet parking. No credit cards accepted. $$$

★★★★Striped Bass
1500 Walnut St., Philadelphia,
215-732-4444;
www.stripedbassrestaurant.com

Set in a former brokerage house, Striped Bass boasts towering 28-foot ceilings, red marble columns and an open kitchen. The menu showcases virtually every fish in the sea, and a magnificent raw bar tempts diners with briny oysters, sweet clams and plump, juicy shrimp. Be sure to go for the raw fish selection: a shimmering array of tartars, ceviches and carpaccios deliciously tinged with Asian, Latin American and Italian flavors.

Seafood menu. Dinner. Bar. Business casual attire. Reservations recommended. Valet parking. $$$

Le Bec-Fin
1523 Walnut St., Philadelphia,
215-567-1000; www.lebecfin.com

Evening-long tasting menus and elaborate table settings are a thing of the past for chef Georges Perrier and his epicurean Philadelphia landmark. After 38 years and international acclaim, Perrier's restaurant, Le Bec-Fin, has loosened its tie, proving that exceptional food doesn't have to carry an outrageous price tag. The room remains opulent with fresh flowers, glass chandeliers and amber lighting. The menu, in contrast, has shifted from a six-course degustation prix fixe to an à la carte parade of enticing flavors such as beef bordelaise with crisp purple sweet potato and wasabi foam, and escargot 'persillade' with almonds, roasted bell peppers and capers. For those who crave the full Perrier experience, Le Bec-Fin's tasting menu is still an option. Whichever route you choose, no meal is complete without a visit from the all-you-can-eat dessert cart. C'est magnifique.

French menu. Lunch, dinner. Closed Sunday. Bar. Reservations recommended. Valet parking. $$$$

MID-ATLANTIC

★
★
★
★

ADAMSTOWN

A CONVENIENT DAY TRIP TO THE NORTHWEST OF PHILADELPHIA, ADAMS-
town is an antique lover's paradise. Home to thousands of vendors specializing in everything from vintage clothing and jewelry to primitives
and dolls, Adamstown provides a scenic country drive and a somewhat
unsuspected haven for antiques.

WHERE TO SHOP

Adamstown Antique Mall
Route 272 (at traffic light),
Adamstown,
717-484-0464
The Adamstown Antique Mall
boasts a fine variety of vintage
finds, ranging from the smallest
china pieces to big and bulky fur-
niture items. Monday, Thursday-
Friday 10 a.m.-5 p.m., Saturday-
Sunday 9 a.m.-5 p.m.; closed
Tuesday-Wednesday.

The Country French Collection
2887 N. Reading Road (Route
272), Adamstown,
717-484-0200;
www.countryfrenchantiques.com
Even the building signifies a step
back in time; housed in a historic
18th-century stone barn, The
Country French Collection is fully
stocked with antique furniture.
The best part? The items here are
all handpicked in France. Daily 10
a.m.-4 p.m.

The Heritage Antique Center
2750 N. Reading Road (Route
272), Adamstown,
717-484-4646;
www.heritageantiquecenter.com
One of the oldest antique shops in
the Adamstown area, Heritage features a wide variety of merchandise from more than 50 dealers,
including glassware, china, collectibles, vintage jewelry, records,
postcards, ephemera and military
items. Daily 10 a.m.-5 p.m.

Mad Hatter Antique Mall
61 Willow St. (at Route 272),
Adamstown,
717-484-4159
Located in a former hat factory
(hence the name), Mad Hatter has
some 100 active dealers specializing in wall hangings, dolls, vintage
advertising, recycled clothing,
retro-modern décor, linens and
much more. Thursday-Monday
10 a.m.-5 p.m.; closed Tuesday-
Wednesday.

Pine Hills Antique Mall
144 Furlow Road (off Routes 272
and 222), Adamstown,
717-484-6313
Housed in a 14,000-square-foot
post and beam building, Pine Hills
boasts some 100 dealers offering a
wide variety of antiques and collectibles, including vintage advertising for those who can't live
without that retro Coca-Cola sign.
Thursday-Monday 10 a.m.-5 p.m.;
closed Tuesday-Wednesday.

ADAMSTOWN

★
★
★
★
★

Stoudt's Clock Tower Antiques and Black Angus Antiques Mall

2800 N. Reading Road (Route 272), Adamstown,
717-484-4386; www.stoudtsblackangusantiques.com

With beautiful, high-quality antiques spanning every field and century, Stoudt's is a beacon for both dealers and private collectors. The Sunday mall draws over 400 dealers to 78,000 square feet of space. Find early American and European furniture as well as fine art, folk art and showcase upon showcase of small collectibles. If all the browsing makes you hungry, stop at the nearby Stoudt's Black Angus Restaurant, which features a German-inspired menu and microbrews on tap. Monday-Tuesday, Thursday-Saturday 10 a.m.-5 p.m., Sunday 7:30 a.m.-4 p.m.; closed Wednesday.

DENVER

THE PERFECT DAY TRIP FROM PHILADELPHIA, DENVER IS ONLY AN HOUR northwest of the city and is choc-a-block full of antiques emporia.

WHERE TO SHOP

Adams Antiques

2400 N. Reading Road (Route 272), Denver,
717-335-3116, 717-335-0001;
www.adamsantiques.com

In addition to a wide variety of vintage fare housed in the 24,000-square-foot store, ranging from clocks to armoires to chandeliers, Adams Antiques also hosts 200 dealers with an ever-changing assortment of merchandise in an outdoor setup every Sunday. Monday-Saturday 10 a.m.-5 p.m., Sunday 8 a.m.-5 p.m.

Adamstown Antique Gallery

2000 N. Reading Road, Denver,
717-335-3435; www.aagal.com

This 20,000-square-foot facility hosts more than 300 dealer showcases with high-quality pieces from 250 dealers, including 20 international ones. Thursday-Tuesday 9 a.m.-4 p.m. or by appointment; closed Wednesday.

Oley Valley Architectural Antiques

2453 N. Reading Road (Route 272), Denver,
717-335-3585;
www.oleyvalley.com

Victorian furniture and reclaimed stained glass and leaded glass windows are just a few of the fine pieces you'll find at Oley Valley. In the market for a fireplace mantel or 19th-century iron gates? This is the place to find them. And if such pieces are sold by the time you arrive, this vast retail outlet is near other area antiques destinations where you can continue the hunt. Thursday-Monday 10 a.m.-6 p.m.; closed Tuesday-Wednesday.

MID-ATLANTIC

The Key Antiques

340 Main St., Denver,
717-335-3585;
www.thekeyantiques.com
The Key Antiques boasts a small-town setting and an accessible owner, Shane Keylor, who also does general appraisals. The shop houses a unique blend of antique furniture, primitives, pottery, glassware, collectibles and electronics, as well as used furniture. Wednesday-Saturday 9 a.m.-5 p.m., Sunday noon-4 p.m.; closed Monday-Tuesday.

COLUMBIA

A CONVENIENT TRIP WEST OF PHILADELPHIA, CHARMING COLUMBIA SITS in bucolic Lancaster County. Founded in the early 1700s by Quakers, the stunning antique wares you'll find here are nearly as old as the town.

WHERE TO SHOP

Burning Bridge Antiques Market

303 Walnut St. (at Route 441),
Columbia,
717-684-7900;
www.burningbridgeantiques.com
You may be stopping by for the antiques, but don't overlook the building: a remarkable architectural gem featuring hardwood floors, a pressed tin ceiling, limestone walls and exquisite chestnut millwork. Monday-Wednesday 10 a.m.-5 p.m., Thursday-Friday 10 a.m.-8 p.m., Saturday 10 a.m.-5 p.m., Sunday noon-5 p.m.

Columbia Rivertowne Antique Center

125 Bank Ave., Columbia,
717-684-8514;
www.rivertowneantiques.com
Housed in a 110-year-old former tobacco warehouse, Rivertowne Antique Center sells a wide range of antiques and collectibles in a dramatic setting that sets the scene for digging up pieces of the past. Wednesday-Monday 10 a.m.-5 p.m.; closed Tuesday.

COLUMBIA

NEW OXFORD

KNOWN AS THE "ANTIQUES CAPITAL OF CENTRAL PENNSYLVANIA," NEW Oxford is a two-and-a-half hour drive west from Philadelphia. It hosts a renowned antique market that takes place the third Saturday of every June.

WHERE TO SHOP

Collector's Choice Antique Gallery
330 W. Golden Lane,
New Oxford, 717-624-1419
With high-style country furniture and accessories, this is the place for serious collectors. Just prepare yourself for sticker shock. Monday-Saturday 10 a.m.-5 p.m., Sunday noon-5 p.m.

Henry's Hideaway
335A Lincolnway West, New Oxford,
717-624-8809
Have a thing for Victorian? Henry's Hideaway sells furniture, lamps, scales, frames, mirrors, wicker and even flax wheels from that eclectic revival era. Saturday-Sunday 11 a.m.-4 p.m.; Monday-Friday "by chance."

Storm's Antiques & Collectibles
1030 Kohler Mill Road,
New Oxford, 717-624-8112
Storm's sports an impressive collection of oak furniture among other antiques treasures. Storm's is located near other area antique dealers as well, so feel free to make an afternoon of it. Daily 8 a.m.-5 p.m.; call before going.

MID-ATLANTIC

WASHINGTON, D.C.

AFTER BROWSING WASHINGTON, D.C.'S MANY ANTIQUE SHOPS IN ITS historic neighborhoods, save time to explore the capital's numerous museums and galleries. Finish off the day with a stellar dinner from one of the city's world-class restaurants or a nightcap on the shores of the Chesapeake Bay.

WHERE TO SHOP

The Brass Knob Architectural Antiques
2311 18th St. NW,
Washington, D.C., 202-332-3370;
www.thebrassknob.com

The Brass Knob specializes in architectural antiques and salvage for restorations and renovations, as well as new construction. You'll find everything here from concrete birdbaths and terracotta finials to decorative iron gates and a quartet of Ionic columns. This is the perfect place if you're looking to pick up such wonderful wares as a nickel-plated toilet paper holder circa 1920 or a brass over-the-tub combination–sponge and soap holder. But the Brass Knob also features outdoor goodies, including Victorian-era wrought-iron andirons, a figural doorknocker and a mechanical doorbell dating from 1880. Monday-Saturday 10:30 a.m.-6 p.m., Sunday noon-5 p.m.

Cherub Antiques Gallery
2918 M St. NW,
Washington, D.C.,
202-337-2224;
www.trocadero.com/cherubgallery

Cherub Antiques Gallery sells an exquisite line of fine Art Nouveau—everything from vases and humidors to candlesticks, including vintage cocktail shakers to mixers—as well as a wonderful selection of porcelain and pottery. A recent score: a gorgeous pair of Art Nouveau candelabras decorated with polished pewter maidens representing day and night. Monday, Saturday 11 a.m.-6 p.m., Sunday 11 a.m.-5 p.m.

Georgetown Flea Market
Clarendon Blvd. at the
Courthouse, Washington, D.C.,
202-775-3532;
www.georgetownfleamarket.com

A favorite of locals for more than 30 years, this outdoor weekend market offers a trove of treasures for those willing to peruse the more than 140 booths. Common finds include vintage glassware, artwork, china and clothing. Open Saturday and Sundays: on Saturdays, you can also shop the nearby farmers' market and park free at 2100 Clarendon Blvd.; on Sundays, the space is dedicated to vintage and antique furnishings.

The Flea Market at Eastern Market

Seventh Street and North Carolina Avenue SE, Washington, D.C.; www.easternmarket.net

The Eastern Market has been an important element in the Capitol Hill community continuously for over a century; besides being a neighborhood market, it's served as a common gathering place. Completed in 1873, the Eastern Market was designed by Adolph Cluss, a prominent local architect who designed many other post–Civil War buildings in the District of Columbia, and is somewhat an antique in itself. There are all sorts of wares here, but if you have an eye for antiques specifically, check out Tom Rall's eclectic finds, including his antique photography, prints and maps. The Market becomes an Arts & Crafts Fair on Saturdays and the Flea Market at Eastern Market on Sundays.

Justine Mehlman Antiques

2824 Pennsylvania Ave. NW, Washington, D.C., 202-337-0613, 800-215-0094; www.justinemehlmanantiques.com

Justine Mehlman Antiques specializes in gold and silver antique jewelry, including rings, cufflinks, necklaces, diamond earrings and brooches. Some specific finds include an Art Deco gold and lapis lazuli bracelet and a glorious Jugendstil green cylindrical

vase that would look terrific on any mantle. Tuesday-Saturday 11 a.m.-5:30 p.m.; closed Sunday-Monday.

Kensington Antique Row

E. Howard and Connecticut Avenues, Kensington, MD, www.kensingtonantiquerow.com

For more than 30 years, this quiet, tree-lined enclave in the blocks surrounding Kensington has played host to a variety of antique shops and galleries, making it a must-stop destination for antique lovers visiting Washington, D.C. Present count lists the number of shops at 80 and the range of goods from art to textiles.

Antique Village

Antique Row, on E. Howard Avenue between Amory and Fawcett Streets, Kensington, MD

This gigantic emporium of all things old and wonderful fills an entire block of Kensington Antique Row and stocks a nice assortment of vintage home furnishings in a range of styles. Here, you're likely to find anything from a full set of vintage Royal Crown Derby china to a classic Chippendale-style breakfront (perfect for displaying your treasures). Come early, though, the shop features some 48 vendors and fills fast. Monday-Saturday 10 a.m.-5:30 p.m., Sunday noon-5:30 p.m.

Arete Bookshop

3760 Howard Ave., Second Floor,
in Antique Village, Kensington,
MD, 301-785-8566

Owners David Johnson and
Charles Burroughs stock a varied
assortment of old, used and rare
books and prints on subjects ranging from children's literature to
Americana. Tuesday-Thursday 11
a.m.-5 p.m., Friday-Saturday 10
a.m.-5 p.m., Sunday noon-5 p.m.

Split Personality Antiques

3760 Howard Ave. in Antique
Village, Kensington, MD,
301-942-4440

"Eclectic" is the best word we
can use to describe Judy Sander's
colorful store, a space filled to
the rafters with everything from
McCoy pottery and 1950s chrome
kitchen sets to vintage bakelite
jewelry, and sturdy wooden tables
and chairs. Monday-Saturday 10
a.m.-5:30 p.m., Sunday noon-5:30
p.m.

The Vintage Vagabond

3776 Howard Ave. in Antique
Village, Kensington, MD

This charming gallery-like shop
sells West German pottery—everything from mainstream brands
like Rosenthal to more obscure
varieties like Hutschenreuther. In
other words, if you're shopping
for a particular piece to add to
your growing collection of mid-
century vessels, you won't want to
miss this spot. Proprietor Anthea
Conlon picks up other mid-century treasures for the shop as well.
Call for hours.

Miller & Arney Antiques

1737 Wisconsin Ave. NW,
Washington, D.C.,
202-338-2369;
www.millerarney.com

Anything but the typical cluttered
antique shop, this Georgetown
fixture since 1973 specializes in
high-end 18th- and 19th-century
American, English and Continental furnishings. Some say the ever-
changing inventory is unrivaled, as
it is known to include such exquisite works as a mahogany and
marble-topped Empire chest with
brass paw feet (circa 1810) and
a fruitwood with inlay German
William III library table. What's
more, everything in the shop is
displayed in tasteful, roomlike
vignettes, so you can easily visualize how to mix and match styles
for an eclectic yet professional
look. Call for hours.

Miss Pixie's Furnishings & Whatnot

1810 Adams Mill Road,
Washington, D.C.,
202-232-8171;
www.misspixies.com

The always-entertaining Miss
Pixie's sells unique and fun items
like fireplace façades, pine farm
tables, wacky sofas and more. Step
inside and savor funky rattan-
and-green vinyl chairs, a white-
painted garden table and chairs
or a 1940s-era black-and-silver
folding screen. New items join the
store's inventory on Thursdays.
Thursday noon-9 p.m., Friday-
Sunday noon-7 p.m.; closed Monday-Wednesday.

27

WASHINGTON, D.C.

Susquehanna Antique Company, Inc.

3216 O St. NW,
Washington, D.C., 202-333-1511;
www.susquehannaantiques.com
This high-end shop specializes in American, English and Continental fine arts and antiques, including 18th- and 19th-century furniture and decorative arts as well as paintings from Old Master works to early 20th-century American artists. A recent find: A George III oyster bucket—perfect for storing all those magazines. Monday, Friday 10 a.m.-6 p.m., Saturday 10 a.m.-5 p.m.

WHERE TO STAY

★★★★★Four Seasons Hotel, Washington, DC

2800 Pennsylvania Ave. NW,
Washington, D.C.,
202-342-0444, 800-332-3442;
www.fourseasons.com/washington
This Four Seasons, located in Washington's historic Georgetown neighborhood, delivers a refined residential experience that extends from your first step in the modern, sophisticated lobby to lights-out in one of the luxuriously appointed guest rooms. Yoga classes, a lap pool and cutting-edge equipment are found in the fitness center, while the seven spa treatment rooms are quiet spots for indulging in signature services like the cherry blossom champagne body wrap. The hotel's restaurant, Seasons, offers a menu with a focus on fresh, regional ingredients, while the

MID-ATLANTIC

Garden Terrace lounge is the capital's top spot for afternoon tea.
211 rooms. Wireless Internet access. Restaurant, bar. Airport transportation available. Fitness center. Pool, whirlpool. Spa. $$$$

★★★★The Hay-Adams

1800 16th St. NW,
Washington, D.C.,
202-638-6600, 800-853-6807;
www.hayadams.com
Set on Lafayette Square across from the White House, this hotel has welcomed notables since the 1920s. The guest rooms are a happy marriage of historic preservation (carved plaster ceilings and ornamental fireplaces) and 21st-century conveniences (high-speed Internet access and CD players). Windows frame views of the White House, St. John's Church and Lafayette Square. All-day dining is available at Lafayette, while the Off the Record bar is a popular watering hole for politicians and hotel guests.
145 rooms. Wireless Internet access. Restaurant, bar. Business center. $$$$

★★★★ Mandarin Oriental, Washington, DC

1330 Maryland Ave. SW,
Washington, D.C.,
202-554-8588, 888-888-1778;
www.mandarinoriental.com
Overlooking the Tidal Basin with views of the Jefferson Memorial, this Washington outpost of the Asian hotel brand delivers a scenic and central location on the Potomac River. Guest rooms mix

an Eastern sensibility with East Coast style—handmade silk tapestries hang above the beds, while reproductions of art from the Smithsonian collections decorate the walls, all blended into tranquil feng shui balance. Contemporary Asian-influenced cuisine is served in the two restaurants, while the Empress Lounge is a more casual alternative with cocktails and small plates like lobster salad BLT. A 10,000-square-foot spa, fitness center and indoor pool offer waterfront views, a full spa menu and on-call personal trainers.

400 rooms. High-speed Internet access. Two restaurants, bar. Airport transportation available. Fitness center. Pool, whirlpool. Spa. Business center. Pets accepted. $$$$

★★★★The Ritz-Carlton, Georgetown

3100 South St. NW,
Washington, D.C.,
202-912-4100, 800-542-8680;
www.ritzcarlton.com

Embassy delegations often stay at the Ritz-Carlton, Georgetown for its contemporary décor and historic setting. Many of the guest rooms offer views of the Potomac River along with feather duvets, goose-down pillows, rich wood accents, contemporary furnishings and marble baths. Sip one of the fire-red martinis in the sleek Degrees Bar and Lounge, then dine on American/Italian cuisine in Fahrenheit. Try a facial at the on-site spa or slip in a workout at the fully equipped fitness center.

86 rooms. Wireless Internet access. Restaurant, bar. Airport transportation available. Fitness center. Spa. Pets accepted. $$$$

★★★★The Ritz-Carlton, Washington

1150 22nd St. NW,
Washington, D.C.,
202-835-0500, 800-542-8680;
www.ritzcarlton.com

The Ritz-Carlton provides noteworthy attention to detail along with innovative amenities. On-call technology butlers assist with computer woes, while frequent visitors can have items stored for their next stay. Even the nightly turndown service is distinctive, and includes a freshly baked brownie left on your pillow. Spacious, comfortable guest rooms provide pleasing vistas of the garden courtyard or various Washington landmarks. Guests are granted access to the Sports Club/LA fitness complex next door.

300 rooms. Wireless Internet access. Two restaurants, bar. Fitness center. Business center. $$$$

★★★Willard InterContinental Washington

1401 Pennsylvania Ave. NW,
Washington, D.C.,
202-628-9100, 877-424-4225;
www.washington.intercontinental.com

Only two blocks from the White House, this legendary Beaux Arts hotel has been at the center of Washington's political scene since 1850. In the Willard's lobby, Lincoln held fireside staff meetings, Grant escaped the rigors of

★
★
★
★

the White House to enjoy brandy and cigars, and the term *lobbyist* was coined. The guest rooms and suites are a traditional blend of Edwardian and Victorian styles furnished in deep jewel tones. The Oval suite is inspired by you guessed it, the Oval Office.

332 rooms. Wireless Internet access. Two restaurants, bar. Fitness center. Spa. Business center. Pets accepted. **$$$$**

WHERE TO EAT

★★★1789 Restaurant
1226 36th St. NW,
Washington, D.C.,
202-965-1789;
www.1789restaurant.com

Located in a restored Federal mansion just on the edge of Georgetown University's campus, this restaurant is a top destination for students with visiting relatives or diners celebrating a special occasion. The restaurant features Victorian décor with fine china, Civil War photos and artifacts, antiques and a gas fireplace. The menu changes seasonally, but the popular rack of lamb is always available. A chef's tasting menu is offered, as well as a pre- and post-theater menu.

American menu. Dinner. Bar. Children's menu. Jacket required. Reservations recommended. Valet parking. **$$$**

★★★★CityZen
1330 Maryland Ave. SW,
Washington, D.C.,
202-787-6006; www.
mandarinoriental.com

Under chef Eric Ziebold, CityZen serves modern American-French cuisine. A new three-course, prix fixe menu every month includes appetizers such as purèe of Savoy cabbage soup with a lobster custard, globe artichoke ravioli, sashimi of Japanese hamachi and broiled Boston mackerel. Desserts include crispy brioche bread pudding, a CityZen peanut butter cup or a chocolate mint julep. Ziebold also offers a multicourse tasting menu, available in a vegetarian option. The restaurant and the lounge, designed by the acclaimed Tony Chi, feel intimate despite the ample space and vaulted ceilings.

American, French menu. Dinner. Closed Sunday-Monday. Bar. Business casual attire. Reservations recommended. Valet parking. **$$$$**

★★★★Michel Richard Citronelle
3000 M St. NW,
Washington, D.C.,
202-625-2150;
www.citronelledc.com

Chef Michel Richard won the James Beard Award for outstanding chef in 2007 for his fresh and bright cuisine. The restaurant is equally uplifting with its colorful mood wall and glass-enclosed open kitchen, which provides a bird's-eye view of the show. The chef manages to wow diners by highlighting the simple flavors of each dish's main component. A la carte entrées may include duck with persimmon and black cherry-anise sauce or squab with macaroni gratin and foie gras-syrah sauce.

French menu. Dinner. Bar. Jacket required. Reservations recommended. Valet parking. Outdoor seating. **$$$$**

★★★★Palena
3529 Connecticut Ave. NW,
Washington, D.C.,
202-537-9250;
www.palenarestaurant.com

Starting with the whole-grain breads baked onsite, chef/owner Frank Ruta's authentic Italian-influenced fare is rustic and exceptional. After working in the White House kitchen in the 1980s with retired pastry chef Ann Amernick, the two opened this small, stylish eatery and were greeted by instantaneous success. The three-, four- or five-course prix fixe menu remains the best way to experience Ruta's culinary expertise, but à la carte dishes, including sea scallops with chestnut purée or gnocchi with roasted endive, turnips, black truffle and shaved pecorino, are no less impressive.

Continental menu. Dinner. Closed Sunday-Monday. Reservations recommended. **$$$**

★★★Restaurant Nora
2132 Florida Ave. NW,
Washington, D.C.,
202-462-5143;
www.noras.com

In this 19th-century grocery store turned organic American eatery, seasonal ingredients are the stars. Chef/owner Nora Pouillon is a pioneer in the organic movement; Restaurant Nora was the first certified organic restaurant in the country (95 percent of the products used are organic). Pouillon integrates flavors from the American South to Spain and from Latin America to Asia and India, and the menu changes daily. The rustic dining room is decorated with dried flowers and museum-quality antique Mennonite and Amish quilts.

International menu. Dinner. Closed Sunday; also late August-early September. Bar. Business casual attire. Reservations recommended. Valet parking. **$$$**

★

★

★

★

★

THE MIDWEST

IF FARM FURNITURE IS YOUR FANTASY—WHETHER OAK, MAHOG-
any, walnut or cherry—then stray from the Midwest's big cities
and shop to your heart's delight in some of the smaller towns
and urban outskirts. If architectural salvage is more to your
liking, then Chicago, Kansas City, and Des Moines, are guaranteed to satisfy your itch. While in Des Moines, be sure to
visit the wonderful David Chipperfield–designed public library
and the Des Moines Art Center, filled with Jeff Koons sculptures and far-flung works by Matisse and Joseph Cornell to get
inspired, before checking out favorite antique malls such as the
Brass Armadillo and the Majestic Lion. Visit Kansas City with
its selection of mid-century furniture by the likes of Dunbar,
Knoll and Eames and St. Louis, where you can browse though
fine furnishings paired with terrific hotels and restaurants. And
while much of what you'll find here has originated in the region,
plenty of dealers specialize in Asian and European antiques, too.
So head to urban hotspots Chicago, Indianapolis and Columbus
(among other major hubs on the prairie), for high culture and
some of the country's best bargains on things of the past.

CHICAGO

THE SO-CALLED WINDY CITY AND THE ARCHITECTURE CAPITAL OF THE United States—with buildings designed by the likes of Louis Sullivan and Mies van der Rohe—Chicago is especially well known for its architectural salvage options. You'll also find plenty of modernist pieces as well as European treasures.

WHERE TO SHOP

Architectural Artifacts, Inc.
4325 N. Ravenswood Ave.,
Chicago, 773-348-0622;
www.architecturalartifacts.com
Housed in a two-building, 80,000-square-foot complex, Architectural Artifacts has delighted locals since 1987 with owner Stuart Grannen's intriguing inventory of doors, windows, columns, balustrades and other architectural works from across the globe. Not to worry if you're not working on a major home renovation; this source for elegant and unusual treasures also stocks a nice assortment of smaller, more manageable home furnishings. Daily 10 a.m.-5 p.m.

Bookworks
3444 N. Clark St., Chicago,
773-871-5318;
www.thebookworks.com
Bookworks has been a fixture on the city's north side since 1984, offering a wide assortment of out-of-print and rare titles as well as recordings, antique photographs and assorted ephemera. Monday-Thursday noon-10 p.m., Friday-Saturday noon-11 p.m., Sunday noon-6 p.m.

Broadway Antique Market
6130 N. Broadway, Chicago,
773-743-5444;
www.bamchicago.com
Less than 30 minutes from downtown, this classic Art Deco building boasts a 20,000-square-foot market of colorful wares from over 75 dealers who specialize in 20th-century art, objects and furniture. Recent finds include a nice selection of George Nelson and Herman Miller furniture, a Jens Rinsom desk and file cabinet, and plenty of exquisite glass, china, pottery, advertising art and other ephemera. Monday-Saturday 10 a.m.-7 p.m., Sunday noon-6 p.m.

33

CHICAGO

★
★
★
★
★

Chicago Antique Market

Randolph Street between Ada St. and Ogden Ave., Chicago, 312-951-9939; www.chicagoantiquemarket.com

This indoor/outdoor market is a favorite among locals in search of vintage clothing, jewelry, collectibles and home furnishings. Likewise, the antique market is frequented by dealers and designers, like the Ralph Lauren store display team members, who are rumored to peruse the stalls regularly in search of one-of-a-kind finds. Both the stock and dealers change on a regular basis, so there's always something new to see. Just be sure to arrive early, because the market is only open on weekends and things disappear quickly. Admission: $10. May-October: last weekend of the month, Saturday 10 a.m.-5 p.m., Sunday 9 a.m.-4 p.m. Check Web site for exact dates.

Colletti Gallery

67 E. Oak St., Chicago, 312-664-6767; www.collettigallery.com

Visit this fabulous emporium for its stellar selection of 19th- and early 20th-century posters by Toulouse Lautrec, Mucha, Cassandre and others, but don't overlook the gallery's equally stunning collection of Belle Epoque and Art Nouveau furnishings. Monday-Saturday 10 a.m.-6 p.m., Sunday noon-5 p.m.; also by appointment.

Douglas Rosin Decorative Arts & Antiques

730 N. Wells St., Chicago, 312-337-6556; www.douglasrosin.com

This River North gallery stocks an impressive, albeit pricey, selection of high-end Art Nouveau, Mission, Arts and Crafts, Art Deco and midcentury modern furnishings and decorative objects. Look for items like a pair of Art Deco ladies from Austria circa 1927 and a silver- and gold-leafed Art Deco mirror dripping with theatrical swags. Tuesday-Saturday 11 a.m.-5:30 p.m.; also by appointment; closed Sunday-Monday.

Jan's Antiques

225 N. Racine Ave., Chicago, 312-563-0275; www.jansantiques.net

A short cab ride from the Loop takes antique enthusiasts to this 18,000-square-foot store specializing in anything antique, from lighting and architectural salvage to fine hand-carved furniture and china. You could say that Jan's has everything but the kitchen sink—except they recently displayed a terrific sink from the 1920s. Wednesday-Friday, 1-7 p.m., Saturday-Sunday 1-6 p.m.; closed Monday-Tuesday.

Jay Roberts Antique Warehouse Inc.

149 W. Kinzie St., Chicago, 312-222-0167; www.jayroberts.com

Located in the River North neighborhood, this 37-year-old,

34

THE MIDWEST

★
★
★
★

50,000-square-foot emporium is renowned for its vast selection of antique clocks sold in working order. In addition, you'll find a wide range of fine period antiques from Chippendale and French Empire to Country Pine, Art Nouveau and Art Deco. A recent find: a wildly ornate English mahogany hall tree with fabulous flourishes. Monday-Saturday 10 a.m.-5 p.m., closed Sunday.

Salvage One
1840 W. Hubbard St., Chicago, 312-733-0098; www.salvageone.com

Since 1979, interior designers, architects and others in the know have been traveling to Salvage One's River West showroom for the best in everything from reclaimed andirons to wrought iron gates. You'll find radiators, stained glass windows, garden statues, fountains, mirrors, and sconces. Make the trip and plan to wander for hours. Monday-Friday, noon-7 p.m., Saturday 9 a.m.-5 p.m., Sunday noon-5 p.m.; also by appointment.

Urban Remains
410 N. Paulina St., Chicago, 312-523-4660, 312-492-6254; www.urbanremainschicago.com

If you're looking for a one-of-a-kind door, fireplace mantel or other architectural gem with a bit of Windy City pedigree, this is the place to head. The shop, located in a converted bottling factory on the Near West Side, deals exclusively in salvage building materials from mid-19th century to late-1930s commercial and residential structures. Visitors to Urban Remains have unearthed a claw-foot tub, a lantern from Chicago's 1934 World's Fair and a streamlined Art Deco medicine cabinet. Daily 11 a.m.-7 p.m.; also by appointment.

WHERE TO STAY

★★★★★Four Seasons Hotel Chicago
120 E. Delaware Place, Chicago, 312-280-8800; www.fourseasons.com/chicagofs

Located in a 66-story building, the Four Seasons Hotel Chicago is in the heart of the city, near the lake, close to restaurants and surrounded by all the best shopping. The guestrooms, decorated with contemporary furniture and soothing, neutral fabrics, are stylish and comfortable and include flat-screen TVs. After a day of scavenging, head to the Roman-columned indoor pool, well-stocked fitness center and full-service spa. Edible indulgences include American and French dishes at Seasons restaurant and international favorites at the Café. The Seasons Lounge, with its working fireplace and live piano, is a favorite gathering spot for cocktails or tea.

343 rooms. Wireless Internet access. Two restaurants, bar. Fitness center. Pool. Spa. Business center. Pets accepted. **$$$$**

CHICAGO

★★★Park Hyatt Chicago

800 N. Michigan Ave., Chicago, 312-335-1234, 800-633-7313; www.parkchicago.hyatt.com

From its stylish interiors to its historic Water Tower Square location, the Park Hyatt is intrinsically tied to the history of Chicago. The public and private spaces feature Mies van der Rohe, Eames and Noguchi furnishings, as well as photography commissioned by the Art Institute of Chicago. Locals flock to the seventh-floor restaurant, NoMI, for the nouvelle cuisine and great views of city life below.

198 rooms. Wireless Internet access. Restaurant, bar. Airport transportation available. Fitness center. Pool. Spa. Business center. $$$$

★★★★★The Peninsula Chicago

108 E. Superior St., Chicago, 312-337-2888, 866-288-8889; www.peninsula.com

An unparalleled level of service and meticulous attention to detail make this hotel a standout. Rooms, with classic and elegant décor, are outfitted with bedside electronic control panels and plush, comfy beds. The sprawling spa and fitness center (and beautiful sky-high indoor pool) feature the most up-to-date equipment and cutting-edge treatments. The hotel's restaurants, including the fine dining Avenues and more casual Shanghai Terrace, are some of the city's most acclaimed.

339 rooms. Wireless Internet access. Four restaurants, bar. Airport transportation available. Fitness center. Pool, whirlpool. Spa. $$$$

★★★★★The Ritz-Carlton, A Four Seasons Hotel

160 E. Pearson St., Chicago, 312-266-1000, 800-621-6906; www.fourseasons.com

Situated on the upper levels of Water Tower Place on the city's Magnificent Mile, this hotel boasts a prized location near world-class shopping, acclaimed restaurants and the shores of Lake Michigan. The lobby is open and airy with a sculptured fountain in the center and opulent floral bouquets. Guest rooms have extra-large picture windows showcasing views of Lake Michigan or the city and rich fabrics. Suites are outfitted with Bulgari toiletries, personalized stationery and fresh-cut flowers. The hotel's full-service spa is one of the city's best.

435 rooms. High-speed Internet access. Two restaurants, two bars. Airport transportation available. Fitness center. Pool. Spa. Business center. Pets accepted. $$$$

★★★The Drake Hotel Chicago

140 E. Walton Place, Chicago, 312-787-2200; www.thedrakehotel.com

A favorite landmark in the Michigan Avenue skyline, The Drake is a classic lakefront hotel offering both spectacular views and a prime Gold Coast location. Built in 1920 as a summer resort, extensive renovations have preserved the ornate, elegant charm of this venerable classic. Amenities include executive floors, an exercise facility, a shopping arcade, and multiple dining options. The clubby Cape Cod Room is famous for its oyster bar and seafood, Drake Bros.' for its lakefront views and delicious steaks, and the Coq d'Or for its piano bar. Afternoon tea in the lobby's Palm Court and 24-hour room service are also offered.

535 rooms. High-speed Internet access. Two restaurants, two bars. Fitness center. Airport transportation available. Business center. $$$

WHERE TO EAT

★★★★★Alinea
1723 N. Halsted St., Chicago, 312-867-0110; www. alinearestaurant.com

A dimly lit corridor provides the dramatic entrance to chef/owner Grant Achatz's popular restaurant. Once inside, you can catch a glimpse of the spotless open kitchen and watch a team of chefs cook with scientific precision. The four intimate dining rooms, appointed with dark mahogany tables, provide the perfect setting for the adventurous cuisine. The restaurant offers two types of menus: a 12- or 24-course degustation feast. Steaming eucalyptus leaves, smoking cinnamon sticks or lavender air-filled pillows are just some of the unusual elements that may be incorporated in the

presentation of some dishes. The knowledgeable and affable wait staff are passionate about every guest's experience and deflate any sense of pretension.

American menu. Dinner. Closed Monday-Tuesday. Business casual attire. Reservations recommended. Valet parking. $$$$

★★★Blackbird
619 W. Randolph St., Chicago, 312-715-0708; www.blackbirdrestaurant.com

The minimalist Blackbird girds style with substance. Like the décor, the food is spare, hitting just the right contemporary notes without drowning in too many flavors. The market-driven menu changes frequently, with seasonal favorites such as homemade charcuterie and braised veal cheeks. Noise levels are high, but the elegantly attired diners who crowd the place consider it simply good buzz.

American menu. Lunch, dinner. Closed Sunday. Bar. Business casual attire. Valet parking. Outdoor seating. $$$

★★★★Charlie Trotter's
816 W. Armitage Ave., Chicago, 773-248-6228; www.charlietrotters.com

Set inside an unassuming brick brownstone, this Lincoln Park legend is an intimate, peaceful place. Upon entry, you are greeted by a well-stocked, two-story bar and a profusion of aromatic floral bouquets. Each of the four dining rooms is light and elegant and remains earnestly unpretentious. The menu features French and Italian influences and seasonal ingredients. Trotter prefers saucing with vegetable juice–based vinaigrettes, light emulsified stocks and purées, and delicate broths and herb-infused meat and fish essences. The result is flavors that are remarkably intense yet light. Staying true to their accommodating reputation, the staff will adjust, adapt and substitute to match personal preferences.

American menu. Dinner. Closed Sunday-Monday. Bar. Jacket required. Reservations recommended. Valet parking. $$$$

★★★★Everest
440 S. LaSalle St., Chicago, 312-663-8920; www. everestrestaurant.com

Perched high atop the city on the 40th floor of the Chicago Stock Exchange building, Everest affords spectacular views and equally fabulous contemporary French cuisine. Chef and owner Jean Joho blends European influences with local, seasonal American ingredients, and he's not afraid to pair noble ingredients like caviar with potatoes or turnips. Everest's dining room is luxuriously decorated with vaulted draped ceilings, mirrored walls, reflective paintings by Adam Seigel and floor-to-ceiling windows.

French menu. Dinner. Bar. Business casual attire. Reservations recommended. Valet parking. $$$$

★★★Gibsons Steakhouse
1028 N. Rush St., Chicago, 312-266-8999; www.gibsonssteakhouse.com

The theme at Gibsons is outsized, from the massive steaks to the stogie-puffing personalities who dine here, a blend of politicians, sports figures, celebrities and conventioneers. Some crave the generous porterhouses, but many also come for the carnival atmosphere. Try the avocado salad and any of the enormous desserts.

Steak menu. Lunch, dinner. Bar. Business casual attire. Reservations recommended. Valet parking. Outdoor seating. $$$

★★Green Zebra
1460 W. Chicago Ave., Chicago, 312-243-7100; www.greenzebrachicago.com

This is chef/owner Shawn McClain's temple to vegetarian cooking. Seasonally modified, the restaurant offers a multitude of small plates that would convert any carnivore. The globally inspired menu includes such dishes as avocado panna cotta with pickled sweet peppers and crimson lentil cake with red pepper jam. A few fish and light meat options are also available. The ever-changing menu is popular, so plan on making reservations far in advance.

American, vegetarian menu. Dinner. Closed Monday. Bar. Casual attire. Reservations recommended. Valet parking. $$

★

★

★

★

★★★★Les Nomades

222 E. Ontario St., Chicago,
312-649-9010;
www.lesnomades.net

Les Nomades is a serene spot tucked away off Michigan Avenue in an elegant turn-of-the-century townhouse. Romantic and intimate with a fireplace, hardwood floors, deep, cozy banquettes and gorgeous flowers, Les Nomades was originally opened as a private club. Chef Chris Nugent has crafted a traditional French menu that features dishes such as white asparagus soup with wild mushrooms and truffle froth.

French menu. Dinner. Closed Sunday-Monday. Bar. Jacket required. Reservations recommended. Valet parking. $$$$

★★★NoMI

800 N. Michigan Ave., Chicago,
312-239-4030;
www.nomirestaurant.com

NoMI is the Park Hyatt's stylish destination for contemporary French cuisine by chef Christophe David. Asian influences are evident in sushi and sashimi selections on the menu. Luxurious materials such as white marble, Italian mosaic tile and leather are combined in the streamlined décor. The wine list is extensive, boasting 3,000 or so bottles. NoMI also serves breakfast and lunch and offers outdoor terrace dining in fair weather.

French menu. Breakfast, lunch, dinner, Sunday brunch. Bar. Business casual attire. Reservations recommended. Valet parking. Outdoor seating. $$$

★★★★Seasons

120 E. Delaware Place, Chicago,
312-280-8800;
www.fourseasons.com/chicagofs

Seasons restaurant has a diverse menu that changes depending upon the availability of fresh ingredients. You might find something like surf and turf tartare, which features American Kobe beef with violet mustard, or ahi tuna with wasabi sorbet and tamarind-soy gelee. Groups of six or more can request the Chef's Table and receive a personally guided eight-course meal with wine pairings. The traditional, hushed dining room features tables set with vintage china. Service is affable and attentive, and every meal ends with freshly made petit fours.

American menu. Breakfast, lunch, dinner, Sunday brunch. Bar. Children's menu. Business casual attire. Reservations recommended. Valet parking. $$$

★★★Shanghai Terrace

108 E. Superior St., Chicago,
312-573-6744;
www.chicago.peninsula.com

Intimate and trimmed in rich hues of ruby red and black lacquer, Shanghai Terrace is housed in the stylish Peninsula Hotel. Start with the refined three-bite dim sum. Save room for flavorful entrées like spicy Szechuan beef and wok-fried lobster. The restaurant adjoins an expansive terrace offering alfresco dining in the summer, six stories above Michigan Avenue.

CHICAGO

★

★

★

★

Chinese menu. Lunch, dinner. Closed Sunday. Bar. Business casual attire. Outdoor seating. $$$

★★★Topolobampo
445 N. Clark St., Chicago,
312-661-1434;
www.fronterakitchens.com

Pioneering chef/owner Rick Bayless is a cookbook author, television personality and perennial culinary award winner with a devoted following. His celebration of the regional cuisines of Mexico is realized at Topolobampo, the upscale counterpart to his famed Frontera Grill (which is next door). The seasonal menu, based on locally produced items, is paired with a tome of premium tequilas and an excellent wine list. Mexican menu. Lunch, dinner. Closed Sunday-Monday. Bar. Children's menu. Business casual attire. Reservations recommended. Valet parking. Outdoor seating. $$$

★★★★Tru
676 N. St. Clair St., Chicago
312-202-0001;
www.trurestaurant.com

Tru's modern, airy dining room is a stunning stage for chef and co-owner Rick Tramonto's progressive French creations and co-owner pastry chef Gale Gand's incredible, one-of-a-kind sweet and savory endings. Tramonto offers plates filled with ingredients that are treated to his unmatched creativity and artistic flair. The wine list, with more than 1,800 selections, is overseen by sommelier Ilana Federman. Museum-quality artwork is on display, including pieces by Andy Warhol, Maya Lin and Gerhard Richter. A lounge area offers a somewhat less formal but no less memorable dining experience. French menu. Dinner. Closed Sunday. Bar. Jacket required. Reservations recommended. Valet parking. $$$$

ST. CHARLES

Located on the Fox River one hour west of Chicago, St. Charles is an affluent suburb with a charming downtown filled with antique and specialty shops housed in historic buildings.

WHERE TO SHOP

Aberdeen Antiques
Antique Market I, 11 N. Third St., St. Charles, 630-377-1868;
www.aberdeenantiques.com

You never know what you'll find at this downtown St. Charles shop. A recent visit unearthed such treasures as Weller and Hull pottery, elaborately carved Victorian furniture and Civil War–era fashions. Daily 10 a.m.-5 p.m.

Artemisia Antiques and Elements

116 Cedar Ave., St. Charles,
630-377-6406;
www.artemisiastyle.com

Housed in an 1850 Italianate home in the city's Century Corners shopping district, this well-edited shop offers a range of antique furnishings for both home and garden. Be sure to check out the vast selection of handcrafted iron lighting fixtures and accessories that would add punch to any home's décor. Open Monday-Saturday 10 a.m.-5 p.m., Sunday noon-5 p.m.

WHERE TO STAY

★★★Hotel Baker

100 W. Main St., St. Charles,
630-584-2100, 800-284-0110;
www.hotelbaker.com

Built in 1928, this hotel has traditionally decorated rooms with Egyptian cotton linens and wireless Internet. The waterfront restaurant hosts everything from wine tastings to a Sunday champagne brunch.

53 rooms. Wireless Internet access. Restaurant, bar. Airport transportation available. $$$

ST. CHARLES

INDIANAPOLIS

THIS SOPHISTICATED YET LOW-KEY CITY IS NIRVANA FOR THOSE WHO can't get their fill of antique malls. Be sure to head to Fountain Square for wonderful architectural salvage items and store after store filled with an eye-popping array of vintage treasures.

WHERE TO SHOP

Antiques on the Square
1056 Virginia Ave., Indianapolis,
317-916-8125
This two-story shop has earned local accolades for its vast assortment of fun and funky finds, ranging from pastel-painted shabby chic furniture to sleek, mid-century modern tables and chairs. Check out the selection of smaller items ranging from '50s kitchenware to vintage textiles and more. Be prepared to be greeted by one of the store dogs; your pooch is welcome, too. Friday-Saturday 10 a.m.-5 p.m., Sunday noon-5 p.m.

Exit 76 Antique Mall
12595 N. Executive Drive,
Edinburgh, 812-526-7676;
www.exit76antiques.com
Located just 30 miles south of Indianapolis off I-65, this massive, 72,000-square-foot mall stocks everything from estate jewelry and rare coins to sports memorabilia, vintage toys and household furnishings. If you can't fit your purchases in the car, the mall offers a pack-and-ship service via UPS. Daily 10 a.m.-6 p.m.

Indianapolis Downtown Antique Mall
1044 Virginia Ave., Indianapolis,
317-635-5336
This 30-dealer, two-story mall boasts a colorful assortment of vintage home furnishings and collectibles. You're bound to find everything from an oversized rolling pin to a set of bright yellow plates from the 1950s that simply scream "Doris Day was here." Monday-Saturday 10 a.m.-5 p.m., Sunday noon-5 p.m.

Midland Arts & Antiques Market
907 E. Michigan St., Indianapolis,
317-267-9005;
www.midlandathome.com
Housed in a four-story brick factory building just off I-65, you'll know Midland by the giant sculpture adorning the front entrance. This urban treasure offers a wonderful lesson in how to mix staid, high-end Victorian furnishings with more modern finds from the 1950s and beyond. Monday-

Saturday 10 a.m.-6 p.m., Sunday noon-5 p.m.

Solomon Jones Antiques and Interiors
1103 E. 52nd St., Indianapolis, 317-475-0203;
www.solomon-jones.com

Since 1973, this 6,000-square-foot gem has stocked an impeccable assortment of Biedermier, Jacobean, Regency, Empire, Neoclassical, Rocco Renaissance and French Provincial furnishings, all handpicked by proprietor Phillip Bennett Solomon, a former decorative arts curator for the Indianapolis Museum of Art. Not sure how to work your recent purchases into your home? Solomon and on-staff designer Ryan Paris are always happy to help. Tuesday-Thursday 10 a.m.-6 p.m., Friday 10 a.m.-5 p.m., Saturday 10 a.m.-4 p.m.

Southport Antique Mall
2028 E. Southport Road, Indianapolis, 317-786-8246;
www.southportantiquemall.net

One step in this decade-old Indianapolis gold mine, not far from I-65, and it's easy to see why it has been featured on HGTV. The 36,000-square-foot shop is bright and welcoming, not to mention packed with a vast assortment of antiques and collectibles, which include highly collectible Roseville pottery, Stickley furniture and the whimsical and offbeat, like a pair of Howdy Doody ear muffs. Monday-Saturday, 10 a.m.-8 p.m., Sunday noon-5 p.m.

White River Architectural Salvage & Antiques
1325 W. 30th St., Indianapolis, 317-924-4000, 800-262-3389;
www.whiteriversalvage.com

Searching for a one-of-a-kind fireplace mantel for your living room or light fixture for your foyer? This well-known Midwest salvage company features a wide variety of these and other architectural treasures like stained glass windows, stonework, ironwork, statuary and more. Don't despair if you can't locate that one-of-a-kind architectural find on your first visit—you can always inquire as to whether White River's Zionsville or Centerville locations have what you are seeking. Monday-Saturday, 10 a.m.-5:30 p.m.; closed Sunday.

WHERE TO STAY

★★★Canterbury Hotel
123 S. Illinois St., Indianapolis, 317-634-3000, 800-538-8186;
www.canterburyhotel.com

Since the 1850s, the Canterbury has been one of Indianapolis' leading hotels. Mahogany furniture and traditional artwork decorate the guest rooms. The restaurant dishes up American and Continental favorites for breakfast, lunch and dinner, while the traditional afternoon tea is a local institution.

99 rooms. Wireless Internet access. Restaurant, bar. Fitness center. Business center. $$$

INDIANAPOLIS

★
★
★
★

★★★Crowne Plaza Hotel–Union Station

123 W. Louisiana St.,
Indianapolis, 317-631-2221,
877-227-6963;
www.crowneplaza.com

Located in historic Union Station, this hotel offers 26 authentic Pullman sleeper train cars for overnight stays, each named for a famous personality from the early 1900s. Full of old-world charm and modern convenience, this hotel is within walking distance of downtown restaurants and sports and cultural hot spots.

273 rooms. High-speed Internet access. Restaurant, bar. Fitness center. Pool. Business center. **$**

WHERE TO EAT

★★★Restaurant at the Canterbury

123 S. Illinois St., Indianapolis,
317-634-3000, 800-538-8186;
www.canterburyhotel.com

Located downtown in the Canterbury hotel, this eatery is decorated more like an English club than a restaurant. Dinner choices include classics like Steak Diane, surf and turf, osso bucco and Dover sole. American, Continental menu. Breakfast, lunch, dinner, Sunday brunch. Business casual attire. Reservations recommended. Valet parking. **$$$**

THE MIDWEST

MISSOURI

KANSAS CITY

SPREAD OUT OVER TWO STATES—MISSOURI AND KANSAS—THIS CITY boasts such architectural gems as The Plaza, the nation's first planned residential community, as well as a terrific museum. The outlying suburbs on the Kansas side include Overland Park and Prairie Village. From flea markets to antique galleries to no-nonsense strip malls, KC knows its vintage valuables.

WHERE TO SHOP

Black Bamboo
1815 Wyandotte St., Kansas City, 816-283-3000;
www.black-bamboo.com
East meets West at this eclectic Crossroads Art District shop, where you'll find a handpicked selection of antique Asian furniture in a variety of styles, finishes and colors all culled from the markets of China and Southeast Asia. In addition to the expected lacquered chests and hand-painted screens, you'll also find a wide assortment of items for both the tabletop and garden. Tuesday-Friday 10 a.m.-6 p.m., Saturday 10 a.m.-5 p.m.; closed Sunday-Monday.

Brass Armadillo Antique Mall
1450 Golfview Drive, Grain Valley, 816-847-5260, 888-847-5260;
www.brassarmadillo.com
Just outside Kansas City and minutes from bustling I-70, this 550-dealer, 42,000-square-foot mega mall stocks everything from sturdy oak furniture to delicate china and crystal. Recent visits have unearthed fabulous tole-painted chandeliers, vintage Baker furniture and several sets of Wedgwood china. This is one of several outposts in the Midwest, so chances are good that if this one doesn't have what you're looking for, another might. Daily 9 a.m.-9 p.m.

Cheep Antiques
500 W. Fifth St., Kansas City, 816-471-0092;
www.kansascityrivermarket.com/cheepantiques
Located in the city's historic River Market district, this affordable antique shop stocks a wide range of 20th-century castoffs (think grandfather clocks and Colonial-style coffee tables) as well as a selection of European goods like French sideboards, armoires and chairs. Restoration services are also available in the event that your purchase requires a little extra TLC. Tuesday-Friday 9

★
★
★
☆
☆

a.m.-3 p.m., Saturday-Sunday 9 a.m.-5 p.m.; closed Monday.

Curious Sofa

3925 W. 69 Terrace,
Prairie Village,
913-432-8969;
www.curioussofa.com

Don't let this store's strip mall exterior fool you: The shop is anything but run-of-the-mill. Inside you'll find a wonderfully eclectic assortment of architectural salvage, painted furniture and rusty chandeliers artfully arranged in an interior that's been painstakingly designed to mimic an old building, right down to the decayed plaster and aged wallpaper. Owner Debbie Dusenberry delights in finding new uses for old things (columns as book stands or dress dummies as coat racks), and her clever ideas may inspire you to do the same. Monday-Saturday 10 a.m.-6 p.m., Sunday noon-5 p.m.

Horsefeathers Antiques

2312 W. 43rd St., Kansas City,
913-677-5566;
www.horsefeathersantiques.com

Piled high with tables, paintings, screens and assorted garden ornaments, this single-dealer shop has the look and feel of a classic antique stall on Portobello Road in London or the Marche aux Puces de St. Ouen in Paris—and with good reason. Owners Steve and Judy Ball make regular trips to Europe in search of fine furniture, accessories and art to stock their shop. There's also a well-edited assortment of classic Ameri-

can furnishings like mahogany highboys, Sheraton bow front chests and the like. By appointment only.

Mission Road Antique Mall

4101 W. 83rd St., Prairie Village,
913-341-7577;
www.missionroadantiquemall.com

If you're an Anglophile, you'll delight in this Tudoresque mall, considered one of the finest in the Kansas City area. Many of the Mission Road Antique Mall's 350 dealers make regular buying trips to both England and France, so there's always a varied selection of overstuffed chairs, highly polished tables and other accoutrements worthy of a country house. But no worries if your tastes are more Colonial than Continental—there's also a nice selection of vintage American finds. The Bloomsbury Bistro serves lunch to hungry antique hunters. Daily 10 a.m.-6 p.m.

The Paris Flee Market

5905 Dearborn St., Mission,
913-362-1300

Driving past The Paris Flee Market, a nondescript brick building with large plate glass windows on one of Mission's main drags, you would never guess the treasures it holds. But do stop, because inside you'll find a wide assortment of vintage furnishings with pedigree—tables, chairs, cabinets and a vast assortment of accessories, all hand-picked by owner Elizabeth Pascoe, who religiously scours antique markets in England and France so you don't have to. Tuesday-Friday 10 a.m.-5 p.m., Saturday 10 a.m.-3 p.m.; closed Sunday.

Retro Inferno
1500 Grand Blvd., Kansas City, 816-842-4004;
www.retroinferno.com
Think George Jetson meets the Brady Bunch, and you'll have a good idea of the sorts of furnishings this store stocks (including cast brass Italian palm tree table lamps). Of course, the quality is slightly more upscale, featuring pieces by such noted 20th-century designers as Josef Hoffman, Verner Panton, Dunbar and Charles and Ray Eames. Monday-Saturday 11 a.m.-6 p.m.; closed Sunday.

River Market Antique Mall
115 W. Fifth St., Kansas City, 816-221-0220;
www.rivermarketantiquemall.com
With a 6,000-square-foot mural of famed exploring duo Lewis and Clark painted on its four-story exterior, this multidealer establishment is hard to miss. Inside you'll find 30,000 square feet of showroom space stocked with an equally impressive selection of furniture, pottery, china and more. Don't miss the vintage clothing and jewelry selection—some of the best vintage finds in the Midwest. Daily 10 a.m.-6 p.m.

Webster House
1644 Wyandotte St., Kansas City, 816-221-4713;
www.websterhousekc.com
Housed in a circa 1885, impeccably restored Romanesque Revival schoolhouse, Webster House is part antique emporium, part restaurant. Visit the store for some of the Midwest's best 18th- and 19th-century European, American and Asian antiques arranged in homey vignettes. When you finish your shopping, have lunch in the restaurant, where you'll find a new American menu featuring such local favorites as warm goat cheese soufflé, house-roasted turkey sandwiches and black truffle-flecked mac and cheese. Monday-Saturday 10 a.m.-5 p.m.; dining room, Monday-Saturday 11 a.m.-2:30 p.m.

WHERE TO STAY

★★Hotel Savoy
219 W. Ninth St., Kansas City, 816-842-3575, 800-728-6922;
www.bandbonline.com
This restored 1888 landmark building features original architectural details such as stained and leaded glass, tile floors and tin ceilings. The Savoy Grille is located on the property, and many attractions are nearby.
22 rooms. Complimentary full breakfast. Restaurant, bar. $

KANSAS CITY

★★★Hotel Phillips
106 W. 12th St., Kansas City,
816-221-7000, 800-433-1426;
www.hotelphillips.com

Located downtown, this boutique hotel is a convenient base for exploring the city. While the historic Art Deco integrity of this 1931 landmark has been preserved, modern amenities have been added to the rooms and suites. Phillips Chophouse has a 1930s feel, and live music can be heard at 12 Baltimore Café and Bar.

217 rooms. High-speed Internet access. Two restaurants, two bars. Airport transportation available. Fitness center. Business center. $$

WHERE TO EAT

★★★★American Restaurant
200 E. 25th St., Kansas City,
816-545-8000;
www.theamericankc.com

The flagship restaurant of the Crown Center, the American has attracted Kansas City diners for 35 years. With a concept designed by the legendary James Beard, the father of American cooking, and Joe Baum, the restaurateur of the former Windows on the World in New York City, the place is as elegant as ever with downtown views, polished service and one of the city's best wine lists. The kitchen staff, led by chef Celina Tio, prepares American fare using local, seasonal produce.

American menu. Lunch, dinner. Closed Sunday. Bar. Children's menu. Business casual attire. Reservations recommended. Valet parking. $$$

★★★Bluestem
900 Westport Rd., Kansas City,
816-561-1101;
www.bluestemkc.com

Bluestem is the product of two acclaimed chefs, Colby and Megan Garrelts, who worked at such restaurants as Aureole in Las Vegas and Tru in Chicago. The space is divided into a 40-seat restaurant, clad in cobalt blue walls and warm candlelight, and an adjacent wine bar that offers more casual fare. A three-, five- or seven-course prix fixe menu is available, as well as a 12-course tasting menu. Entrées might include a torchon of foie gras, wild Tasmanian salmon with oxtail or LaBelle duck with sweet potato gnocchi and apple emulsion. Desserts are outstanding, simplistic in their approach but full of intense flavors.

American menu. Dinner, brunch. Bar. Business casual attire. Reservations recommended. $$$

★★★Tatsu's
4603 W. 90th St., Prairie Village,
913-383-9801, www.tatsus.com

This quiet French restaurant grew from a small pastry and lunch shop opened by chef/owner Tatsu Arai in 1980. Since then, it has become a top Kansas City dining destination. The classic French cuisine includes dishes such as beef bourguignon, poached salmon with champagne sauce or lemon butter sauce and roasted boneless duck breast with peppercorn cream sauce.

French menu. Lunch, dinner. Bar. $$

ST. LOUIS

HOME TO THE GATEWAY ARCH AND THE PLACE WHERE HOT DOGS WERE invented in 1906, St. Louis has an up-and-coming historic district as well as a thriving antiques community, thanks to the influx of a young, hip crowd seeking a mix of mid-century and more traditional finds.

WHERE TO SHOP

Cherokee Antique Row
Cherokee Street between Jefferson and Lemp Avenues; www.cherokeeantiquerow.net
St. Louis residents with a nose for antiques will always tell out-of-towners to head for Cherokee Row, a six-block area within the Cherokee-Lemp historic district that is on a par with the likes of Brimfield, Round Top and other large fairs. Given that the area covers such a vast expanse, there are simply too many stores to list individually. Here are a few favorites:

China Finders
2125 Cherokee St., St. Louis, 314-776-5900, 800-900-2557; www.chinafinders.com
This shops stocks a nice range of vintage furnishings, but the real reason to visit is for the china and crystal selections. Want to add pieces to a vintage set? The store offers a replacement service. Tuesday-Saturday 10 a.m.-4 p.m., Sunday noon-4 p.m.

HearthBeats Vintage Kitchen Wares
2001 Cherokee St., St. Louis, 314-771-2600; www.hearthbeats.com
The name says it all. This shop specializes in kitchenware—primarily glassware, cookware, cookbooks, furniture and fixtures from the 1940s, '50s and '60s. Saturday 10 a.m.-6 p.m., Sunday noon-4 p.m.; also "by chance" or by appointment.

Jasper's Antique Radio Museum
2022–24 Cherokee St., St. Louis, 314-421-8313; www.jaspers-stl-mo.com
Part museum, part store, Jasper's has the largest selection of vintage radios and radio-related para-phernalia we've ever seen under one roof. Monday-Saturday 8 a.m.-4 p.m.; closed Sunday.

Lady Jane's
2110 Cherokee St., St. Louis, 314-773-3205
Lady Jane prides itself on a won-derful assortment of antique hardware, but don't overlook the large selection of mantles, doors, wrought iron and other architec-tural salvage. Tuesday-Sunday 10 a.m.-4 p.m.; Monday "by chance."

ST. LOUIS

South Country Antique Mall

13208 Tesson Ferry Road, Sappington, 314-842-5566; www.southcountyantiquemall.com

Housed in an old Kroger supermarket, this 300-plus dealer mall in the southwest suburbs stocks a varied assortment of intriguing finds—everything from old advertising art to painted wood tables and chairs. It may require several hours combing through booths, but the bargains on the likes of vintage state plates and retro furniture are worth the effort. Daily 10 a.m.-6 p.m.

Warson Woods Antique Gallery

10091 Manchester Road, St. Louis, 314-909-0123; www.warsonwoodsantiques.com

Stop by and walk this mall's 26,000 square feet of showroom space stocked by some 300 dealers who sell everything from rustic Colonial antiques to delicate European china and crystal. Past customers have walked away with quite a range: everything from framed prints of British country estates to blue-and-white porcelain vases. Daily 10 a.m.-6 p.m.

WHERE TO STAY

★★★Chase Park Plaza

212 N. Kingshighway Blvd., St. Louis, 314-633-3000; www.chaseparkplaza.com

This historic hotel in St. Louis's Central West End has guest rooms decorated with period furnishings. A resortlike feel pervades the establishment, which has a five-screen movie theater, spa and salon, courtyard with an outdoor pool and 24-hour concierge.

250 rooms. High-speed Internet access. Four restaurants, five bars. Fitness center. Pool. Spa. Business center. $$

★★★★The Ritz-Carlton, St. Louis

100 Carondelet Plaza, Clayton, 314-863-6300, 800-241-3333; www.ritzcarlton.com

Nestled in the upscale Clayton neighborhood, this sophisticated hotel is conveniently located near the city's business district as well as bustling restaurants and cultural landmarks. The rooms are spacious and polished with plush furnishings, large marble bathrooms and private balconies offering views of the city skyline. A comprehensive fitness center includes lap and hydrotherapy pools, a steam room and sauna. The Wine Room is a unique spot for sampling one of the hotel's more than 7,000 bottles.

301 rooms. Wireless Internet access. Two restaurants, bar. Airport transportation available. Fitness center. Pool, whirlpool. Business center. Pets accepted. $$$$

★★★Seven Gables Inn

26 N. Meramec Ave., Clayton, 314-863-8400, 800-433-6590; www.sevengablesinn.com

Surrounded by upscale shops, galleries and restaurants, this inn offers a blend of old-world charm and modern conveniences. The inn was inspired by sketches in Nathaniel Hawthorne's novel *The House of Seven Gables*.

32 rooms. Complimentary continental breakfast. Restaurant, bar. Airport transportation available. $

WHERE TO EAT

★★★The Grill
100 Carondelet Plaza, Clayton, 314-863-6300, 800-241-3333; www.ritzcarlton.com

Located in the Ritz-Carlton, St. Louis hotel, this upscale dining room serves up contemporary interpretations of American classics. The décor includes extensive mahogany paneling and woodwork, overstuffed leather banquettes, dramatic lighting and a marble fireplace. Nightly entertainment is featured (piano or acoustic guitar), and on weekends, there's live music (jazz, blues or swing) in the lounge.

American menu. Dinner. Bar. Business casual attire. Reservations recommended. Valet parking. $$$

★★★★Tony's
410 Market St., St.Louis, 314-231-7007; www.tonysstlouis.com

Italian food may bring to mind images of pasta with red sauce, but at Tony's, you'll find a menu of authentic Italian fare prepared with a measured and sophisticated hand. Expect appetizers like smoked salmon with mascarpone cheese and asparagus and Belgian endive, and entrées like tenderloin of beef with foie gras in a port wine demi-glaze. The room has an urban, postmodern style with sleek, low lighting; linen-topped tables; and glossy, wood-paneled walls. The chef's tasting menu is a nice choice for gourmands with healthy appetites.

Italian menu. Dinner. Closed Sunday; also first week of January and first week of July. Bar. Jacket required. Reservations recommended. Valet parking. $$$

★
★
★
★
★

OHIO

CINCINNATI

LOCATED IN THE SOUTHERN CLIMES OF OHIO, CINCINNATI MIXES BIG BUSIness with old money, thereby attracting a well-shod selection of upscale antique shops.

WHERE TO SHOP

Duck Creek Antique Mall
3715 Madison Road, Cincinnati,
513-321-0900;
www.duckcreekantiquemall.com
Housed in a restored former bakery, this two-level shop features an outstanding selection of estate jewelry, Rookwood pottery, Americana and European porcelain and ceramics. Monday-Saturday 10 a.m.-5 p.m., Sunday noon-5 p.m.

Federation Antiques
2124 Madison Road, Cincinnati,
513-321-2671;
www.federationantiques.com
This stately Cincinnati shop stocks a fine assortment of English and American period furniture (with rare exception, nothing later than 1840 is offered for sale). There's also a carefully edited selection of ceramics, including Chinese export wares of the late 18th and 19th centuries, Staffordshire figures and other pieces from makers like Derby and Worcester. Tuesday-Saturday 10 a.m.-5 p.m.; closed Sunday-Monday.

Greg's Antiques
1404 Main St., Cincinnati,
513-241-5487;
www.gregsantiques.com
If you're lucky enough to catch Greg while he's in town, you'll find his Main Street shop stocked with a wonderful assortment of Victorian wrought iron and stone furnishings for the garden, as well as some interior items, including chandeliers and mantles. You can also find his wares at shows across the Midwest and South; details at the Web site. By appointment only.

Main Auction Galleries
137 W. Fourth St., Cincinnati,
513-621-1280;
www.mainauctiongalleries.com
Generations of Cincinnati residents have furnished their homes or started collections with purchases from this 126-year-old auction gallery. Sales take place every Tuesday with lots posted on the gallery's Web site the week prior. Though you never know what you'll find, if past auctions are any indication, there's always a plentiful stock of china, porce-

lain, American and European furniture and artwork.

Wooden Nickel Antiques

1400–1414 Central Parkway,
Cincinnati, 513-241-2985;
www.woodennickelantiques.net

This 32-year-old Cincinnati staple specializes in heavy, ornate American and European furniture from 1830 to 1900. There's also a good assortment of architectural salvage (antique bars are a common find) and iron, bronze, terracotta, cast stone and marble garden items. Monday-Saturday 10 a.m.-5 p.m.; closed Sunday.

WHERE TO STAY

★★★★The Cincinnatian Hotel

601 Vine St., Cincinnati,
513-381-3000, 800-942-9000;
www.cincinnatianhotel.com

Open since 1882, the Cincinnatian was one of the first hotels in the world to have elevators and incandescent lighting and now is listed on the National Register of Historic Places. The accommodations are lovingly maintained and incorporate modern technology, like high-speed Internet access. Furnishings lean toward the contemporary, while some rooms feature balconies and fireplaces. The eight-story atrium of the Cricket Lounge serves afternoon tea and evening cocktails. The fine dining and impeccable service at the Palace Restaurant make it one of the top tables in town.

146 rooms. High-speed Internet access. Restaurant, bar. Fitness center. $$

WHERE TO EAT

★★★★Jean-Robert at Pigall's

127 W. Fourth St., Cincinnati,
513-721-1345; www.pigalls.com

Jean-Robert at Pigall's serves the sort of inventive, high-quality food that has fans, who pay $75 for three courses, feel as though they've scored a bargain. Chef Jean-Robert de Cavel reinvigorated the hoary Pigall's with fresh, sophisticated décor and a lively new menu. Changing to reflect the season, Pigall's French cuisine is typified by cauliflower vichyssoise with truffles, crab and melon salad with caviar and bacon-wrapped guinea fowl. The chef engenders goodwill by frequently issuing surprise plates on the house.

French menu. Dinner. Closed Sunday-Monday. Bar. Casual attire. Reservations recommended. Valet parking. $$

★★★Precinct

311 Delta Ave., Cincinnati,
513-321-5454, 877-321-5454;
www.jeffruby.com/preinct.html

This restaurant, housed in a former police precinct that was used from the 1900s to the 1940s, offers steakhouse classics—from aged Angus beef to the perfect rib eye—broiled to perfection and seasoned with a secret spice mix. At night, the exterior of this historic building is bathed in neon light. Dishes such as steak Diane, fettuccine

CINCINNATI

★

★

★

★

★

and bananas Foster are prepared tableside.

American menu. Dinner. Bar. Business casual attire. Reservations recommended. Valet parking. **$$$$**

★★★The Phoenix
812 Race St., Cincinnati,
513-721-8901; www.thephx.com
Built in 1893, this traditional restaurant serves dinner in the wood-paneled President's Room, while the rest of the historic building, which is adorned with two elegant chandeliers, is used for weddings or special events. The menu features steaks and other classics like the grilled pork chop with walnut stuffing and sage buerre blanc.

American menu. Dinner. Closed Sunday-Tuesday. Bar. Business casual attire. Reservations recommended. Valet parking. **$$$**

54

THE NORTHEAST

TRAVELING FROM THE ESTABLISHED SHOPS IN BOSTON'S distinct neighborhoods toward Portland, Maine, you can detour from Interstate 95 and experience a scenic journey along Route 1 north to Wells. Wind your way past clam and lobster shacks and retro motels to explore some of the region's best antique outposts: You'll find everything from funky antique malls to top-tier shops featuring rare pieces picked up in Marseille and Parisian flea markets. And be sure to veer off to explore such favorite finds as Old House Parts in Kennebunk, Maine, with its unparalleled selection of antique doorknobs, windows and other salvage finds. Or head for the fall foliage in Vermont and tour old barns brimming with vintage farm tools, Vaseline glass and myriad chairs piled up by the dozen. If your trip allows a few days in New England, make time for a stop at the thrice-annual Brimfield antique market near Sturbridge, Massachusetts, where you will encounter acre after acre of wonderful treasures paired with a state fair–like feeling. Grab a turkey sandwich piled high on a roll with cranberry sauce—it's a specialty—find a picnic table and watch the colorful goings-on as you savor your delicious finds. Wrap up a weekend in the area by heading west to Connecticut for some of the most picturesque towns boasting antiques stores with pricey, museum-worthy articles—all within close proximity of charming inns and classic restaurants!

CONNECTICUT

GREENWICH

ONE OF THE STATE'S MOST TALKED-ABOUT TOWNS, GREENWICH HAS long been home to hedge fund barons, ladies who lunch and other moneyed folk. Less than 30 miles from New York City, take at least an afternoon to stroll Greenwich's leafy 18th-century streets and visit the numerous antique outposts that dot the byways off the town's glittering main drag.

WHERE TO SHOP

Estate Treasures
1162 E. Putnam Ave. (Post Road), Greenwich, 203-637-4200;
www.estatetreasures.com
This charming shop sells a variety of antique china, silver, furniture and reproductions. Look for items like a Chinese export dinnerware set and full silver tea service in addition to reproduction furniture imported from England, Italy and Holland. Estate Treasures can also provide custom furniture-making services for that special nook in your home. Monday-Saturday 10 a.m.-5:30 p.m.; Sunday noon-5:30 p.m.

Guild Antiques
384 Greenwich Ave., Greenwich, 203-869-0828;
www.guildantiques.com
Those hunting for 18th- and 19th-century English furniture, Chinese export porcelain, and other antique accessories undoubtedly will be wooed by Guild Antiques.

Look for treasures, including a pair of large Chinese cinnabar lamps, an English brass coal bucket (could work wonderfully for storing towels) and an English oak and brass umbrella stand. Call for hours or for an appointment.

Quester Gallery
119 Rowayton Ave., Rowayton, 203-523-0250;
www.questergallery.com
The gallery in this cozy oceanfront town specializes in 18th-, 19th- and 20th-century marine paintings from such notables as James E. Buttersworth and Montague Dawson and prides itself on its collection of high-end marine art and antiques. Look for the wonderfully simple and sublime pine sailor's chests that are painted in pale colors and feature intricate rope detailing. Open Monday-Saturday 10 a.m.-6 p.m. or by appointment.

Rue Faubourg St. Honoré

44 Putnam Ave., Greenwich,
203-869-7139

Rue Faubourg St. Honoré offers fine home-furnishing antiques, including lighting fixtures and fireplace accents. Pick up a pair of pristine fireplace andirons to add punch to your living room. Open Monday-Saturday 9:30 a.m.-5-p.m.

WHERE TO STAY

★★★De La Mar on Greenwich Harbor

500 Steamboat Road, Greenwich,
203-661-9800, 866-335-2627;
www.thedelamar.com

The award-winning De La Mar looks more like a Lake Como mansion than an old Connecticut retreat. Its sprawling cream-colored façade hides an interior rich with original artwork, sparkling chandeliers, ornate sconces and a plethora of marble. Overlooking the Greenwich Marina, the property has 82 rooms filled with up-to-date electronics, luxe Italian linens and cast-iron tubs. Even pooches get pampered here—the resort's "sophisticated pet" program includes a doggie bed, a personalized ID tag, food and water bowls and a Pet Services menu.

82 rooms. Wireless Internet access. Restaurant, bar. Fitness center. Spa. $$$

★★★Homestead Inn

420 Field Point Road, Greenwich,
203-869-7500;
www.homesteadinn.com

The rooms at the Homestead Inn aren't called rooms—they're called "chambers." And the lodging at this renovated 1799 inn is anything but average: second- and third-floor suites have imported furniture, Frette linens, original artwork and heated bathroom floors. Renovated by Greenwich hoteliers Thomas and Theresa Henkelmann, the inn—and its accompanying restaurant—is a study in old-school sumptuous elegance.

18 rooms. Closed two weeks in March. Children over 12 only. Restaurant, bar. $$$$

WHERE TO EAT

★★★Jean-Louis

61 Lewis St., Greenwich,
203-622-8450;
www.restaurantjeanlouis.com

Sophisticated and elegant with professional service to match, this cozy restaurant has a menu grounded in the precision of French Classicism. Its décor is decidedly Parisian—the serving china and candle lamps were all custom-made in France. The chef works directly with local farmers to acquire the freshest ingredients and, in addition to the á la carte menu, the restaurant offers tastings, petit tastings and vegetarian and vegan menus.

French menu. Lunch (Monday-Friday), dinner. Closed Sunday;

GREENWICH

★
★
★
★
★

also first two weeks of August. Business casual attire. Reservations recommended. $$$

★★★L'Escale
500 Steamboat Road, Greenwich, 203-661-4600;
www.lescalerestaurant.com

This French-Mediterranean restaurant earns its stars by re-creating the Mediterranean on the North Atlantic shore, importing a stone fireplace and terra-cotta floors to warm the dining room and setting up light-filtering thatched bamboo to shade the patio. The menu from François Kwaku-Dongo includes a salad of caramelized leeks and chanterelles, apple- and prune-paired foie gras, and crispy duck breast. The eatery has become quite a gathering place for locals and travelers, and it's no wonder—L'Escale allows guests to sail to dinner and tie up their yachts at its waterfront dock.

French, Mediterranean menu. Breakfast, lunch, dinner, Sunday brunch. Bar. Business casual attire. Reservations recommended. Valet parking. Outdoor seating. $$$

★★★Thomas Henkelmann
420 Field Point Road, Greenwich, 203-869-7500;
www.homesteadinn.com

Located in the historic Homestead Inn, this fine dining restaurant featuring the cuisine of chef/owner and namesake Thomas Henkelmann provides a cozy setting for enjoying inventive dishes based around seasonal ingredients. German- and Geneva-trained Henkelmann serves up multiple courses that rely on French influences—pâté of duck with truffles and pistachios, goat cheese beignet and oven baked loin of rabbit, to name a few. Enjoy the fine cuisine among the comforts of home as the dining rooms feature fireplaces, upholstered chairs, exposed beams and upscale country décor.

French menu. Breakfast, lunch, dinner. Closed Sunday; also two weeks in March. Bar. Jacket required. Reservations recommended. Valet parking. $$$$

58

THE NORTHEAST

MAINE

KENNEBUNK & KENNEBUNKPORT

THESE QUINTESSENTIAL AMERICAN COASTAL COMMUNITIES ARE LOADED with shopping, hotels and fine restaurants, serving as a terrific base from which to set out and explore southern Maine's myriad antique offerings, many of which are located along Route 1. Note that many of these emporia are only open in season, from May through Thanksgiving, due to Maine's unpredictable winter weather.

WHERE TO SHOP

Americana Workshop
111 York St., Kennebunk,
207-985-8356, 877-619-0903;
www.americanaworkshop.com
At this rustic former barn, you'll find a wide selection of country antiques, antique documents, paintings, carvings and decorative signs—perfect for repurposing into contemporary interior décor. The emphasis here is on the Colonial period (think decoys and restored oak furniture). Monday-Saturday 10 a.m.-5 p.m., Sunday noon-5 p.m.

Antiques on Nine
81 Western Ave., Kennebunk,
207-967-0626
Over 12,000 square feet of show space accommodates the vast collection of English, Continental and American furniture at Antiques on Nine. Also here

are decorative accessories, lighting, quilts, garden ornaments . . . You can practically decorate your entire house—inside and out—at this far-reaching emporium. Winter: Thursday-Saturday 10 a.m.-5 p.m. Call for summer hours.

Arundel Antiques
1713 Portland Road (Route 1 at Log Cabin Road), Arundel,
207-985-7965
This Route 1 must-see stocks everything from paintings to pottery. During the peak summer/fall season (May-November), there's a bonus: an outdoor flea market on the grounds. As many as 100 dealers on the weekends, fewer on weekdays, sell everything from secondhand paperbacks to fine Victorian furniture. Daily 10 a.m. to 5 p.m. Late May to mid-October: Monday-Friday 10 a.m.-5 p.m., Saturday-Sunday 8 a.m.-6 p.m.; mid-October to late May: daily 10 a.m.-5 p.m.

Old House Parts

1 Trackside Drive, Kennebunk, 207-985-1999; www.oldhouseparts.com

You've hit a jackpot at this sprawling 1872 warehouse which stocks an endless array of vintage hardware, doors, windows, moldings, fireplaces and everything else to gussy up your retro-leaning home. With an emphasis on finds from the 1730s to 1930s, Old House Parts boasts a collection of big stuff but doesn't leave out the little things. You'll find doorknobs, knockers, hinges, latches, mantles, molding and plenty of other miscellanny. Monday-Saturday 9 a.m.-5 p.m., Sunday 11 a.m.-5 p.m.

WHERE TO STAY

★★★The Kennebunkport Inn

1 Dock Square, Kennebunkport, 207-967-2621, 800-248-2621; www.kennebunkportinn.com

Conveniently located in the heart of the historic seaport town of Kennebunkport, this inn is an easy walk to the harbor and all the shops and galleries of Dock Square. This Victorian mansion, built by a wealthy tea and coffee merchant in 1899, was renovated into an inn in 1926. Guest rooms feature period antiques and reproductions, elegant fabrics and floral carpeting. Many of the beds are high four-posters—perfect for Victoriana buffs.

49 rooms. Wireless Internet access. Complimentary conti-

nental breakfast. Restaurant, bar. Pool. Spa. $$$

★★★★The White Barn Inn & Spa

37 Beach Ave., Kennebunkport, 207-967-2321; www.whitebarninn.com

This cluster of cottages, restored barns and a circa-1860s house make up the White Barn Inn, a quaint spot that delivers quiet luxury on the coast. The charming rooms and suites are decorated with antiques and feature wood-burning fireplaces, whirlpool tubs and flat-screen TVs with DVD and CD players. Simple pleasures include relaxing by the stone swimming pool, riding a bike along the coast, experiencing a spa treatment and having afternoon tea by the fire in the comfortable sitting room. The inn has one of the region's most acclaimed restaurants, which serves New England cuisine in a rustic, candlelit setting.

27 rooms. Wireless Internet access. Complimentary continental breakfast. Restaurant, bar. Pool. Spa. $$$$

WHERE TO EAT

★★★Stripers

131-133 Ocean Ave., Kennebunkport, 207-967-5333; www.thebreakwaterinn.com

With an appealing menu, a lovely setting and great attention to each detail, Stripers offers a relaxed fine-dining experience. The décor is that of a contemporary seaside cottage, with steel-rimmed table-tops, a see-through aquarium wall that divides the entry from the main dining room and views of the river. The seafood cuisine includes options such as local Kennenunkport oysters, farm-raised stiped bass, halibut, and scallops.

Seafood menu. Dinner, brunch. Bar. Business casual attire. Reservations recommended. Valet parking. Outdoor seating. **$$$**

★★★★★The White Barn Inn Restaurant

37 Beach Ave., Kennebunkport, 207-967-2321;
www.whitebarninn.com

A New England classic, this charming candlelit space inside the White Barn Inn is filled with fresh flowers and white linen-topped tables. Chef Jonathan Cartwright creates delicious regional dishes expertly accented with a European flair. The four-course prix fixe menu changes weekly, highlighting seafood from Maine's waters as well as native game and poultry. The vast wine selection perfectly complements the cuisine, and a rolling cheese cart offers some of the best local artisans' products.

American menu. Dinner. Closed three weeks in January. Bar. Jacket required. Reservations recommended. Valet parking. **$$$$**

PORTLAND

FUN AND FUNKY, PORTLAND HAS A WONDERFUL RANGE OF ATTRACTIONS—
from the historic Old Port neighborhood, former sea captains' mansions and a bustling waterfront to modern, world-class restaurants and antique shops filled with maritime relics as well as classic American furnishings.

WHERE TO SHOP

F. Barrie Freeman Antiques & Rare Books

Quaker Point Road, West Bath, 207-442-8452

F. Barrie Freeman specializes in New England decorative arts prior to 1840, including (but not limited to) glass, ceramics, metals, wood, textiles and fine arts, plus it has a massive collection of rare old books and maps. Call for hours or for an appointment.

Geraldine Wolf Antiques & Estate Jewelry

26 Milk St., Portland, 207-774-8994

You'll find the ultimate in antique, estate and costume jewelry and sterling silver flatware at Geraldine Wolf Antiques. Keep your eyes peeled for interesting and unexpected silver pieces like the set of sterling chargers found on a recent visit. Your dinner parties

★

★

★

★

might never be the same again. By appointment only.

Heller Washam Antiques
1235 Congress St., Portland,
207-773-8288

Heller Washam provides visitors a visually enticing journey through 18th- and early 19th-century American furniture, accessories, paintings, folk art, textiles and garden furnishings. Past visits have uncovered everything from a pair of antique globes to a tall maple Chippendale chest. By appointment only.

JL'Antiquaire Antiques & Decoration
94 Neal St., Portland,
207-780-0181;
www.antiquaireusa.com

Here you'll find "all things French"—antique and decorative accessories from the 18th and 19th centuries, including furniture, quilts, textiles, pottery and garden pieces. Check out the selection of rustic garden furniture and pots as well as the hand-blown vintage vinegar bottles; they make for pretty vases on any kitchen table. By appointment only.

Nelson Rarities
2 Monument Square, Portland,
207-775-3150, 800-882-3150;
www.nelsonrarities.com

If you're thinking about popping the question, Nelson Rarities is the place to head; it specializes in antique and estate jewelry from the Art Deco, Art Nouveau and Victorian periods, as well as vintage engagement rings. There's something for every jewelry lover here, from the colorful and ornate to the more subdued and simple. You'll find engagement rings and estate pieces spanning the ages and the globe. By appointment only.

WHERE TO STAY

★★★Portland Harbor Hotel
468 Fore St., Portland,
207-775-9090, 888-798-9090;
www.portlandharborhotel.com

Located in the Old Port district of downtown Portland, a fully restored area of Victorian buildings now flourishes with restaurants, shops and galleries, just a block from the waterfront. This hotel exudes European style and charm and the amenities are first-rate. An enclosed garden patio with a fountain is just off the lobby dining room. Guest rooms feature toile spreads, custom mattresses with fine linens, feather pillows and duvets and a two-level desk with a leather chair.

97 rooms. Wireless Internet access. Restaurant, bar. Airport transportation available. Fitness center. $$

★★★Portland Regency Hotel & Spa
20 Milk St., Portland,
207-774-4200, 800-727-3436;
www.theregency.com

This small, European-style hotel is located in Portland's Old Port waterfront district, surrounded by galleries, shops and restaurants.

★

★

★

★

★

A circular brick driveway leads guests to the historic red brick building, which was built in 1895. The lobby and public rooms hold true to the hotel's heritage with mahogany woodwork, Victorian furnishings and a "map room" with burgundy leather chairs. The period décor in the guest rooms includes two- or four-poster beds and antique or reproduction dressers, tables and desks. The spa offers a complete selection of treatments to help you relax after a day digging for vintage treasures.

95 rooms. Wireless Internet access. Restaurant, bar. Airport transportation available. Fitness center. Spa. **$$**

★★★Black Point Inn
510 Black Point Road, Scarborough, 207-883-2500; www.blackpointinn.com

This seaside resort, dating from 1878, is located on a hill at the tip of Prout's Neck, with the natural rugged beauty of the Maine coast on three sides. Each guest room has period wallpaper and both porcelain and crystal lamps, and many of the antiques are original to the inn. Enjoy the geothermally heated pool during the warmer months and miles of beaches year-round.

25 rooms. Restaurant, bar. Fitness center. Tennis. Golf. Beach. Pool. Airport transportation available. **$$$**

WHERE TO EAT

★★★Back Bay Grill
65 Portland St., Portland, 207-772-8833; www.backbaygrill.com

Located in downtown Portland in a restored pharmacy (1888), this local favorite offers innovative cuisine and an intimate dining room while the pressed-tin ceiling adds to the ambience of the cozy rooms. The daily menu features the freshest locally sourced foods and emphasizes high-quality ingredients. Special dinners are offered with a prix fixe menu (wine tastings, wine dinners, lobster evenings).

International menu. Dinner. Closed Sunday. Bar. Business casual attire. Reservations recommended. **$$$**

★★★Street & Co.
33 Wharf St., Portland, 207-775-0887

Located in the Old Port District on a cobblestone street, this 19th-century building, formerly a fish warehouse, has an upscale rustic look with its exposed bricks, original plank hardwood flooring and beamed ceilings. A fully open kitchen is opposite the center dining room, where large windows open to the street. Only seafood is served, along with the freshest seasonal organic produce.

Seafood menu. Dinner. Bar. Casual attire. Reservations recommended. Outdoor seating. **$$$**

PORTLAND

★

★

★

★

WELLS

HEAD SOUTH FROM KENNEBUNK TO EXPLORE THIS BUSTLING COASTAL community with its myriad motels, clam shacks and roadside antique shops and malls filled with bric-a-brac for all tastes.

WHERE TO SHOP

The Farm
294 Mildram Road, Wells,
207-985-2656;
www.thefarmantiques.com

This very elegant emporium specializes in fine English period furniture of the 17th, 18th and 19th centuries and a far-reaching selection of accessories to go with it. Standouts spotted on a recent visit include a pair of English Regency hall chairs circa 1815 and a colorful Ming Dynasty glazed pottery tomb figure. May to mid-June and Labor Day-Christmas: Friday-Sunday 10 a.m.-4 p.m. or by appointment; mid-June to Labor Day: Thursday-Tuesday 10 a.m.-4 p.m; winter: by appointment only; April: closed.

Macdougall-Gionet Antiques & Associates
2104 Post Road (Route 1), Wells,
207-646-3531;
www.macdougall-gionet.com

Macdougall-Gionet Antiques specializes in American furniture, as well as porcelain, metal ware, glass, folk art, toys and scrimshaw. If you seek outstanding American painted pieces—like a mustard-colored dressing table or a grain-painted corner cabinet—you won't want to pass by Macdougall-Gionet's beautifully restored,

bright red barn shop without stopping to peruse the collection. Tuesday-Sunday 10 a.m.-5 p.m.; closed Monday.

R. Jorgensen Antiques
502 Post Road (Route 1), Wells,
207-646-9444;
www.rjorgensen.com

Renowned for traditional antiques from the Federal, Sheraton, Hepplewhite, Chippendale and Queen Anne periods, this well-respected dealer offers a vast collection. You'll find everything from barometers to gilt-framed mirrors, all housed in two buildings on a spectacular New England National Historic Registered property dating from the late 17th century. Monday-Saturday 10 a.m.-5 p.m., Sunday noon-5 p.m.

Reeds Antiques & Collectibles
1773 Post Road (Route 1), Wells,
207-646-8010;
www.reedsantiques.com

This 4,000-square-foot shop houses some 100-odd dealers selling antiques and collectibles that range from Meissen to Mickey Mouse. The numerous showcases are filled with tiny treasures, including a wonderful array of pottery and glassware as well as vignettes that incorporate everything from dining tables to old telephones. Daily 10 a.m.-5 p.m.

THE NORTHEAST

★
★
★
★

WISCASSET

A MUST-VISIT SPOT FOR ANTIQUE LOVERS WITH ENDLESS EMPORIA FOR browsing and buying, Wiscasset is a scenic, one-hour drive along the coast northeast from Portland. Be sure to visit www.shopwiscasset antiques.com for a complete listing of dealers.

WHERE TO SHOP

Avalon Antiques Market
536 Bath Road (Route 1),
Wiscasset, 207-882-4029;
www.avalonantiquesmarket.com
This 10,000-square-foot shop has more than 100 dealers who sell a wide range of goods from pottery and glass to fine china. Avalon may have you heading home with blue-and-white porcelain, an oversized foo dog to place in the loo or frisky French teapots. June 1-Labor Day: daily 9 a.m.-7 p.m.; Labor Day-May: daily 9 a.m.-5 p.m.

Blythe House Antiques
161 Main St. (Route 1),
Wiscasset, 207-882-1280;
www.blythehouseantiques.com
Dating from 1799, this charming country house hosts the wares of some 17 dealers who sell everything from nautical finds to folk art and photography. Painted floor cloths and rustic objects (like the miniature log cabin found on a recent trip) make for interesting conversation pieces. April-November: daily 10 a.m.-5 p.m.

Louwers Antiques
54D Water St., Wiscasset,
207-882-6567, 207-882-7774;
www.louwersantiques.com
This charming shop owned by the delightful Dennis and Natalie Louwers specializes in artwork from fine to folk in addition to myriad metal ware items in tin, pewter, copper and bronze. May-October: daily 10 a.m.-5 p.m.; November-April: "by chance" or by appointment.

65

WELLS/WISCASSET

BOSTON

IT'S NO SURPRISE THAT ONE OF AMERICA'S OLDEST CITIES BOASTS SOME of its most spectacular antiques. Boston serves up shops that offer everything from the sophisticated and museum-quality to the retro kitsch and downright kooky. Most stores are clustered around quaint Charles Street, which also has plenty of cafés and restaurants to supply sustenance for serious shoppers.

WHERE TO SHOP

Alberts-Langdon, Inc.
126 Charles St., Boston,
617-523-5954;
www.alberts-langdon.com
If you're a fan of Asian antiques, beeline it to elegant Alberts-Langdon, Inc. in the heart of Beacon Hill, where you will unearth such treasures as a Qing Dynasty bronze censer or an olive glazed melon ewer. Tuesday-Friday 11 a.m.-5:00 p.m., Saturday noon-4:00 p.m.; also by appointment; closed Sunday.

Autrefois Antiques
130 Harvard St., Brookline,
617-566-0113, 866-966-0113;
www.autrefoisantiques.com
Some 15 minutes outside of downtown Boston in leafy Brookline, Autrefois Antiques offers an ever-changing selection of collectibles ranging from Venetian lanterns to 19th-century marble busts and French grain buckets. Tuesday-Thursday, Saturday 11 a.m.-6

p.m., Friday, Sunday 11 a.m.-4 p.m.

Brodney Antiques & Jewelry
145 Newbury St., Boston,
617-536-0500;
www.brodney.com
Open since 1939, Brodney sells everything from estate jewelry to porcelain and Orientalia. Fine estate jewelry is one specialty at this downtown establishment; you might also go home with a marble bust of William Shakespeare or a French malachite-and-brass clock. Monday-Saturday 10 a.m.-6 p.m.; closed Sunday.

Cadia Vintage
148 Salem St., Boston,
617-742-1203;
www.cadiavintage.com
Fun and funky describe the finds at the always-magical (albeit tiny) Cadia, where you're likely to unearth everything from vintage jewelry to a stash of retro *Playboy* magazines or antique china and

66

THE NORTHEAST

porcelain. Located in Boston's North End, with close access to dozens of Italian eateries, this "purveyor of kitsch" boasts new merchandise on a daily basis. Saturday-Sunday, noon-5 p.m.; closed Monday-Friday.

Devonia Antiques for Dining
43 Charles St., Boston,
617-523-8313;
www.devonia-antiques.com

This über-specialized Beacon Hill shop with proximity to other antique stores features a wide array of antiques for dining: Colorful English and American porcelain and stemware selections fill the shelves. You'll find all sorts of hand-blown glass and hand-painted china options, including a set of plates with sea creatures swimming about without a care in the world. Devonia even offers a wedding registry for brides looking to fulfill their "something old." Monday-Saturday 11 a.m.-5 p.m., Sunday noon-5 p.m.

Light Power
59 Wareham St., Boston,
617-423-9790;
www.genuineantiquelighting.com

As the name implies, this 3,000-square-foot showroom displays more than 250 antique chandeliers, lights and sconces. A vintage lighting paradise, Light Power offers something for every taste, from simple schoolhouse fixtures to ornate chandeliers and Moravian stars. Saturday 10 a.m.-5 p.m.; Tuesday-Friday by appointment; closed Sunday-Monday.

Small Pleasures
142 Newbury St., Boston,
617-267-7371;
www.small-pleasures.com

A wonderful assortment of vintage jewelry can be found at this Back Bay staple (there's also a branch downtown on State Street). You won't find furniture here, but you will find a range of antiques from glittering diamond rings and cameos to gold Victorian necklaces. Monday-Saturday 11 a.m.-6 p.m.; closed Sunday.

WHERE TO STAY

★★★★Boston Harbor Hotel
70 Rowes Wharf, Boston,
617-439-7000, 800-752-7077;
www.bhh.com

Occupying an idyllic waterfront location, this quietly luxurious, hotel is situated across from Boston's financial district along a stretch of land that was once dominated by an elevated highway but now is poised to become the new Rose Kennedy Greenway. The staff at this full-service property take care of every possible need. Rooms and suites are beautifully appointed in rich colors, and it's worth paying extra for a room with a view. In summer, live music, dancing and a movie night take place on the outdoor patio. The hotel's Meritage restaurant is the domain of chef Daniel Bruce, who dreams up seasonal dishes based on the freshest local ingredients and pairs them with imaginative wines by the glass or bottle from around the world. The Rowes

BOSTON

★
★
★
★
★

Wharf water taxi whisks guests straight to the airport, avoiding Boston's notorious traffic.

230 rooms. High-speed Internet access. Three restaurants, two bars. Airport transportation available. **$$$$**

★★★The Eliot Hotel

370 Commonwealth Ave., Boston, 617-267-1607, 800-443-5468; www.eliothotel. com

This 95-room, European-style boutique hotel is located just off the Mass Turnpike in the Back Bay, convenient to shopping, entertainment and cultural sites. A quiet elegance pervades the lobby, and most of the newly renovated accommodations are spacious suites with pull-out sofas, French bedroom doors, Italian marble baths and down comforters. The Eliot is also home to the critically acclaimed Clio and Uni restaurants, which serve contemporary French-American and Japanese cuisine, respectively.

95 rooms. Wireless Internet access. Restaurant, bar. **$$$**

★★★★★Four Seasons Hotel Boston

200 Boylston St., Boston, 617-338-4400, 800-330-3442; www.fourseasons.com

This hotel offers its guests a prime location overlooking the Public Garden and Boston Common. The recently renovated contemporary lobby, complete with a dramatic yellow marble and black granite floor, gleams. Antiques, fine art, sumptuous fabrics, period furniture and sleek technology, such as flat-screen televisions and wireless Internet access, bring the guest rooms and suites up-to-date, while impeccable and attentive service heightens the experience. The Bristol Lounge is where Boston's power players come to celebrate their successes, or where you can toast your purchases.

273 rooms. Wireless Internet access. Two restaurants, two bars. Airport transportation available. **$$$$**

★★★Hyatt Regency Boston Financial District

1 Avenue de Lafayette, Boston, 617-912-1234, 800-233-1234; www.hyatt.com

When Hyatt took over this former Swisshôtel, it wisely kept much of the elegant décor (as well as its discounted weekend packages). The hotel sits a block off Boston Common at the intersection of the financial and theater districts. Public areas suggest old-world refinement with antique furniture, marble floors and Waterford crystal chandeliers. Many upper-level corner suites have city views, and the trendy restaurants and nightclubs of the Ladder District are just a few steps away.

498 rooms. Wireless Internet access. Restaurant, bar. **$$$**

THE NORTHEAST

★★★Nine Zero Hotel
90 Tremont St., Boston,
617-772-5800, 866-646-3937;
www.ninezero.com

When Kimpton bought out this downtown boutique hotel last year, Nine Zero lost some of its independent character. The chain has, however, done an admirable job of sprucing up the property's rooms and introducing a menu of quirky amenities. The lobby and suites are a modern mix of nickel, chrome, stainless steel and glass, and the property is completely wired with Internet access, stereo sound systems and flat-screen TVs. Luxe trappings include Frette linens, goose down comforters and pillows, and local beauty guru Mario Russo's bath products.
189 rooms. Wireless Internet access. Restaurant, bar. $$$

★★★Omni Parker House
60 School St., Boston,
617-227-8600, 800-843-6664;
www.omnihotels.com

The Parker House, which invented its eponymous dinner rolls and Boston cream pie, is the oldest continuously operating hotel in the United States. The plush lobby and dining room, which date from just before World War I, are good examples of Edwardian excess. The guest rooms are up to modern standards, as are the sleek fitness room and private, convenient business center.
551 rooms. High-speed Internet access. Restaurant, bar. Business center. $$$

★★★★The Ritz-Carlton, Boston Common
10 Avery St., Boston,
617-574-7100, 800-241-3333;
www.ritzcarlton.com

In a town known for its historic buildings, this contemporary hotel is a fresh and stylish alternative. Located near the city's theater district and overlooking the country's oldest public space, the Ritz-Carlton, Boston Common is convenient for business and leisure travelers alike. The guest rooms and suites have a distinctly serene feel with muted tones and polished woods. After a night of indulgence, guests often head to the massive Sports Club/LA, the city's most exclusive health club.
193 rooms. High-speed Internet access. Restaurant, bar. Pets accepted. $$$$

★★★★Taj Boston
15 Arlington St., Boston,
617-536-5700, 877-482-5267;
www.tajhotels.com

A 1920s landmark hotel perched at the end of Newbury Street and across from the Public Garden, this hotel seduces with its "wedding cake" ceiling details, elaborate moldings, lavish carpets and graceful marble staircases. The guest rooms are heavenly with feather beds, soft robes, Molton Brown amenities and luxe marble bathrooms (suites include wood-burning fireplaces with butler service). Even the hotel's oldest tradition of proper afternoon tea is still going strong.
273 rooms. High-speed Internet access. Restaurant, two bars. $$$$

69

BOSTON

★
★
★
★

★★★★XV Beacon

15 Beacon St., Boston,
617-670-1500, 877-982-2226;
www.xvbeacon.com

This turn-of-the-century Beaux Arts building on Beacon Hill belies the sleek décor found within. Original artwork commissioned specifically for the hotel by well-known artists fills the walls. The eclectic guest rooms and suites are decorated in a palette of chocolate brown, black and cream. Rooms feature canopy beds with luxurious Italian linens and gas fireplaces covered in cool stainless steel. Completed in crisp white with simple fixtures, the bathrooms are a modernist's dream. A new steakhouse called Mooo occupies the hotel's ground floor.

63 rooms. High-speed Internet access. Restaurant, bar. Airport transportation available. Fitness center. Pets accepted. **$$$$**

WHERE TO EAT

★★★★Aujourd'hui

200 Boylston St., Boston,
617-338-4400, 617-423-0154;
www.fourseasons.com

With floor-to-ceiling windows overlooking Boston's Public Garden, Aujourd'hui is a beautiful spot for lunch or an intimate dinner. Tables are set with Italian damask linens and decorated with antique plates and fresh flowers. The kitchen aims to please with an innovative selection of seasonal modern French fare prepared with regional ingredients. The predominantly American wine list complements the delicious food. A lighter menu of more nutritional choices is also available.

French menu. Dinner, Sunday brunch. Bar. Children's menu. Business casual attire. Reservations recommended. Valet parking. **$$$**

★★★★Clio

370 Commonwealth Ave.,
Boston, 617-536-7200;
www.cliorestaurant.com

Chef/owner Ken Oringer treats ingredients like notes in a melody—each one complements the next, and the result is a culinary symphony. Fresh fish plays a big role on the menu, and for those who prefer their seafood raw, Clio has a separate sashimi bar, Uni, which features a pricey selection of rare fish from around the world. Each meal begins with Oringer's signature tomato water martini, a palate-awakening concoction that takes the flavor of the fruit to its most honest essence. Where you go from there depends on what's in season but might include toro tartare, St. Pierre in crisped bread or spiced pear "biscuit coulant." The rooms are perpetually packed with Boston's media and financial elite.

French, pan-Asian menu. Breakfast, dinner. Bar. Business casual attire. Reservations recommended. Valet parking. Closed Monday. **$$$**

★★★★L'Espalier
30 Gloucester St., Boston,
617-262-3023;
www.lespalier.com

Housed in a charming 19th-century townhouse, L'Espalier feels like a Merchant-Ivory film come to life. The place captures the elegance of another era, while the French-influenced New England recipes are completely modern. Chef Frank McClelland prepares prix fixe and tasting menus, as well as a caviar special for those feeling indulgent. A monster of a wine list offers an amazing variety of vintages with many great choices under $50. The afternoon teas are a favorite with the local ladies who lunch.

French menu. Dinner, Saturday tea. Closed Sunday-Monday January-April and July-October. Bar. Children's menu. Business casual attire. Reservations recommended. Valet parking. $$$$

★★★Locke-Ober
3 Winter Place, Boston, 617-542-1340; www.lockeober.com

Established in 1875, Boston's famed Locke-Ober is a city icon. Once a stomping ground for various foodies, financiers, politicians and local glitterati (women were even excluded until the 1970's), the restaurant, under the skilled leadership of chef/co-owner Lydia Shire, makes traditional American fare feel exciting. Even slightly passé dishes, like beef Stroganoff made with hand-cut egg noodles and onion soup gratine, taste fresh. Don't miss the signature Indian pudding for dessert.

American menu. Lunch, dinner. Bar. Business casual attire. Reservations recommended. Valet parking. Closed Sunday. $$$

★★★★Meritage
70 Rowes Wharf, Boston,
617-439-3995, 800-752-7077;
www.bhh.com

Fulfilling chef Daniel Bruce's quest to pair great wine with food, Meritage is an oenophile's playground where more than 900 varities of wine are on hand to enhance the flavors of the seasonal menu. Bruce matches his eclectic dishes with wine flavors rather than varietals, progressing from light to heavy and usually offering tastes of each grape by the glass. Fennel-cured smoked salmon is matched with sparkling wines, while herb- and mustard-marinated filet comes with a pairing of robust reds. All menu items are available as large or small plates.

International menu. Dinner, Sunday brunch. Bar. Business casual attire. Reservations recommended. Valet parking. Closed Monday. $$$

★★★★No. 9 Park
9 Park St., Boston,
617-742-9991;
www.no9park.com

In the shadow of the State House on historic Beacon Hill sits chef/owner Barbara Lynch's No. 9 Park. Her effort to support top-of-the-line local producers is evident on the seasonal menu, where many ingredients are identified by farm. Perfectly prepared with a healthy dose of flavor and style, Lynch's sophisticated, tempting modern European fare includes beef, fish, venison and pheasant. Lynch is particulary known for her masterful hand at preparing fresh gnocchi, which usually appears on the menu with seared foie gras and Vin Santo glaze. Wine Director Cat Silirie selects a thoughtful and unique list and trains the friendly wait staff to be as knowledgeable as she is.

Continental menu. Lunch, dinner. Bar. Business casual attire. Reservations recommended. Valet parking. Closed Sunday. **$$$**

THE NORTHEAST

NEW YORK

THE HAMPTONS

A TWO-HOUR DAY TRIP FROM MANHATTAN, THE HAMPTONS SERVE AS A summertime playground for New York's upper crust. But dig beneath the surface, and you will find many layers underneath the glitz and glam veneer. Come here to discover amazing offerings for art lovers—from the Pollock-Krasner House & Study Center in The Springs to the Parrish Art Museum in Southampton and Napeague's Art Barge—as well as world-class shopping and restaurants, charming hostelries and some spectacular antique outposts, of course.

WHERE TO SHOP

English Country Antiques
26 Snake Hollow Road,
Bridgehampton, 631-537-0606;
www.ecantiques.com

Wander the 10,000 square feet of overflowing goodies in this charming Bridgehampton shop, where you're likely to unearth a Chinese-styled bed or fine French and English dining chairs, as well as items from as varied origins as Sweden and India. After shopping, visit the nearby Candy Kitchen for a grilled cheese sandwich paired with a decadent milkshake. And keep your eyes open for visiting celebrities: Martha Stewart and Christie Brinkley have reportedly passed through here. Monday-Saturday 9 a.m.-5:30 p.m., Sunday 10 a.m.-5:30 p.m.

Good Ground Antique Center
52 W. Montauk Highway,
Hampton Bays, 631-728-6300

Situated on the main drag in sleepy but up-and-coming Hampton Bays, Good Ground offers a wonderful mishmash of styles, encompassing everything from Federal-style mirrors emblazoned with gold American eagles to mid-century cocktail shakers, all at reasonable prices. Head to the side yard should you be looking for '60s-era wrought iron garden furniture, from glass-topped tables to chaise lounges emblazoned with vintage daisy-printed fabrics. Monday-Friday 10 a.m.-5 p.m., Saturday-Sunday 11 a.m.-5 p.m.; also by appointment; closed Tuesday.

Jed
27 Washington St., Sag Harbor,
631-725-6411

Charming Jack Deamer has a terrifically edited selection of theatrical antiques at this tiny outpost in the former whaling village of Sag Harbor. We've coveted everything from a Chinese lacquered cabinet to a Dorothy Draper-style pair of sconces crafted of plaster and a pair of gorgeous mid-century chairs. Call for hours.

Laurin Copen Antiques

1703 Montauk Highway, Bridgehampton, 631-537-2802; www.laurincopenantiques.com

Housed within a fabulous 1791-era home on bustling Route 27, Laurin Copen stocks an eclectic—but expertly selective—collection of 18th-, 19th- and 20th-century antiques, including glorious finds for the garden. Monday-Saturday 11 a.m.-5:30 p.m., Sunday noon-5 p.m.

The Yard Sale

66 Newtown Lane (rear parking lot), East Hampton, 631-324-7048

You might have spotted The Yard Sale's wildly charismatic owner, Vincent Manzo, on *The Martha Stewart Show* discussing his amazing collection of antiques, ranging from stained glass windows to fountains, urns, midcentury modern chairs, costume jewelry and botanical prints. This is a fabulous place to spend an afternoon rummaging about and picking up finds before the interior designer set descends to stock up en masse for their glittering clients. Saturday-Sunday 11 a.m.-5 p.m.; also by appointment.

THE NORTHEAST

WHERE TO STAY

★★★The 1770 House

143 Main St., East Hampton, 631-324-1770; www.1770house.com

This restored 18th-century house boasts antique furnishings and a prime location close to East Hampton's stellar shopping and restaurants. The rooms are sumptuous and elegant with Frette linens and flat-screen TVs.

7 rooms. Children over 12 years only. Restaurant, bar. $$$

★★★Maidstone Arms

207 Main St., East Hampton, 631-324-5006; www.maidstonearms.com

The Osborne family built this estate as a private residence in the 1750s, and the terrifically situated property has been operating as an inn since the 1870s. Enjoy the bustle of the Hamptons during the summer months or settle in by the fireplaces during cozy winter stays.

19 rooms. Complimentary full breakfast. Restaurant, bar. $$$

WHERE TO EAT

★★★Della Femina

99 N. Main St., East Hampton, 631-329-6666; www.dellafemina.com

This happening eatery boasts a sunken bar area complete with caricatures of famous regulars. On the menu, you'll find such favorites as yellowfin tuna tartare, maple-soy pork loin chops, roasted chicken with rosemary jus and pan-roasted day-boat halibut. The sizable wine list includes many premium wines and a number of boutique and handcrafted selections.

American menu. Dinner. Closed Wednesday (off-season). Bar. Casual attire. Outdoor seating. **$$$**

NEW YORK CITY

SPRAWLING NEW YORK CITY, WITH SO MANY FAR-FLUNG SHOPS IN ITS FIVE boroughs, attracts everyone from flea market-goers, who head to Park Slope in Brooklyn for modernist finds paired with a dash of funk, to a glittering crowd who seek the world's finest treasures for their palatial homes and apartments.

WHERE TO SHOP

Alan Moss
436 Lafayette St., New York, 212-473-1310;
www.alanmossny.com
An alluring selection of 20th-century lighting and furnishings await at this charming West Village shop. Items, which range from streamlined lighting from the 1920s and 1930s to a wonderful selection of furniture pieces by Billy Haines, Rene Herbst and the like, are sourced from France, England, Germany, Italy and across the United States, so you'll always be surprised here. Recent finds include a pair of shell-shaped console tables by famed French atelier Jansen. Monday-Saturday 11 a.m.-6 p.m., Sunday noon-5 p.m.

Buck House
1264 Madison Ave., New York, 212-828-3123;
www.buckhouse.biz
Shop owner, designer and artist Deborah Buck considers her Madison Avenue boutique to be part antique shop and part art gallery. On the antique front, Buck deals primarily in mid–20th century furnishings from both the States and abroad, including pieces from South America and Eastern Europe. On the gallery front, she organizes themed shows ("flowers" was a recent theme), where she showcases both emerging and internationally acclaimed artists and demonstrates how art and antique can live harmoniously side by side. Monday-Friday 10 a.m.-6 p.m., Saturday noon-5 p.m.; closed Sunday.

Donzella
17 White St., New York, 212-965-8919;
www.donzella.com
This Tribeca shop specializes in modern 20th-century furniture

by such notable designers as Paul Frankl, Paul Laszlo, Tommi Parzinger, T. H. Robsjohn-Gibbings and Edward Wormly, so you can generally count on finding at least a few pieces in stock by one of these heavy hitters. For those interested more in the design of the piece than the person who created it, there's also a wide selection of significant mid–20th century designs and an ever-changing assortment of art. Monday-Saturday 11 a.m.-6 p.m.; closed Sunday.

John Rosselli Antiques
523 E. 73rd St., New York,
212-772-2137;
www.johnrosselliantiques.com
A New York institution for more than 50 years, John Rosselli Antiques offers a stunning selection of European and American furnishings chosen for what Rosselli calls their "timeless styling and their ability to add distinctive personality to a room." While the pieces Rosselli sells—like a black lacquer flip-top table with chinoiserie decoration or a mahogany-framed recamier—are important and carry an equally important price tag, the vibe here is far from stuffy. Call for an appointment.

Las Venus
163 Ludlow St., New York,
212-982-0608;
www.lasvenus.com
Walking into this Lower East Side institution is like stepping back in time 30, even 40, years. That's because everything in this fun and funky shop was made after 1950 but before 1980. Stock includes

such unexpected room staples as a vintage 1970s four-piece orange sectional or a 1960s rosewood Danish bar. There's also a much smaller but equally enticing outpost at ABC Carpet & Home at 888 Broadway. Monday-Saturday, noon-9 p.m., Sunday noon-8 p.m.

Liza Sherman
37 Bedford St., New York,
212-414-2684;
www.lizashermanantiques.com
This tiny West Village shop stocks an eclectic assortment of truly unusual antiques, including plates from pinball machines (great wall art), Swedish arm chairs, beehives and a suite of black-and-white inlaid bone and ebonized wood Indian chests from the 1940s. Monday-Saturday 11 a.m.-6 p.m.; closed Sunday. Call first.

Lost City Arts
18 Cooper Square, New York,
212-375-0500;
www.lostcityarts.com
One of the best sources in the city for mid-century furnishings, Lost City Arts deals in lighting, seating, tables, storage and objects produced from 1900 onward. Owner James Elkind handpicks every item in the shop with an eye toward its importance in the role of design. Favorites include pieces by such design luminaries as Vladimir Kagan, Charlotte Perriand, Gio Ponti and Florence Knoll, to name a few. Monday-Friday 10 a.m.-6 p.m., Saturday-Sunday noon-6 p.m.

★
★
★
★

Malmaison

343 E. 74th St., New York,
212-288-7569;
www.malmaison.1stdibs.com

Fine French antiques by the likes of Maison Jansen, Bagues and Serge Roche abound at this charming Upper East Side emporium. Jansen devotees will rejoice when perusing the selection of items known to include a directoire-style mirrored-top desk and a set of ten Louis XV dining chairs covered in a vibrant shade of emerald green. By appointment only.

Todd Merrill

65 Bleecker St., New York,
212-673-0531;
www.merrillantiques.com

It seems only fitting that this Soho shop, which specializes in 20th-century design, would find itself inside the historic Bayard-Condict building, the city's only structure designed by esteemed 20th-century architect Louis Sullivan. Come for the glamorous mix of furniture, lighting and accessories by such landmark names as Venini, Murano, LaVerne, Parzinger and more. And while you're at it, don't forget to take a look at the famed building design. Monday-Saturday 10 a.m.-7 p.m.; Sunday by appointment.

Yale R. Burge Antiques, Inc.

315 E. 62nd St., New York,
212-838-4005;
www.yaleburge.com

This 7,000-square-foot gallery specializes primarily in 18th-, 19th- and 20th-century English and French antiques. Here, you'll find such staples as Louis XV fruitwood needlepoint chinoiserie fireplace screens, French Empire mahogany fauteuils and English coromandel and brass-trimmed storage boxes. Monday-Friday 9 a.m.-5 p.m.; closed Saturday-Sunday.

WHERE TO STAY

★★★★The Carlyle, A Rosewood Hotel

35 E. 76th St., New York,
212-744-1600, 888-767-3966;
www.thecarlyle.com

Discreetly tucked away on Manhattan's Upper East Side, the Carlyle has maintained the allure of being one of New York's best-kept secrets for more than 70 years. A favorite of movie stars, presidents and royals, the Carlyle feels like an exclusive private club. Its art collection is extraordinary, from Audubon prints and Piranesi architectural drawings to English country scenes by Kips. Frequented by power brokers and socialites, the Carlyle Restaurant defines elegance. Bemelmans Bar proudly shows off its murals by *Madeline* creator Ludwig Bemelmans, while Café Carlyle is one of the city's most beloved piano bars.

179 rooms. Wireless Internet access. Two restaurants, bar. Airport transportation available. Fitness center. Spa. Business center. Pets accepted. **$$$$**

★

★

★

★

★★★★Four Seasons Hotel New York

57 E. 57th St., New York, 212-758-5700; 800-545-4000; www.fourseasons.com

Designed by legendary architect I. M. Pei, the Four Seasons is the tallest hotel in New York. An opulent tone is set immediately by an entry foyer boasting 33-foot ceilings and massive marble columns. The rooms and suites have a chic style with neutral tones, English sycamore furnishings and state-of-the-art technology. Floor-to-ceiling windows showcase the dazzling city skyline or the verdant swath of Central Park. Some rooms offer furnished terraces so that guests can further admire the views. Frette linens and blackout blinds guarantee a restful night's sleep. But it's the service that defines the Four Seasons experience: The staff is wonderfully helpful and courteous.

370 rooms. Wireless Internet access. Restaurant, bar. Airport transportation available. Fitness center. Spa. Business center. Pets accepted. $$$$

★★★The Gramercy Park Hotel

2 Lexington Ave., New York, 212-920-3300; www.gramercyparkhotel.com

A legendary hotel that's hosted the likes of Babe Ruth, Madonna and David Bowie, this long-neglected hostelry was reborn in 2006 under the direction of famed hotelier Ian Schraeger and the design of artist Julian Schnabel. With the hefty price tag of a room comes access to keys to the adjacent very exclusive and very private Gramercy Park. Rooms can be petite, but details like iPod players, plush beds and plasma TVs make up for any shortcomings. The Rose Bar, with its Andy Warhol and Damien Hirst paintings, fireplaces and cozy chairs, is a prime spot for a cocktail, though the newly opened private roof club and garden is the toughest velvet rope to cross in town.

183 rooms. Wireless Internet access. Restaurant, two bars. Fitness center. Spa. Business Center. Pets accepted. $$$$

★★★★The Pierre New York, a TAJ Hotel

2 E. 61st. St., New York, 212-838-8000, 866-969-1825; www.tajhotels.com/pierre

Regal and luxurious, this is the definition of a grand old hotel. Although guest rooms are undergoing a massive renovation, slated for completion in early 2009, banquet and meeting rooms are still available. The Pierre has been a city landmark since its construction in 1930. Rooms and suites have a traditional bent thanks to floral prints and antique reproductions. The Rotunda, where breakfast, lunch and afternoon tea are served, has a ceiling of trompe l'oeil murals.

201 rooms. Wireless Internet access. Two restaurants, bar. $$$$

★★★Library Hotel
299 Madison Ave., New York,
212-983-4500, 877-793-7323;
www.libraryhotel.com

As the name suggests, this unique Midtown hotel was inspired by the New York City Public Library, which sits one block away. Each of the ten floors is dedicated to one of the ten categories of the Dewey Decimal System, which include languages, literature, history, the arts and religion. Guest rooms are stocked with books and art relevant to the floor's particular topic. In keeping with this theme, the hotel houses a reading room and a poetry garden with a terrace for relaxing and reading.

60 rooms. High-speed Internet access. Complimentary continental breakfast. Restaurant, bar. Airport transportation available. **$$$**

★★★London NYC
151 W. 54th St., New York,
866-690-2029;
www.thelondonnyc.com

This recently opened boutique hotel is luxurious, sophisticated and chic. With interiors by designer David Collins, the space has been updated with quietly contemporary and glamorous furnishings, artwork and luxury touches like Waterworks bathrooms, Egyptian cotton linens, iPod docking stations and flatscreen TVs. The hotel is the location of British star chef Gordon Ramsey's first U.S. restaurant, which serves delicious takes on French-influenced contemporary cuisine (think lobster ravioli with celery root cream and shellfish vinaigrette.) The property also boasts a concierge desk manned by Quintessentially, the renowned international service that can handle requests for anything from a private jet to tickets to the city's hottest show.

561 rooms. Wireless Internet access. Restaurant, bar. **$$$$**

★★★★The Lowell
28 E. 63rd St., New York,
212-838-1400, 800-221-4444;
www.lowellhotel.com

Located in a landmark 1920s building on the Upper East Side, the Lowell captures the essence of an elegant country house with a delightful blend of English prints, floral fabrics and Chinese porcelains. Many suites boast woodburning fireplaces. All rooms are individually decorated, and the Lowell's specialty suites are a unique treat. The glamour of the 1930s silver screen is recalled in the Hollywood Suite, while the English influences extend to the Pembroke Room, where a proper tea is served, as are breakfast and brunch. The clubby Post House, a well-respected New York steakhouse, serves terrific chops.

70 rooms. Wireless Internet access. Complimentary continental breakfast. Two restaurants, bar. Airport transportation available. **$$$$**

★

★

★

★

★

★★★★★Mandarin Oriental, New York

80 Columbus Circle, New York, 212-805-8800, 866-801-8880; www.mandarinoriental.com/newyork

This luxury hotel occupies 54 floors high atop the Time Warner Center, offering spectacular views of Central Park, the Hudson River and the city skyline. Guest rooms are serene and relaxing. Outside your room, take a swim in the 36th-floor pool or have a Balinese body massage at the spa. The hotel's Asian theme carries over into Asiate, which serves French and Japanese fusion cuisine, and MObar, which features drinks like the East Meets West, a combination of pear- and cinnamon-infused brandy, chilled champagne and a sugar cube. Want to be dazzled by one of the world's best chefs? Make reservations at one of the much-talked-about restaurants in the Time Warner Center, including Thomas Keller's Per Se and Masa Takayama's Masa.

248 rooms. Wireless Internet access. Two restaurants, bar. Fitness center. Pool. Spa. Business Center. $$$$

★★★The Mercer

147 Mercer St., New York, 212-966-6060; www.mercerhotel.com

Catering to a fashion-forward crowd and situated in SoHo, the Mercer Hotel epitomizes relaxed chic with its exposed brick, steel beams and hardwood floors. French designer Christian Liaigre, darling of the minimalist décor movement, crafted a sophisticated look for the hotel with simple furnishings and serene, neutral colors. The lobby also serves as a lending library stocked with favorite books and videos, and the nearby Crunch Gym is available for guests' use. Mercer Kitchen and Bar serve comfort food under the direction of Jean-Georges Vongerichten.

75 rooms. Wireless Internet access. Restaurant, bar. $$$$

★★★★The New York Palace

455 Madison Ave., New York, 212-888-7000, 800-804-7035; www.newyorkpalace.com

Return to the Gilded Age at the New York Palace. Marrying the historic 1882 Villard Houses with a 55-story contemporary tower, this hotel brings the two worlds together under one roof. The glorious public rooms are masterfully restored and recall their former incarnations as fin-de-siècle ballrooms and sitting areas. The Palace's rooms and suites are a blend of contemporary flair and period décor, while the restaurant, Gilt, serves exceptional food in a dramatic modern yet classic setting.

897 rooms. Wireless Internet access. Restaurant, bar. Spa. Airport transportation available. $$$$

★★★★The Peninsula New York

700 Fifth Ave., New York, 212-956-2888, 800-262-9467; www.newyork.peninsula.com

The lobby of this turn-of-the-century Beaux Arts landmark hotel is magnificent with a sweep-

★

★

★

★

ing staircase and elegant bar. Bellhops in crisp white uniforms escort guests to rooms and suites where lush fabrics and warm tones create a soothing ambience. A few rooms overlook the famed St. Patrick's Cathedral. Though the décor exudes old-world charm, modern amenities abound, including flat-screen plasma TVs, wireless Internet access and silent in-room fax machines. The glass-enclosed fitness center, overlooking the city, is a favorite among those in the know. With its views above the city, the Pen-Top Terrace and Bar is a prime spot for a drink.

239 rooms. Wireless Internet access. Two restaurants, three bars. Airport transportation available. Fitness center. Spa. Business Center. **$$$$**

★★★★The Ritz-Carlton New York, Battery Park

2 West St., New York,
212-344-0800, 800-542-8680;
www.ritzcarlton.com

Watch the world from the Ritz-Carlton New York, Battery Park. While only a five-minute walk from Wall Street and the Financial District, the Ritz-Carlton seems removed from the fray thanks to its staggering views of the Hudson River, the Statue of Liberty and Ellis Island. The 38-story glass and brick tower is a departure from the traditional Ritz-Carlton European style, and inside are contemporary artwork and modern furnishings. The service, however, is distinctly Ritz-Carlton with exceptional concierge ser-

vice and bath butlers, who create special concoctions for bath time. The view takes center stage throughout the hotel, whether you're gazing through a telescope in a harbor view room, enjoying a cocktail at Rise (the 14th-floor bar with outdoor space) or savoring a meal at 2 West.

298 rooms. Wireless Internet access. Restaurant, two bars. Fitness center. Spa. Business center. Pets accepted. **$$$$**

★★★★★The Ritz-Carlton New York, Central Park

50 Central Park S., New York,
212-308-9100; 800-542-8680;
www.ritzcarlton.com

Rising above Central Park, this hotel has one of the most coveted locations in town and is exquisite down to every last detail, from the priceless antiques and artwork in the glamorous lobby to the floral displays. The rooms and suites have sumptuous fabrics and plush furnishings. No detail is overlooked; rooms facing the park include telescopes for closer viewing. The white-glove service makes this a top choice of well-heeled travelers. The hotel includes an outpost of the renowned European La Prairie Spa and star chef Laurent Tourondel's BLT Market.

261 rooms. Wireless Internet access. Restaurant, bar. Airport transportation available. Fitness center. Spa. Business center. **$$$$**

NEW YORK CITY

★
★
★
★
★

★★★★★The St. Regis
2 E. 55th St., New York,
212-753-4500, 888-625-4988;
www.stregis.com/newyork
Located just off Fifth Avenue, the St. Regis reigns as New York's grande dame. Opened in 1904, this Beaux Arts landmark defines elegance with its gleaming marble, glittering gold leafing and sparkling chandeliers. The guest rooms are elegantly decorated in soft pastel colors with Louis XVI–style furnishings. The Astor Court is the perfect place to enjoy traditional afternoon tea. Renowned for its famous Red Snapper cocktail and bewitching Maxfield Parrish mural, the King Cole Bar is a favorite of hotel guests and locals alike. Be sure to ask the bartender why crafty Old King Cole is smirking.
229 rooms. Wireless Internet access. Restaurant, bar. Airport transportation available. Fitness center. Spa. Business center. $$$$

★★★★Trump International Hotel & Tower
1 Central Park W., New York,
212-299-1000, 888-448-7867;
www.trumpintl.com
Occupying an enviable site across from Central Park and the Time Warner Center on Manhattan's Upper West Side, the 52-story Trump International Hotel and Tower delivers glitz and glam. The guest rooms and suites reflect a contemporary European flavor, while the floor-to-ceiling windows focus attention on the views of Central Park and Columbus Circle. All suites and most rooms feature kitchens, and in-room chefs are available to craft memorable meals. Room service comes courtesy of top chef Jean-Georges Vongerichten, whose restaurant, Jean Georges, sits just off the lobby. The personal attaché service provides an apt pair of hands to take care of life's little details.
176 rooms. Wireless Internet access. Restaurant, bar. Airport transportation available. Spa. $$$$

★★★The Waldorf-Astoria
301 Park Ave., New York,
212-355-3000, 800-925-3673;
www.waldorfastoria.com
Enjoy a taste of old New York at this landmark, 1931 Art Deco hotel, which has played host to countless U.S. presidents and international luminaries. The lobby features murals, mosaics and a piano that once belonged to Cole Porter. The rooms are individually decorated, elegant and traditional in style. The Bull & Bear steakhouse has a 1940s feel and attracts a sophisticated, steak-loving crowd.
1,416 rooms. Wireless Internet access. Two restaurants, two bars. Airport transportation available. Spa. $$$$

WHERE TO EAT

★★★'21' Club
21 W. 52nd St., New York,
212-582-7200; www.21club.com
This one-time speakeasy is as much part of New York culture as pretzels and yellow taxis. The bus-

★

★

★

★

tling restaurant with its clubby, brass-railed bar, linen-topped tables and old photos hung on wood-paneled walls, is always full of Wall Street investment bankers, media power players, ladies who lunch and everyone in between. The chef turns out stellar, seasonal American fare. The Upstairs at '21' is a restaurant within a restaurant and provides a more intimate dining experience. Dress sharp: It's coat and tie at dinner, and no jeans. American menu. Lunch, dinner. Closed Sunday; three weeks in August. Bar. Jacket required in Upstairs at 21. Reservations recommended. $$$

★★★Aquavit
65 E. 55th St., New York,
212-307-7311;
www.aquavit.org
Chef/partner Marcus Samuelsson introduced New York to his splashy brand of modern Scandinavian cuisine a decade ago at Aquavit. After ten years and a move to the ultramodern Park Avenue Tower, the restaurant has a sleek, sophisticated vibe, and the cuisine is even more spectacular. While ingredients like herring, lamb, salmon, caviar and dill show up with regularity, the food is more uniquely Samuelsson than anything else. A shot of smooth yet decidedly potent aquavit complements dinner nicely, as does a selection from the impressive wine list.
Scandanavian menu. Lunch, dinner, Sunday brunch. Bar. Business casual attire. Reservations recommended. $$$$

★★★★Asiate
80 Columbus Circle, New York,
212-805-8800; www.
mandarinoriental.com
Asiate offers a spectacular view of Central Park and a modern Franco-Asian menu on the 35th floor of the Mandarin Oriental Hotel. World-renowned restaurant designer Tony Chi was the creative force behind this stunning space, which features a jeweled tree branch sculpture that hangs from the cathedral-style ceiling. Like the ambience, Chef Noriyuki Sugie's inspired menu impresses even the most sophisticated traveler, borrowing from both Old Europe and New Asia. Highlights include the seafood yuzu ceviche, surf clam salad and pickled vegetables; grilled Maine lobster with cuttlefish noodles and goji berries; and chocolate fondant cake with raspberry compote.
Asian, French menu. Breakfast, lunch, dinner, brunch. Business casual attire. Reservations recommended. Valet parking. $$$$

★★★★Aureole
34 E. 61st St., New York,
212-319-1660;
www.charliepalmer.com/aureole_ny
Hidden inside an elegant brownstone on Manhattan's Upper East Side, Aureole is a luxurious space bathed in cream tones and warm lighting and furnished with overstuffed, wine-colored banquettes. (An enclosed courtyard garden opens for warm-weather dining.) The restaurant is friendly and cozy and suited for just about any

83

NEW YORK CITY

★
★
★
★

occasion, from couples looking for romance to colleagues seeking a luxe business dinner. Owner and celebrity chef Charlie Palmer offers his guests a wonderfully prepared menu of what he calls "progressive American" fare. There are always two tasting menus—one vegetarian and another inspired from the market—in addition to a parade of terrific à la carte selections. The extensive and celebrated wine program includes bold wines from California, Spain and Italy.

American menu. Lunch, dinner. Closed Sunday. Bar. Jacket required. Reservations recommended. Outdoor seating. $$$$

★★★Balthazar
80 Spring St., New York, 212-965-1785; www.balthazarny.com

From the attractive crowds at the bar to the attractive folks who squeeze into the restaurant's tiny tables—you'll be seated as close to a stranger as is possible without becoming intimate—Balthazar is a dazzling, wonderfully chaotic destination. It sports a menu of brasserie standards like frisée aux lardons, pan bagnat, steak frites and a glistening raw bar platter, not to mention fresh-baked bread from the Balthazar bakery next door. Pick up a bag of croissants, a couple of baguettes and a dozen tarts on your way out for breakfast or lunch the next day.

French menu. Breakfast, lunch, dinner, brunch. Bar. Business casual attire. Reservations recommended. $$$

★★★Barbetta
321 W. 46th St., New York, 212-246-9171; www.barbettarestaurant.com

This classic Italian restaurant opened its doors in 1906 and is still owned by the same family, the Maioglios. Located in a pair of historic early 19th-century townhouses, this restaurant is all about elegant, old-world dining. The menu doesn't aim anywhere other than where its heart is—Italy—but don't expect just pasta. The kitchen offers a great selection of seafood, poultry and beef prepared with seasonal ingredients and lively flavors.

Italian menu. Lunch, dinner. Closed Monday. Bar. Business casual attire. Reservations recommended. Outdoor seating. $$$

★★★★Bouley
120 W. Broadway, New York, 212-964-2525; www.bouleyrestaurants.com

Acclaimed chef David Bouley mans the stoves at this temple of haute French gastronomy. Housed in the renovated and impeccably decorated space that was once his more casual bistro, Bouley appeals to an epicurean-minded crowd. The elegant space is packed with well-heeled foodies, fashionistas, political pundits and celebs who understand that a night in Bouley's care is nothing short of perfection. The service is charming, the seasonal ingredients shine, the French technique is impeccable and the food is nothing short of brilliant. Indulge in the chef's

THE NORTHEAST

★

★

★

★

canapé tasting menu or opt for succulent à la carte dishes, including seared foie gras with Pruneaux d'Agen and apple-rosemary purée and tea-smoked organic duckling with vanilla glazed baby turnips and porcini mushrooms.

French menu. Lunch, dinner. Jacket required. Reservations recommended. **$$$$**

★★★Carlyle Restaurant

35 E. 76th St., New York, 212-744-1600;
www.rosewoodhotels.com

This lavishly decorated restaurant is housed in the elegant Carlyle Hotel. From the plush velvet walls covered with rare 19th-century prints to the crystal chandeliers and unique floral arrangements, guests will delight in the atmosphere. Meticulous attention is paid to the visual presentation of the gourmet dishes served by a wonderfully attentive staff. Live entertainment includes a pianist and jazz trio.

French menu. Breakfast, lunch, dinner, brunch. Children's menu. Business casual attire. Reservations recommended. Valet parking. **$$$**

★★★★Country

90 Madison Ave., New York, 212-889-7100;
www.countryinnewyork.com

Housed in a Beaux Arts building that includes the Carlton Hotel, this creation of chef Geoffrey Zakarian (with design by David Rockwell) combines classic Manhattan elegance with contem-porary flair in both décor and cuisine. The seasonal, French-influenced menu comes in three-course pretheater, four-course or six-course chef's tasting versions. Entrées change daily and might include everything from Berkshire pork with apple jam, chestnut and polenta to snapper with clams and lemon. The space also includes a more casual café, which serves breakfast, lunch and dinner, as well as a Champagne lounge.

French, American menu. Breakfast, lunch, dinner. Bar. **$$$**

★★★★Daniel

60 E. 65th St., New York, 212-288-0033;
www.danielnyc.com/daniel

Daniel is a dining experience that begins when you enter the palatial front room and continues as you sip an old-fashioned cocktail in the romantic, low-lit lounge. From there, it's on to the formal dining room, where superstar chef Daniel Boulud serves sublime cooking in the most gracious of settings overflowing with flowers. Potato-crusted sea bass is a signature dish: A crisp, golden coat, fashioned from whisper-thin slices of potatoes, wraps the fish while it cooks and seals in the flavor. After dessert, there are petit fours and then the pièce de résistance: warm madeleines.

French menu. Dinner. Closed Sunday. Bar. Children's menu. Jacket required. Reservations recommended. **$$$$**

★★★★Danube

30 Hudson St., New York, 212-791-3771;
www.thedanube.net

Danube is the creation of David Bouley, the inspired chef who has created many notable New York establishments. A stunning place to spend an evening, Danube has the feel of an old Austrian castle, with dark wood, plush banquettes and soft, warm lighting. Austrian-inspired dishes are interspersed with seasonal new American ones. Bouley's food is spectacular, though not for those who fear taking risks. The staff offer refined service, and the wine list is eclectic and extensive. As you would expect, it includes some gems from Austria.

Continental, American menu. Dinner. Closed Sunday. Bar. Business casual attire. Reservations recommended. **$$$$**

★★★DB Bistro Moderne

55 W. 44th St., New York, 212-391-2400;
www.danielnyc.com/dbbistro

This cool, sexy, ultrastylish Midtown bistro is Daniel Boulud's most casual outpost. His signature DB Burger is an excellent example of creative interpretation. Boulud builds a juicy round of beef and stuffs it with short ribs and sinful amounts of foie gras and truffles. He serves it on a homemade Parmesan brioche bun with house-stewed tomato confit (instead of ketchup) and a big vat of fries, perfect for sharing.

American, French menu. Lunch, dinner. Business casual attire. Reservations recommended. **$$$$**

★★★Del Posto

85 Tenth Ave., New York, 212-497-8090;
www.delposto.com

A dream team of star chefs—Joe Bastianich, Lidia Bastianich and Mario Batali—is behind this Italian restaurant, which has a menu that spans the many regions of the country and features dishes that range from classic to contemporary. The garganelli is topped with a ragú Bolognese any nonna would be proud of, while the rare tuna with bresaola is a more modern offering. The grand tasting menu (the whole table must participate to try it) offers seven courses and is a great way to sample this establishment's varied dishes. Service is polished and polite, and the presentation is pleasing. The enoteca serves reasonably priced portions of the menu's more simple dishes like spaghetti and house-made gelati. Be sure to reserve a table well in advance—Del Posto requests a one-month notice.

Italian menu. Lunch, dinner. Bar. Business casual attire. Reservations recommended. **$$$$**

★★★Eleven Madison Park

11 Madison Ave., New York, 212-889-0905;
www.elevenmadisonpark.com

Located across from the leafy, historic Madison Square Park, Danny Meyer's grand new American restaurant is a wonderful, soothing spot. The magnificent dining room boasts old-world charm with vaulted ceilings, clubby banquettes, giant floor-to-ceiling windows and warm, golden lighting. The crowd is equally stunning: a savvy blend of sexy, power-suited types and chic, fashion-forward New Yorkers. The contemporary seasonal menu, created by Chef Daniel Humm, features updated American classics as well as a smart selection of dishes that borrow accents from Spain, France and Asia.

American menu. Lunch, dinner, brunch. Bar. Business casual attire. Reservations recommended. $$$

★★★Firebird

365 W. 46th St., New York, 212-586-0244;

www.firebirdrestaurant.com

Set in a lavish double townhouse, this restaurant and cabaret is furnished like a majestic Russian palace, with ornate antique furniture, intricate china and etched glass, old-world oil paintings and 19th-century photographs. The extravagance extends to the food, with Russian classics like blinis with sour cream and caviar, *zakuska* (the Russian equivalent of tapas), borscht made with pork, and dill and sturgeon baked in puff pastry.

Eastern European menu. Lunch, dinner. Closed Monday. Bar. Business casual attire. Reservations recommended. Outdoor seating. $$$

★★★★Gilt

455 Madison Ave., New York, 212-891-8100.

www.giltnewyork.com

When the staff at New York's celebrated Le Cirque 2000 packed up their knives in 2004, foodies everywhere wondered what would take the restaurant's place in the New York Palace Hotel's historic Villard Mansion. The answer: the opulent Gilt, whose name pays homage to the late 19th-century's Gilded Age, when the mansion was created. The 55-seat space, with carved-wood and gilded walls, cathedral ceilings and marble fireplaces, features contemporary elements that give the dining room a modern twist while retaining its historic beauty. Chef Christopher Lee's menu features new American options like crispy sea bass with chorizo, red bliss potatoes, garlic aioli and saffron mussel broth. Wine is a large part of the experience, and Gilt offers an expansive (and expensive) selection to complement each dish.

New American menu. Dinner. Closed Sunday-Monday. Bar. Jacket required. Reservations recommended. Valet parking. $$$$

★★★★Gordon Ramsay at the London

151 W. 54th St., New York, 212-468-8888;

www.thelondonnyc.com/gordon_ramsay

The culinary world's mad genius now has a stateside playground in which to romp at the recently opened London NYC hotel. The menu is French influenced and

★

★

★

★

sophisticated, and the room, designed by David Collins, matches that aesthetic. Chef de Cuisine Josh Emmett interprets Ramsay's recipes when the star chef is away, and dishes include everything from filet of beef with braised oxtail, baby onions and creamed mushrooms to pan-fried John Dory with eggplant, tomato and zucchini. Service is crisp and polished, and the wine list complements the cuisine perfectly.

French, continental menu. Lunch, dinner. Reservations recommended. $$$$

★★★★Gramercy Tavern
42 E. 20th St., New York, 212-477-0777;
www.gramercytavern.com

Owner Danny Meyer's perpetually bustling New York eatery is warm and charming without a smidge of pretension. In the glorious, rustic main room, you can choose from a pair of seasonal tasting menus or a wide array of equally tempting à la carte selections. The duck terrine smothered with onion and pistachio marmalade is an effusion of sweet and savory, and the smoked lobster on a bed of saffron-fennel strozzapreti and pancetta is not to be missed. If you don't have a reservation, stroll in, put your name on the list and you'll have the chance to sample some spectacular food at the bar. There's a terrific house cocktail list, too.

American menu. Lunch, dinner. Bar. Business casual attire. Reservations recommended. $$$

★★★★Jean Georges
1 Central Park W., New York, 212-299-3900;
www.jean-georges.com

Perfection is the word that comes to mind when speaking of meals at Jean Georges. Located in the Trump International Hotel and Tower, Jean Georges is a shrine to haute cuisine. Drawing influences from around the world, the menu is conceived and impeccably executed by celebrity chef/owner Jean-Georges Vongerichten. Prix fixe dishes include young garlic soup with thyme and sautéed frog's legs and mouth-watering Arctic char with miso-potato purée in a Granny Smith apple-jalapeño juice. If you can't secure a table at the restaurant, try your luck at Nougatine, the popular on-site café. It has a simple bar menu but will give you a taste of Vongerichten's cuisine. The bar is also a lovely place to meet for an aperitif or a cocktail before dinner or a walk through the park.

Continental, French menu. Breakfast, lunch, dinner, brunch. Bar. Business casual attire. Reservations recommended. Valet parking. Outdoor seating. $$$$

★★★★L'Atelier de Joël Robuchon
57 E. 57th St., New York, 212-758-5700;
www.fourseasons.com/newyork

Housed in the Four Seasons Hotel, this offering from star French chef Joël Robuchon—his first in New York—delivers an intimate, sophisticated dining experience. The name means "artist's workshop," and this concept, with outposts in Las Vegas, Paris and Tokyo, is a space for Robuchon and his well-trained staff to churn out small plates of perfectly executed culinary art. Diners sit at a 20-seat bar or at one of the 26 seats arranged around the dining room's tables and sample creations like truffled mashed potatoes or sea urchin in lobster gelée with cauliflower cream. Service is precise and professional, which allows the food in all its glory to take center stage.

French. Lunch, dinner. Reservations recommended. Formal attire. **$$$$**

★ ★ ★ ★ ★ Le Bernardin
155 W. 51st St., New York,
212-554-1515;
www.le-bernardin.com

This fabled restaurant has impressed foodies and newbies alike since it moved from Paris to Manhattan in 1986. Le Bernardin is very civilized and sophisticated, and it's certainly not the place for a quick bite. Enjoying service that is both precise and impeccably understated, diners can turn their full attention to their taste buds. Chef Eric Ripert's food is light, aromatic and perfectly balanced, and the presentations are museum-worthy. Seafood is the star, and the menu features such knockout dishes as poached halibut with marinated grapes and cherry tomatoes and organic Chilean turbot in a lemon-miso broth. The wine list is equally exquisite.

French, seafood menu. Lunch, dinner. Closed Sunday. Bar.

Jacket required. Reservations recommended. **$$$$**

★ ★ ★ ★ ★ Masa
10 Columbus Circle, New York,
212-823-9808;
www.masanyc.com

You need deep pockets to indulge at Masa. This is the high roller's table for gourmands, given that you've already committed to spending $400 just by walking through the 2,500-year-old Japanese cedar door—before you've had a drink, tacked on tax or paid the gratuity. Chef/owner Masa Takayama creates a different dining experience each day based on market offerings. A mere shiitake mushroom, for example, is raised to shrine-worthy status. Every detail at Masa is aesthetically exquisite, from the amazing cuisine to the top-flight service.

Japanese, sushi menu. Lunch, dinner. Closed Sunday. Bar. Business casual attire. Reservations recommended. **$$$$**

★ ★ ★ Nobu
105 Hudson St., New York, 212-219-0500;
www.myriadrestaurantgroup.com

Nobu's lively dining room on an otherwise quiet corner of Tribeca has a serene vibe despite the high-energy, high-fashion crowd that packs in nightly for famed chef Nobu Matsuhisa's spectacular sushi and unique brand of Asian-Latin–inspired seafood. Lime, soy, chiles, miso, cilantro and ginger are frequently employed to accent many of the chef's succulent creations. A signature dish is

★

★

★

★

the almost-melting black cod with miso. The omakase (chef's choice) menu is an option for those with an adventurous palate. If you can't get a reservation (call well in advance and be prepared for a busy signal), you can always try for a seat at the sushi bar.

Japanese menu. Lunch, dinner. Casual attire. Reservations recommended. $$$

★★★★★per se
10 Columbus Circle, New York, 212-823-9335; www.perseny.com

Thomas Keller, the chef at the fabled French Laundry, calls his restaurant in the Time Warner Center "per se" because it's not exactly The French Laundry, per se. Both restaurants embrace rich copper floors; a harmonious mix of wood, marble and granite; and a signature blue door. What's missing is the bucolic setting of the Napa Valley, but in its place are eye-popping views and equally incredible cooking. The best way to enjoy per se is to order the ever-changing nine-course tasting menu and settle in for three hours of culinary surprises exemplified by small dishes, such as truffles and custard in an eggshell and foie gras accompanied by various salts. Custom-made china and pristine table settings speak to the equally outstanding service details.

American, French menu. Lunch, dinner. Closed two weeks late July to early August. Business casual attire. Reservations recommended. Valet parking. $$$$

★★★★Picholine
35 W. 64th St., New York, 212-724-8585

Located on Manhattan's Upper West Side, Picholine is an obvious choice for dinner if you are attending an opera, ballet or play at Lincoln Center. But chef/owner Terrance Brennan's lovely, serene restaurant is also wonderful for any special occasion. Redesigned in 2006 to reflect the contemporary sensibilities of its tantalizing Mediterranean fare, the interior boasts hues of rich violet and boysenberry, impressive ten-foot velvet curtains and custom-made mirrors. The menu changes with the seasons, and the chef uses organic and local ingredients to create such dishes as the olive oil-poached halibut and morel and rabbit risotto.

French, Mediterranean menu. Lunch, dinner. Bar. Jacket required. Reservations recommended. $$$

★★★Rosa Mexicano
61 Columbus Ave., New York, 212-977-7700; www.rosamexicano.com

One of the first restaurants to introduce New Yorkers to authentic Mexican cuisine, Rosa Mexicano was founded by Chef Josefina Howard in the early '80s. It remains an essential stop for anyone who craves strong, ice-cold margaritas and knockout bowls of guacamole mixed tableside to your desired level of heat (mild to scorching). The menu is a tribute to the regional home cooking of Mexico—steamy pork tamales;

chicken in a rich, savory blanket of mole; terra-cotta cazuelas brimming with shrimp, tomatoes, garlic and chiles; and a longtime entrée signature, budin Azteca, a wonderful tortilla casserole with layers of shredded chicken and cheese.

Mexican menu. Lunch, dinner, brunch, late-night. Bar. Casual attire. Reservations recommended. Outdoor seating. **$$**

NEW YORK CITY

FLORIDA

MIAMI

FROM ART DECO DELIGHTS TO THE ALFRESCO ACTION AT THE LINCOLN Road market, Miami mixes colorful and eclectic finds in a Technicolor, Latin-flavored setting.

WHERE TO SHOP

Alhambra Antiques
2850 Salzedo St., Coral Gables, 305-446-1688, 866-446-1688; www.alhambraantiques.com
Alhambra Antiques houses a variety of furnishings that reflect exquisite craftsmanship and European 18th- and 19th-century elegance. It will have antiquers fantasizing about new uses for a green faux bamboo garden table and an antique drum equipped with leather strap. Monday-Saturday noon-6 p.m.; also by appointment; closed Sunday.

Bonnin Ashley Antiques, Inc.
4707 SW 71st Ave., Miami, 305-666-7709; www.bonninashleyantiques.com
Covering two floors, this gorgeous shop has an incredible selection of light and dark English and French wood furniture, as well as a few little somethings from the 21st century, including new linens and embroidered pillows to adorn the centuries-old wares. Open Tuesday-Saturday 11 a.m.-5 p.m.; closed Sunday-Monday.

Lincoln Road Outdoor Antique & Collectible Market
Lincoln Road Mall between Lenox and Michigan Avenues, Miami Beach Art Deco District, 305-673-4991; www.antiquecollectiblemarket. com
Some 125 vendors line this charming pedestrianized shopping street in the heart of South Beach to display antiques, including jewelry, china, vintage clothing, posters, furniture and more. Keep your eyes peeled for lots of '50s and '60s finds that look like they were plucked from a Palm Beach manse—like a faux bamboo wrought iron chandelier painted blue or pink. There's also overwrought iron patio furniture with seahorse and seashell motifs. January-May: every other Sunday 8 a.m.-5 p.m.

Miami Twice
6562 Bird Road, Miami, 305-666-0127; www.miami-twice.com
Miami Twice is a must-visit for groovy vintage clothing and accessories, from delicate, bejeweled flapper dresses to well-thumbed

THE SOUTH

vintage magazines and show-stopping boas in rainbow colors. Truly fitting for the setting, this shop pays homage to its Miami location. Monday-Saturday 10 a.m.-7 p.m., Sunday 11 a.m.-6 p.m.

Midori Gallery & Antiques

3168 Commodore Plaza, Miami, 305-443-3399

In addition to an impressive collection of art from China and Japan, Midori Gallery & Antiques has everything from 35,000-year-old neolithic ceramics to folk art. Monday-Saturday 11 a.m.-6 p.m.; closed Sunday.

Stoneage Antiques

3236 NW South River Drive, Miami, 305-633-5114; www.stoneage-antiques.com

If you have been searching for an antique cannon, anchor or lantern from a sunken Spanish galleon, you're in luck (there are 15 cannons here). With a truly versatile collection of nautical antiques, South Florida is the perfect setting for this antique shop. Monday-Saturday 9 a.m.-5 p.m.; closed Sunday.

Valerio Antiques & Art Deco

250 Valencia Ave., Coral Gables, 305-448-6779; www.valerioartdeco.com

Valerio Antiques specializes in jazzy Art Deco lamps and furnishings as well as finely wrought metalwork and more. You might leave with a museum-quality marquetry cabinet with ivory inlay for your kitchen or a dramatic Art Deco–era sculpture of an aviator for the front lawn. Monday-Saturday 10 a.m.-5 p.m.; closed Sunday.

WHERE TO STAY

★★★★Four Seasons Hotel Miami

1435 Brickell Ave., Miami, 305-358-3535, 800-332-3442; www.fourseasons.com

This contemporary hotel is located in downtown Miami's newly buzzing Brickell neighborhood. Guest rooms and suites are decorated with cool earth tones and distinctive artwork. The 50,000-square-foot Splash Spa at the onsite Sports Club/LA has ten treatment rooms, including a Turkish steam room. The hotel features a fine dining restaurant, Acqua, which serves up Latin-inspired fare, and two lounges, including the sky-top, poolside Bahia where locals and travelers gather for cocktails.

305 rooms. High-speed Internet access. Restaurant, two bars. Airport transportation available. Fitness center. Pool. Spa. Business center. Pets accepted. $$$$

★★★★Mandarin Oriental, Miami

500 Brickell Key Drive, Miami, 305-913-8288, 866-888-6780; www.mandarinoriental.com

With its waterfront location and contemporary interior design, this hotel is an island of calm in the middle of downtown Miami. Located on tiny Brickell Key opposite the city center, this outpost of the Asian hotel group is a favorite for its skyline views, Azul

★
★
★
☆

restaurant and man-made white sand beach. Guests can sign up for the hotel's South Beach Experience, which includes transportation to South Beach, a private beach cabana and access to the pool and restaurant at the famed South Beach mansion turned private club Casa Casuarina. Come back to one of the luxurious guest rooms decorated in a contemporary Asian-influenced style with bamboo hardwood floors, simple furnishings and white fabrics.

327 rooms. High-speed Internet access. Two restaurants, two bars. Airport transportation available. Fitness center. Beach. Pool, whirlpool. Spa. Business center. Pets accepted. **$$$$**

★★★★The Ritz-Carlton Coconut Grove
3300 SW 27th Ave., Miami, 305-644-4680, 800-241-3333; www.ritzcarlton.com

This palatial hotel is recognized for its impeccable service—technology, travel, bath and even pet butlers cater to your every whim. Rooms are classically decorated and offer views of the city and Biscayne Bay. The spacious spa offers dozens of treatments, and a shimmering pool with views over Coconut Grove is a prime spot for sunbathers and people-watchers. The lobby lounge serves cocktails and afternoon tea, while Bizcaya Grill offers steaks prepared to perfection.

115 rooms. High-speed Internet access. Restaurant, three bars. Airport transportation available.

Fitness center. Pool. Spa. Business center. **$$$$**

WHERE TO EAT

★★★★Azul
500 Brickell Key Drive, Miami, 305-913-8358; www.mandarinoriental.com

Mediterranean and Asian flavors marry at Azul at the Mandarin Oriental, Miami, where Chef Clay Conley crafts a menu made from the day's fresh catch and seasonal ingredients. Miso-marinated hamachi is accompanied by edamame rice, shrimp dumplings and sake butter sauce, while a grilled lamb chop might rest alongside a harissa-marinated lamb loin with smoked eggplant. Wash down these delicacies with an exclusive wine from a selection that boasts more than 700 bottles. Views through the huge windows overlooking Biscayne Bay make the restaurant's bar a prime spot for lingering with after-dinner drinks.

Japanese menu. Lunch, dinner. Bar. Children's menu. Business casual attire. Reservations recommended. Valet parking. Outdoor seating. **$$$$**

★★★Baleen
4 Grove Island Drive, Miami, 305-858-8300; www.groveisle.com

An eclectic, contemporary, seafood-centered menu is served at this intimate restaurant, a serene oasis set in a vista of plush outdoor greenery, complete with waterfront views. Inventive fish

THE SOUTH

dishes include fried Chinese-style snapper with coconut rice and sweet-tart black bean sauce and wood-roasted day-boat scallops.

International menu. Breakfast, lunch, dinner, Sunday brunch. Bar. Business casual attire. Reservations recommended. Valet parking. Outdoor seating. $$$

SARASOTA

SARASOTA MIXES A RELAXED SENSIBILITY WITH TERRIFIC HOTELS AND restaurants, as well as numerous antique shops where you can load up on everything from Bakelite bracelets with candy-colored fruit to rattan sofas upholstered in tropical-themed fabrics.

WHERE TO SHOP

Antiques & Chatchkes
1542 Fruitville Road, Sarasota, 941-906-1221
If you're in the market for American furniture or pottery, head to Sarasota's Antiques & Chatchkes. You'll find a variety here—aside from the larger pieces, look for the selection of sterling jewelry. Monday-Saturday 10 a.m.-5 p.m., Sunday noon-4 p.m.

Crissy Galleries
640 S. Washington Blvd., Sarasota, 941-957-1110, 800-367-0313; www.crissy.com
Crissy Galleries specializes in 18th- through 20th-century furniture, porcelains, cut glass and paintings. One showroom features pieces with a decorative flair, the other works for serious collectors. Look for pieces spanning the ages from a Royal Worcester coiled dragon lamp to a fantastical 19th-century console outfitted with blackamoors. Monday-Friday 10 a.m.-5 p.m., Saturday, 10 a.m.-4 p.m.; closed Sunday.

Elizabeth Rice, Inc. Fine Art & Antiques
1467 Main St., Sarasota, 941-954-8575; www.elizabethrice.com
This upscale shop spans many eras and styles from Biedermeier antique furniture to contrasting contemporary and modern art. Recent visits have sent shoppers crazy over cantilever chairs from Thonet and a pair of mid-century Murano glass lamps. Monday-Friday, 10 a.m.-5 p.m.; also by appointment.

Jack Vinales Antiques
539 Pineapple Ave. S., Sarasota, 941-957-0002; www.jackvinalesantiques.com
Jack Vinales specializes in mid-20th-century modern, 1950s, Art Deco and 1960s pop design. There's always a terrific selection of Heywood-Wakefield furnish-

SARASOTA

ings, as well as plenty of Herman Miller, Knoll and Eames. If you are a fan of Bakelite jewelry, you'll find colorful bananas, cherries and coral plastics adorning everything from necklaces to napkin holders. Monday-Saturday, 11 a.m.-5 p.m.; first Friday of every month 11 a.m.-9 p.m.; closed Sunday.

Sharalyn's Faded Rose Fine Antiques & Vintage Linens
1472 Fruitville Road, Sarasota, 941-364-5156

As the name suggests, Sharalyn's houses a wide selection of vintage linens, crystal, silver and neat costume jewelry. From classic to funny to all-out weird, you never know what you might find. Daily 10:30 a.m.-4:30 p.m.

WHERE TO STAY

★★★★The Ritz-Carlton, Sarasota
1111 Ritz-Carlton Dr., Sarasota, 941-309-2000, 800-241-3333; www.ritzcarlton.com

Located in the city's cultural district overlooking Sarasota Bay, the Ritz-Carlton is close to the boutiques and galleries of the city but maintains a resort feel. The hotel's lobby sets an elegant tone—think rich marble floors and crystal chandeliers—that carries throughout the property. Rooms feature rich colors, sumptuous fabrics and antiques. The hotel also offers an 18-hole Tom Fazio–designed golf course. From the technology butlers on call to assist with computer woes to the bath menu drawn by the bath butlers, the service here is superlative.

266 rooms. High-speed Internet access. Four restaurants, two bar. Airport transportation available. Fitness center. Beach. Pool, whirlpool. Golf. Tennis. Business center. Pets accepted. $$$

WHERE TO EAT

★★★Bijou Café
1287 First St., Sarasota, 941-366-8111; www.bijoucafe.net

This noisy, eclectic restaurant with country French décor is housed in a converted 1930s gas station. If you're headed to the nearby Opera House, dine pretheater on hearty options like grilled rack of lamb with roasted shallot and mint demi-glacé.

International menu. Lunch, dinner. Closed Sunday in summer. Bar. Business casual attire. Reservations recommended. Valet parking. Outdoor seating. $$

★★★Vernona Restaurant
1111 Ritz-Carlton Drive, Sarasota, 941-309-2008, 800-241-3333; www.ritzcarlton.com

The ambience at this restaurant inside the Ritz-Carlton resembles that of a Tuscan villa, complete with crystal chandeliers and elegantly arched windows. The menu, though, is contemporary American and features locally sourced organic ingredients. Signature favorites include lobster macaroni and cheese, roasted ratatouille soup, sage-orange braised veal short ribs and olive oil-poached prime beef tenderloin. Be sure to save room for the Sarasota key lime pie.

American menu. Breakfast, lunch, dinner, Sunday brunch. Bar. Children's menu. Casual attire. $$$

TAMPA

WITH ITS MINARETS OVERLOOKING THE HILLSBOROUGH RIVER AND eclectic Ybor City neighborhood, Tampa mixes a dash of Old Florida with a splash of Cuban élan. Antique lovers should head straight for the Seminole Heights neighborhood before exploring south Tampa with its eclectic shops interspersed among quaint cafés.

WHERE TO SHOP

Janet's Antiques
2545 Central Ave.,
St. Petersburg, 727-823-5700
Located in sleepy downtown St. Petersburg, Janet's boasts plenty of decorative objects and also does appraisals. Not all the items here are antiques in the traditional sense; look for unexpected finds, like a giant pineapple made of porcelain. Tuesday-Sunday 10 a.m.-5 p.m.

Palma Ceia Antiques & Books
1802 S. MacDill Ave., Tampa,
813-254-7149;
www.tampaantiquesandbooks.com
This quaint, pink Spanish '20s house showcases antique art pottery from the American Arts & Crafts and Art Deco periods and European and Japanese porcelain from the 19th and 20th centuries. After browsing through the vintage book collection, perhaps your eye will be drawn to the Rookwood and Roseville pottery or the Royal Doulton china. Monday-Saturday 11 a.m.-5 p.m.

Peddler's Village
14330 Seventh St., Dade City,
352-518-0600
Located 30 minutes from Tampa, Peddler's Village is the largest antique mall in Dade City, hosting some 75 vendors in more than 7,000 square feet of show space. From hand-carved furnishings in pristine condition to rusty old radios and from fossils to silver and antique glass, come prepared to dig. Monday-Saturday 10 a.m.-5 p.m.; closed Sunday.

Seminole Heights Antiques & Consignments
4713 N. Florida Ave., Tampa,
813-237-5850;
www.seminoleheightsantiques.com
Seminole Heights Antiques is a multidealer mall with 25 dealers and 7,500 square feet. We have unearthed everything from groovy 1970s-era plates to a mid-century buffet and Hollywood Regency–styled lighting in acid-hued colors. Monday 11 a.m.- 6 p.m., Sunday noon-5 p.m.

TAMPA

★
★
★
★
★
★

Sherry's Yesterdaze Vintage Clothing & Antiques

5207 N. Florida Ave., Tampa, 813-231-2020;
www.yesterdazevintage.com

Located in historic Seminole Heights, Sherry's Yesterdaze offers a large range of clothing, accessories and jewelry dating from the late 1800s to early 1980s. Here, you're likely to uncover pins shaped like overblown flowers and rattan sofas upholstered in brown cotton with white welting. Pick up a baroque white-plaster mirror that is sure to add drama to any foyer or hall. Tuesday-Saturday 11 a.m.-6 p.m., Sunday noon-6 p.m.; closed Monday.

World Famous Gaslight Antiques

3616 Henderson Blvd., Tampa, 813-870-0934

With 31 years of experience, Gaslight specializes primarily in 18th- and 19th-century furniture and is the largest antiques-only store in Hillsborough County. We love the selection of vintage office furniture, including file cabinets and desks from the 1940s. Even if you leave empty-handed, a trip back in time before computers were desktop mainstays is an entertaining treat. Monday-Saturday 10:30 a.m.-5 p.m., Sunday noon-4 p.m.

WHERE TO STAY

★★★Grand Hyatt Tampa Bay

2900 Bayport Drive, Tampa, 813-874-1234, 800-633-7313;
www.grandtampabay.hyatt.com

Situated on a 35-acre wildlife preserve on the shores of Tampa Bay, this hotel boasts the finest views in the city. The lobby is airy and decorated in pastel tones, and the guest rooms feature comfortable bedding, overstuffed chairs and work desks. Armani's, an upscale northern Italian restaurant located on the top floor of the hotel, is a sophisticated spot with exceptional views, and Oystercatcher's, the hotel's seafood dining outlet, has the best brunch in Tampa.

445 rooms. Wireless Internet access. Three restaurants, three bars. Airport transportation available. Fitness center. Pool. Tennis. Business center. Pets accepted. $$

WHERE TO EAT

★★★Armani's

2900 Bayport Drive, Tampa, 813-207-6800;
www.armanisrestaurant.com

Perched high atop the Grand Hyatt Tampa Bay, Armani's offers views of the sunset over Tampa Bay as well as of planes taking off and landing at the nearby airport. The outdoor terrace is the perfect spot for a twilight cocktail, and the restaurant is formal and refined. The centerpiece of the restaurant is its antipasto bar, which features an extensive selection of grilled vegetables, smoked meats, pastas, olives, cheeses and other Italian treats. Armani's impressive northern Italian menu includes something for everyone—poultry, lamb, beef and fish—though the kitchen is known for its veal dishes. Classico scaloppine, Armani's veal scaloppine sautéed with wild mushrooms and cognac

in a creamy black truffle sauce, is
the signature of the house.
Italian menu. Dinner. Closed Sunday. Bar. Business casual attire.
Reservations recommended. Valet
parking. Outdoor seating. **$$$**

★★★Columbia Restaurant
**2117 E. Seventh Ave., Tampa,
813-248-4961;
www.columbiarestaurant.com**
Opened in 1905, this is Florida's
oldest restaurant. Owned and
operated by the fourth and fifth
generations of the Hernandez/
Gonzmart family, the extensive
Spanish menu includes both tapas
and full entrées. There is a $6 cover
charge for the dining room when
the flamenco show is performed.
A jazz band in the lounge enter-
tains Tuesday through Saturday
evenings. The wine cellar features
California and Spanish reds.
Spanish menu. Lunch, dinner. Bar.
Children's menu. Casual attire.
Reservations recommended. Valet
parking. **$$**

99

TAMPA

ATLANTA

SURE THERE'S PLENTY OF URBAN SPRAWL, BUT ATLANTA ALSO BOASTS world-class antique shopping with everything from garden ornaments to architectural salvage and French finds.

WHERE TO SHOP

14th Street Antiques Market
530 14th St. NW, Atlanta,
404-325-4600;
www.14thstreetantiques.com
Nationally known as one of the country's best, this 70,000-square-foot, 175-dealer showplace has just about anything one could ever want—from oil paintings of "soon-to-be ancestors" to sleek Saarinen marble-topped tables. Our favorite feature: the Market's on-site lighting and furniture restoration shop. If your finds are in need of a little restorative boost, there's no need for you to haul your purchases elsewhere. Monday-Saturday 10 a.m.-6 p.m., Sunday noon-6 p.m.

Anne Flaire Antiques
996 Huff Road, Atlanta,
404-352-1960;
www.anneflaireantiques.com
An institution in the Atlanta design world, Anne Flaire Antiques is the city's go-to source for all things French—from Art Deco to Louis to Provençal, they carry it all. And they don't just carry furniture. You're also likely to find plenty of decorative items for your garden or outdoor living space, such as a handsomely carved stone fountain or a pair of urns that serve perfectly as flower planters. Monday-Friday 9:30 a.m.-5p.m, Saturday noon-4 p.m.; closed Sunday.

Belvedere
996 Huff Road, Atlanta,
404-352-1942;
www.belvedereinc.com
When we're in need of a movie star moment we head immediately for Belvedere. And with good reason: The name, not to mention the stock—a well-preserved assortment of mid-20th century furnishings—conjures up images of Judy Garland, Frank Sinatra and other movie stars of yesteryear sitting poolside at the Beverly Hills hotel drinking martinis. Look for inspiring items like a pair of curved-front silver leaf dressers, but be warned: The stock here changes so rapidly, there's no telling what you may discover on your next visit. Tuesday-Saturday 11 a.m.-5p.m

100

THE SOUTH

★
★
★
★

The Bennett Street Market Design District

2100 block of Peachtree Road;
www.buckhead.net/bennettstreet

Take a detour from the city's famed Peachtree Road at the 2100 block, and you'll land square in the center of what locals fondly refer to as the Market Design District, a collector's haven in the heart of Buckhead teeming with so many antique shops and art galleries, you can easily spend a day or two just roaming the neighborhood. A few highlights:

Designer Antiques

25 Bennett St., Atlanta,
404-352-0254, 800-261-0283;
www.designerantiques.com

This is the store to shop if you're looking to infuse your home with European flare. Designer Antiques imports a variety of mid- to late-1800s English, Irish and French antique furniture and accessories with an understated, casual feel. The selection of antique dressers is known for its quality, and the same goes for the assortment of chests. Monday-Saturday 10:30 a.m.-5 p.m.

Cadeaux

25 Bennett St., Atlanta,
404-355-5550

This charming shop stocks an eclectic assortment of 18th- and 19th-century furnishings, architectural elements and garden gear. Call for hours.

Interiors Market

55 Bennett St., Atlanta,
404-352-0055, 800-375-9963;
www.interiorsmarket.com

You'll find everything from architectural accents to silver at this 200-dealer market. Come for the wide and varied assortment of Asian accessories and furnishings or for the solid range of European furnishings. Don't worry about buying too much—Interiors market will be happy to ship your purchases. If you can't find what you want here, ask them to contact one of their other two locations in Birmingham, Alabama, or Jackson, Mississippi. Monday-Saturday 10 a.m.-5 p.m.; closed Sunday.

The Stalls Bennett Street Antique Market and Café

116 Bennett St. NW, Atlanta,
404-352-4430;
www.thestalls.com

The curiously named Stalls Bennett Street Antique Market and Café is reminiscent of European antique haunts Portobello Road and Bermondsey in London and the Marche aux Puces de Saint-Ouen in Paris. At this stateside market, you'll find some 60 dealers specializing in international design, ranging from Italian tables to country French furnishings. Monday-Saturday 10 a.m.-5 p.m.; closed Sunday.

ATLANTA

★

★

★

★

★

Foxglove Antiques

669 Miami Circle, Atlanta,
404-233-0222;
www.foxgloveantiques.com

Known locally as one of the city's top antique stores, Foxglove stocks a stellar selection of English, French, Swedish and Italian wares. And while the furnishings, which range in scope from armoires to upholstery, are always worth a look, the real treat is digging through the accessories, including the likes of a terra-cotta statue of a whippet. After browsing the stock, take a breather and relax in the store's Café at Pharr while munching on the tasty walnut chicken salad and a glass of wine. Monday-Saturday 10 a.m.-5 p.m.; also by appointment; closed Sunday.

Great Gatsby's Antiques

Atlanta Expo Centers, 5070
Peachtree Industrial Blvd.,
Atlanta, 770-457-1903;
www.greatgatsbys.com

For more than 20 years, the folks at Great Gatsby's have been shopping the world and shipping their finds back to a 100,000-square-foot showroom, a veritable Aladdin's cave of American and European antiques and treasures. Great Gatsby's sells everything from Louis XVI chairs to ornately carved fireplace mantels, and if you're still feeling energetic after touring the showrooms, head outside to find three acres of garden benches, urns, statuary and gazebos. Monday-Saturday 9 a.m.-5 p.m.; closed Sunday.

J. Tribble Antiques

747 Miami Circle, Atlanta,
404-846-1156, 888-652-6116;
www.jtribbleantiques.com

Sure, you'll find a vast collection that encompasses everything from Art Deco and Biedermeier furnishings to African sculptures, but the real reason to love this place is that it's one of the few antique shops to offer antique or antique-inspired bases for kitchen islands, wet bars and bathrooms. Monday-Friday 9:30 a.m.-5:30 p.m., Saturday 11 a.m.-4 p.m.; closed Sunday.

Pieces, Inc.

3234 Roswell Road NW, Atlanta,
404-869-2476;
www.piecesinc.com

Pieces, Inc. specializes in fashionable home furnishings and accessories from chic glassware to bark rope pillows. Owner Lee Kleinhelter, a former associate of Dan Carithers, one of the city's legendary interior designers, opened the shop in May of 2004. In the four years since, Lee has been wowing locals and home décor gurus with her fresh take on vintage finds, like a pair of black trellis dining chairs she upholstered in hot pink or a vintage Morroccanesque lantern painted daffodil yellow. At Pieces, it's all about seeing vintage finds in a new light. Monday-Friday 10 a.m.-6 p.m., Saturday 10 a.m.-5 p.m.; closed Sunday.

THE SOUTH

★

★

★

★

Scott Antiques Market

Atlanta Expo Centers, 3650
Jonesboro Road, Atlanta,
740-569-4112;
www.scottantiquemarket.com

Billing itself as the "world's largest indoor antiques shows," the Scott Antiques Market is a treasure hunter's paradise, with more than 2,400 vendors offering a huge selection of gold and silver jewelry, antique pottery, glassware and furniture. It's going to take some time to sort through the stands, so put on a pair of comfortable shoes, bring a tote bag to carry your loot and come early so you can escape before the midday crowd descends. June-December: second weekend of every month, Friday-Saturday 9 a.m.-6 p.m., Sunday 10 a.m.-4 p.m.

William Word Fine Antiques

707–709 Miami Circle, Atlanta,
404-233-6890;
www.williamwordantiques.com

Over the past 52 years, William Word Antiques has grown from a small basement furniture restoration business to a full-fledged antiques dealer with 16,000 square feet of showroom space and a wide selection of elegant furnishings (with prices to match). Expect a variety of antiques ranging from exquisite Biedermeier armoires and burled wood linen presses to 19th-century iron garden gates and Regency-period mahogany stools. In addition to the expected American, English and French furnishings, William Word also stocks a nice range of goods from

Germany and Holland. Monday-Friday 10 a.m.-5 p.m., Saturday 11 a.m.-5 p.m.; closed Sunday.

WHERE TO STAY

★★★★★Four Seasons Hotel Atlanta

75 14th St., Atlanta,
404-881-9898, 800-332-3442;
www.fourseasons.com

This Neoclassical tower rises over Atlanta's Midtown, where world-class culture, flourishing businesses and enticing stores line the streets. This hotel offers its guests fine accommodations and flawless, intuitive service. Earth tones and polished woods set a relaxed elegance in the rooms and suites. The state-of-the-art fitness center is complete with an indoor pool and sun terrace. Park 75's fresh approach to American cuisine earns praise from locals and hotel guests alike. Service is top-notch, from the twice-daily turn-down service to the affable staff at the door.

244 rooms. High-speed Internet access. Restaurant, bar. Fitness center. Pool. Business center. Pets accepted. $$$$

★★★★InterContinental Buckhead

3315 Peachtree Road NE, Atlanta,
404-946-9000, 800-972-2404;
www.intercontinental.com

This luxe hotel is within walking distance of Lenox Square, the largest shopping mall in the Southeast, as well as the upscale Phipps Plaza.

ATLANTA

Guest rooms have pillow-top bedding, floor-to-ceiling windows and large marble bathrooms. This establishment also boasts the only day spa in an Atlanta hotel. The lovely grounds add to the property's Southern elegance. Early risers are treated to a complimentary breakfast from 5 to 7 a.m.

422 rooms. Wireless Internet access. Complimentary breakfast. Restaurant, bar. Spa. **$$$**

★★★★The Ritz-Carlton, Buckhead

3434 Peachtree Road NE, Atlanta,
404-237-2700, 800-241-3333;
www.ritzcarlton.com

This hotel in one of the city's most fashionable neighborhoods offers a warm and luxurious experience. A recent renovation made way for updated rooms with antique furnishings and amenities like pillow-top mattresses and flat-screen TVs. Bay windows in each room or suite showcase views of the downtown skyline. Afternoon tea in the Lobby Lounge is a great way to relax, especially after a day of perusing the area's shops, and the Café is a popular gathering place for casual fare. After an extensive kitchen overhaul, The Dining Room has reopened under acclaimed Chef Arnaud Berthelier and serves award-winning French cuisine.

533 rooms. Wireless Internet access. Restaurant, bar. Airport transportation available. Fitness center. Pool, whirlpool. Business center. Pets accepted. **$$$**

WHERE TO EAT

★★★★Bacchanalia

1198 Howell Mill Road, Atlanta,
404-365-0410;
www.starprovisions.com

Set in a renovated factory complex, this urban dining room has a sleek, industrial feel. The dramatic vaulted ceiling and exposed brick-trimmed factory windows are the perfect foil to the long, low-lit, sexy bar. Chefs Anne Quatrano and Clifford Harrison create vibrant, seasonal American menus that change daily based on whatever organic and small-farm produce is available. Plates are presented with little fuss but lots of flavor. The wine list includes a thoughtful collection of food-friendly choices by the bottle or the glass.

American menu. Dinner. Bar. Business casual attire. Reservations recommended. Outdoor seating. **$$$**

★★★★★The Dining Room

3434 Peachtree Road NE, Atlanta, 404-237-2700, 800-241-3333; www.ritzcarlton.com

Prepare for an extraordinary experience when dining in the masterful hands of Chef Arnaud Berthelier, who creates menus influenced by the lively flavors of France, Spain and northern Africa at The Dining Room in the Ritz-Carlton, Buckhead. The restaurant closed in early 2008 for three months of kitchen renovations. During that time, the chef was dispatched to Spain and the sommelier to California to find new inspiration for the restaurant's menus. Dishes served in the classically elegant room (think deep, tufted banquettes cloaked in Victorian green silk) include sweetbread kebobs with tomato confit, lobster and citrus cocotte, or truffle-stuffed guinea hen. After dessert and a cheese course, sample the petit fours, which arrive in numbers.

French menu. Dinner. Closed Sunday-Monday. Jacket required. Reservations recommended. Valet parking. **$$$$**

★★★★Park 75
75 14th St. NE, Atlanta,
404-253-3840, 800-332-3442;
www.fourseasons.com

Located in the Four Seasons Hotel, Park 75 is a classic choice for tranquil and comfortable fine dining. The serene, pale-yellow room is warmed by iron candelabras, custom lighting and oversized watercolor murals. The cross-cultural menu takes its cue from the season, offering the finest local vegetables, meats and fish. The signature Park 75 surf and turf combines butter-braised Maine lobster with milk-fed veal filet and foie gras. The wine list is mostly American, with some boutique and international selections. For a special treat, reserve the chef's table and enjoy an eight-course menu with wines to match.

American menu. Breakfast, lunch, dinner, Sunday brunch. Bar. Children's menu. Business casual attire. Reservations recommended. Valet parking. **$$$**

★★★★Quinones at Bacchanalia
1190 Howell Mill Road, Atlanta,
404-365-0410;
www.starprovisions.com

Quinones at Bacchanalia has a cozy dining area—there are only 11 tables—and an intimate atmosphere with pressed Irish linens and oil lamps on the tabletops. A ten-course prix fixe contemporary American menu features new creations daily. Sample Southern-influenced dishes, such as squab with turnips, turnip greens and butter beans or flounder with local pecans, apples and butternut squash. Desserts are elegant takes on Southern classics like the pecan tart with vanilla bean ice cream.

Contemporary American menu. Dinner. Closed Sunday-Tuesday. Business casual attire. Reservations recommended. **$$$$**

KENTUCKY

LOUISVILLE

HOME OF THE KENTUCKY DERBY, LOUISVILLE ALSO PLAYS HOST TO A BUS-tling antiques scene—think everything from architectural salvage to high-quality European pieces—as well as stunning hostelries and terrific dining options.

WHERE TO SHOP

Architectural Salvage
614–618 E. Broadway, Louisville,
505-589-0670;
www.architecturalsalvage.com
Architectural Salvage hosts a vast inventory of antique light fixtures, mantels, entryways and backbars, as well as a constant stock of unusual items. You could go home with everything from delicious 1910 medallions that originally decorated Louisville's Milner Hotel to doorknobs richly festooned with vines and flowers and handfuls of colorful milk glass drawer pulls. Monday-Friday 9 a.m.-5 p.m., Saturday 10 a.m.-3:30 p.m.; closed Sunday.

Joe Ley Antiques
615 E. Market St., Louisville,
502-583-4014; www.joeley.com
Located in a former schoolhouse, Joe Ley covers two acres of space with antique toys, carousel animals, vintage signs and the occasional clown. You'll go crazy for all of the terrific finds here, including doorstops, intricate hall trees and ornate chairs, including a Gothic-style sanctuary chair that would make a dramatic impression in the corner of any living room. Tuesday-Saturday 8:30 a.m.-5 p.m.; closed Sunday-Monday.

Kentucky Flea Market
Kentucky Fair and Expo Center,
Louisville, 502-456-2244;
www.stewartpromotions.com
The 25-year-old Kentucky Flea Market hosts over 1,000 booths at each monthly fair, and you never know what you'll find. Admission to most fairs is free. Check Web site for exact show dates. Friday noon-7 p.m., Saturday 10 a.m.-7 p.m., Sunday 11 a.m.-5 p.m; Memorial Day and Labor Day Monday 10 a.m.-5 p.m.

Schumann Antiques
4545 Taylorsville Road, Louisville,
502-491-0134;
www.schumannantiques.com
Schumann Antiques carries a large selection of English, French and American antiques with an emphasis on furniture and superb craftsmanship. Looking for high-

THE SOUTH

boys? Check. You like lowboys? Check. Lamps, glassware, chandeliers, chests and artwork. It's all inside. Monday-Friday 8 a.m.-5 p.m., Saturday 11 a.m.-4 p.m.; closed Sunday.

Trace Mayer Antiques
3700 Lexington Road, Louisville, 502-899-5335;
www.tracemayer.com

Trace Mayer sells a variety of decorative and fine arts. You'll find period English, Continental and American items here. From Victorian-era mother-of-pearl card cases and a 19th-century burl and yew snuff box to American handblown glasses dating from 1820–40, the vintage prizes are aplenty. Tuesday-Saturday 10 a.m.-5 p.m.; closed Sunday, Monday.

WHERE TO STAY

★★★21c Museum Hotel
700 W. Main St., Louisville, 502-217-6300, 877-217-6400;
www.21cmuseumhotel.com

This award-winning museum-hotel hybrid puts a premium on good design. Sprinkled throughout the hotel are photographs, paintings and sculptures from some of the world's top contemporary artists (one guest room even boasts a Chuck Close portrait); the 9,000-square-foot museum is funded by the International Contemporary Art Foundation. Rooms are appropriately loaded with 21st-century amenities, including oversized plasma TVs and iPods (customized prearrival with your favorite music) as well as luxuri-

ous Malin and Goetz amenities. The hotel includes an onsite spa and fitness center as well as the acclaimed restaurant Proof on Main.
90 rooms. Wireless Internet access. Restaurant, bar. Fitness center. Spa. **$$**

★★★The Seelbach Hilton Louisville
500 Fourth Ave., Louisville, 502-585-3200, 800-333-3399;
www.seelbachhilton.com

Elegant and historic, the Seelbach Hotel provides a luxurious home-away-from-home. Built in 1905 by brothers Otto and Louis Seelbach, this landmark in the heart of downtown Louisville is immortalized in F. Scott Fitzgerald's *The Great Gatsby* as the site of Tom and Daisy Buchanan's wedding. Magnificent Belle Époque architecture and glittering interiors reflect an era long past, but the Seelbach offers all the amenities a contemporary traveler could want. The rooms and suites are charming with 18th-century period reproductions and rich fabrics. Don't miss the sensational Oakroom restaurant.
321 rooms. High-speed Internet access. Two restaurants, bar. Airport transportation available. Pets accepted. **$$**

LOUISVILLE

★

★

★

★

★

WHERE TO EAT

★★★ Le Relais

2817 Taylorsville Road, Louisville, 502-451-9020;
www.lerelaisrestaurant.com

This romantic French bistro is tucked away in the historic Administration Building in Bowman Field. Its comfortable and elegant Art Deco dining room, wonderful service and creative French menu has made Le Relais one of the most beloved restaurants in Louisville. Fresh, seasonal ingredients fill the menu in dishes like herb-encrusted venison rack with braised cabbage, carrots and potatoes; certified Angus beef filet with roasted potato and root vegetables; and duck confit with sage polenta cake, flageolet beans and baby brussel sprouts. A well-crafted wine list beautifully complements every dish.

French menu. Dinner. Closed Monday. Business casual attire. Reservations recommended. Outdoor seating. $$$

★★★ Proof on Main

702 W. Main St., Louisville, 502-217-6360;
www.proofonmain.com

Art collectors and Kentucky philanthropists Steve Wilson and Laura Lee Brown (heir to a liquor fortune built by brands such as Jack Daniels) launched this cutting-edge restaurant in 2006. Along with the adjacent 21c Museum Hotel, Proof on Main (the name is a nod to their bourbon past) is a prime spot for showcasing top-notch contemporary art and food. Executive chef Michael Paley sources local ingredients and puts them to good use in dishes such as Kentucky bison tenderloin with buttered leeks and fingerling potatoes or smoked chicken with grain mustard and roasted string beans. Desserts include twists on Southern classics such as bread pudding (this version comes in chocolate with sea salt-caramel gelato).

American, Italian menu. Breakfast, lunch, dinner. Bar. Valet parking. Outdoor seating. $$

108

THE SOUTH

NEW ORLEANS

REBOUNDING FROM THE DEVASTATION OF HURRICANE KATRINA, NEW Orleans is bustling once again, and its glorious antique shops are attracting a far-flung clientele with far-reaching offerings in a wildly romantic setting.

WHERE TO SHOP

Bush Antiques
2109 Magazine St., New Orleans, 504-581-3518; www.bushantiques.com

This charming shop specializes in elegant Continental furniture, such as antique beds (many with their original paint) and clerical items—if you need a bronze and brass crucifix from France dated 1860, you know where to go. There are also fun and wacky accessories like a silk-lined snake charmer's basket dating from 1900 and a set of four deep-blue English ginger beer bottles dating from 1930 that are terribly posh. Monday-Saturday 10 a.m.-5 p.m.; closed Sunday.

French Antique Shop
225 Royal St., New Orleans, 504-524-9861, 866-524-9861; www.gofrenchantiques.com

Founded by a Parisian couple who share a passion for antiques, the French Antique Shop has a sizable selection of 18th- and 19th-century country and sophis-ticated furnishings, as well as an extensive display of marble mantels and gold leaf mirrors, bronze statues and Continental and Oriental porcelains. This is ornate, overwrought merchandise full of gorgeous details but not necessarily for the modernist looking for clean lines and minimalist furnishings. Standout items include a 19th-century Napoleon III gilt bronze and Baccarat chandelier and a Louis XV desk with ormolu desks and a tooled leather top. Monday-Saturday 9:30 a.m.-4:30 p.m.; closed Sunday.

French Market Community Flea Market
1008 N. Peters St., New Orleans, 504-522-2621; www.frenchmarket.org

What began as a Native American trading post now offers everything from a farmers' market to a bric-a-brac-filled flea market. Whether it's a pair of vintage jeans from the 1970s or a set of plates emblazoned with cavorting monkeys, it's unlikely you'll go home empty-handed. Daily 9 a.m.-6 p.m.

109

NEW ORLEANS

★

★

★

★

Ida Manheim Antiques

409 Royal St., New Orleans,
504-620-4114, 888-627-5969;
www.idamanheimantiques.com
Founded by a master cabinet-maker, Ida Manheim Antiques specializes in cabinets and European furnishings. The collection boasts numerous museum-quality pieces, such as a monumental William and Mary walnut chest on a stand dating back to 1690 and a highly carved Louis XV oak wedding armoire. Monday-Saturday 9 a.m.-5 p.m.; closed Sunday.

Magazine Street

Magazine St., New Orleans,
504-342-4435, 866-679-4764;
www.magazinestreet.com
Fun and funky, Magazine Street offers six miles of clothing retailers, antique establishments, gift shops, eateries and more. Most of the businesses are housed in 19th-century buildings or brick-faced cottages, which help the area maintain its otherworldly charm. You can stroll from the French Quarter to the Audubon Zoo, picking up a piece of jewelry, some furniture, a book or a bite to eat along the way. Make a point to stop off at the Magazine Arcade, a mini mall that houses eclectic shops offering antique household items, music boxes and musical instruments, period medical equipment, and dolls and their furnishings. Most shops open daily 10 a.m.-5 p.m.

M. S. Rau Antiques

630 Royal St., New Orleans,
504-523-5660, 800-544-9440;
www.rauantiques.com
Internationally known names such as Paul Revere, Meissen, Faberge, Wedgwood, Tiffany and Chippendale are represented in the 25,000-square-foot showroom and extensive catalogue. You can also pick up fabulous diamonds, jewelry, silver and objets d'art among the vast array of American and European antiques. Monday-Saturday 9 a.m.-5:15 p.m.; closed Sunday.

Rothschild Antiques

321 Royal St., New Orleans,
504-523-5816;
www.rothschildsantiques.com
Rothschild is a fourth-generation antique shop with jewelry, chandeliers, mantels and furniture. You'll love wandering through Rothschild's vast display space and feasting on the exclusive merchandise. But come prepared for equally exclusive price tags. Monday-Saturday 10 a.m.-5 p.m.; closed Sunday.

WHERE TO STAY

★★★Dauphine Orleans Hotel

415 Dauphine St., New Orleans,
504-586-1800, 800-521-7111;
www.dauphineorleans.com
This hotel offers guests quiet luxury and a few good stories. May Baily's Place, the hotel's bar, was once a popular 19th-century bordello in the city's red light district. Guests and staff members have claimed to see ghosts—perhaps

the bawdy kind—lurking around here. And John James Audubon, famous naturalist and artist, painted his well-known "Birds of America" series from 1821-22 in the hotel's main meeting room (which used to be a cottage). In addition to all the history, the charming boutique hotel serves guests a complimentary welcome cocktail, continental breakfast and afternoon tea.

111 rooms. Complimentary continental breakfast. Bar. $$

★★★Hotel Monteleone
214 Rue Royale, New Orleans, 504-523-3341; www.hotelmonteleone.com

The French Quarter's oldest and largest hotel has been rolling out the red carpet for its guests since 1886. Katrina broke windows, so the rooms have recently been renovated, and though they vary in size and style, they're comfortable and well appointed. For decades, locals have favored the Monteleone's Carousel Bar, where some seats revolve around the room (hence the watering hole's name). After cocktails, take a seat inside the Hunt Room Grill for fine dining. For recreation, head up to the rooftop for a dip in the pool or a workout in the well-equipped fitness center, which offers splendid views of the French Quarter and the Mississippi River.

600 rooms. Restaurant, bar. $$

★★★Lafitte Guest House
1003 Bourbon St., New Orleans, 504-581-2678, 800-331-7971; www.lafitteguesthouse.com

Want to feel as though you're in the mid-19th century, visiting with some friends? This three-story bed and breakfast should do the trick. Each room has its own Victorian flair, and the ground-floor sitting room will make you want to linger, sipping a mint julep. Best of all, breakfast is delivered to wherever you choose: your room, your balcony or the courtyard. Most of the guest rooms have private balconies with views of Bourbon Street or the French Quarter.

14 rooms. Complimentary continental breakfast. $

★★★Le Pavillon Hotel
833 Poydras St., New Orleans, 504-581-3111

This historic hotel has seen it all: wars, prohibition and the birth of the horseless carriage. The Crystal Suite contains a hand-carved marble bathtub, a gift from Napoleon to a wealthy Louisiana plantation owner—just like the one in the Louvre. But this hotel isn't too stuffy; peanut butter-and-jelly sandwiches, milk and chocolates are offered in the lobby after hours.

226 rooms. Restaurant, bar. Airport transportation available. $

NEW ORLEANS

★

★

★

★

★★★International House
221 Camp St., New Orleans,
504-553-9550, 800-633-5770;
www.ihhotel.com

At this top-rated boutique hotel, the décor is a winning blend of New Orleans style and contemporary chic. The charming folk art and handmade furniture created by Louisiana artisans serve as a pleasant reminder of Cajun country tradition, but the stainless steel and marble accents give the intimate hotel a cosmopolitan feel. Get in touch with the spirits at Loa (the Voodoo word for deities), a dark bar lighted only by candles.

119 rooms. Restaurant, bar. $$

★★★The Ritz-Carlton, New Orleans
921 Canal St., New Orleans,
504-524-1331, 800-241-3333;
www.ritzcarlton.com

The Ritz-Carlton brings its luxury brand to the edge of the French Quarter and offers the refined elegance travelers expect from the Ritz. The guest rooms have a timeless elegance, topped off by feather beds and deep-soaking tubs, and the spa is renowned for its unparalleled services, delivered in a gorgeous setting. If all this relaxing makes you hungry, try the bistro-style FQB for its casual setting or Victors for its dazzling setting and refined cuisine. The exquisite lounge offers an unrivaled afternoon tea set to the gentle strains of a harp.

527 rooms. Restaurant, bar. Airport transportation available. $$

★★★Royal Sonesta Hotel New Orleans
300 Bourbon St., New Orleans,
504-586-0300

Gabled windows. French doors. Wrought iron lace balconies. Gilded mirrors. Furniture reminiscent of 18th-century France. Tranquil, beautifully landscaped courtyards. This property occupies a full block right on Bourbon Street, and it looks like it belongs in this historic district. If you crave a gourmet meal, sample the contemporary French and Creole cuisine served at Begues Restaurant. For something more casual, opt for the Desire Oyster Bar, where the chefs cook up both Creole and seafood dishes. Party at the Mystick Den cocktail lounge or the Can-Can Café and Jazz Club. If you just want to rest and relax, lounge out by the pool on an appealing third-floor terrace.

484 rooms. Two restaurants, two bars. Pool. $$$

★★★St. James Hotel
330 Magazine St.,New Orleans,
504-304-4000, 888-856-4485;
www.saintjameshotel.com

The St. James has the look of a distinguished older property because it occupies a renovated building from the 1850s. The building has wrought iron balconies and some rooms feature exposed-brick walls. Rooftop terraces overlook a small pool in a charming courtyard. Cuvée restaurant offers contemporary Creole cuisine and more than 500 wine choices.

90 rooms. Restaurant, bar. Airport transportation available. $$

★★★W New Orleans
333 Poydras St., New Orleans,
504-525-9444, 800-522-6963;
www.whotels.com
This style-soaked chain is designed for savvy business travelers, but leisure guests won't mind the down comforters, Aveda products and great fitness center. Zoe Bistro offers creative French food and the lobby's Whiskey Blue bar delivers a dose of Randy Gerber-style nightlife.
423 rooms. Restaurant, bar. $$$

★★★★Windsor Court Hotel
300 Gravier St., New Orleans,
504-523-6000, 888-596-0955,
www.windsorcourthotel.com
Located in the city's business district and a short walk from the historic French Quarter, the Windsor Court brings a bit of the English countryside to New Orleans. Guest rooms feature traditional English furnishings and artwork, Italian marble bathrooms and elegant touches, such as complimentary imported chocolates or pralines at turndown. Balconies or bay windows provide scenic views of the city and the Mississippi River from every room. This full-service hotel also includes a pool, sundeck, business and fitness centers and terrific restaurants.
324 rooms. High-speed Internet access. Restaurant, bar. Fitness center. Pool. Business center. Pets accepted. $$

WHERE TO EAT

★★★★Bayona
430 Dauphine St., New Orleans,
504-525-4455; www.bayona.com
A little slice of the romantic Mediterranean awaits you at Bayona, a jewel of a restaurant tucked into a 200-year-old Creole cottage in the heart of the French Quarter. The cozy room is often set with fresh flowers and warmed by sunny lighting and bright colors. Chef Susan Spicer serves up her own interpretation of New Orleans cuisine, blending the ingredients of the Mediterranean with the flavors of Alsace, Asia, India and the Southwest. You'll find an outstanding waitstaff eager to guide you and answer questions about the menu. The restaurant has a great selection of beers, including several local brews, plus an extensive wine list.
International menu. Lunch, dinner. Closed Sunday-Monday, Mardi Gras. Business casual attire. Reservations recommended. Outdoor seating. $$$

★★★Cuvee
322 Magazine St., New Orleans,
504-587-9001;
www.restaurantcuvee.com
Foodies love this restaurant for its innovative menu and excellent advice on wine and food pairings. Opened in 1999 and considered an upstart in this city of decades-old dining establishments, Cuvee has gained a reputation as one of New Orleans' finest gourmet restaurants. With just 85 seats, the

NEW ORLEANS

intimate restaurant is housed in a landmark 1833 building whose age strangely complements its nouveau New Orleans cuisine (think sugar cane–smoked duck breast and crispy confit leg served with Hudson Valley foie gras and Roquefort-pecan risotto).

Creole menu. Lunch, dinner. Closed Sunday. Bar. Business casual attire. Reservations recommended. Valet parking. $$$

★★★ Emeril's Restaurant
800 Tchoupitoulas St.,
New Orleans, 504-528-9393,
800-980-8474; www.emerils.com

Emeril's is a chic and stylish hotspot located in the Central Business District—and not only that, it's the place that started it all for celebrity chef Emeril Lagasse. With lofty ceilings, an open kitchen and a towering wooden wine wall, the restaurant is a dynamic space that suits its urban Warehouse District neighborhood. The slick food bar is a fun spot to take in the buzzing see-and-be-seen crowd. The room can get loud, but the vibe is good. The menu employs a world of herbs, spices and chilies that awaken the palate with a bam!

Cajun/Creole menu. Dinner. Closed Sunday. Bar. Business casual attire. Reservations recommended. Valet parking. $$$

★★★★ The New Orleans Grill
300 Gravier St., New Orleans,
504-522-1994, 888-596-0955;
www.windsorcourthotel.com

Dining at The New Orleans Grill (located inside the Windsor Court Hotel) may be one of the most luxurious ways to spend an evening in this city. With a menu that changes monthly and features locally grown and organic foods whenever possible, the restaurant is known for its fabulous contemporary American cuisine. Gumbo is taken to a new level here with locally raised organic chicken and native-grown rice. Enjoy live music on Friday nights in the lounge.

French-influenced menu. Breakfast, lunch, dinner. Bar. Children's menu. Jacket required. Reservations recommended. Valet parking. $$$

★★★ Restaurant August
301 Tchoupitoulas St.,
New Orleans, 504-299-9777;
www.rest-august.com

Step into this converted 18th-century townhouse, and you're sure to be greeted with a hearty welcome. August's warm, exposed-brick room features vaulted ceilings and old-world antiques. Dining at August is all about being pampered, and chef Jon Besh does a wonderful job of spreading the love from the kitchen with an innovative and delicious menu of dishes that marry robust ingredients from Spain and France with regional flavors. His menu changes seasonally, but two flawless signatures are the Moroccan-spiced duck with polenta and tempura dates, and the BLT, made from meaty fried Buster crabs, lettuce and heirloom tomatoes on a slab of brioche.

French menu. Lunch, dinner. Closed Sunday. Business casual attire. Reservations recommended. Valet parking. **$$$$**

NEW ORLEANS

CHARLOTTE

THIS BANKING CAPITAL HAS A VARIED RANGE OF ANTIQUE EMPORIA, FROM classic American finds to more Continental creations.

WHERE TO SHOP

Antique Kingdom, Inc.

700 Central Ave., Charlotte,
704-377-5464;
www.antiquekingdom.biz
Walking through the front door of Antique Kingdom, a charming white two-story house with a signature Southern-style columned front porch, is like stepping into the home of a favorite great-aunt who never discarded a thing. Here you'll find a vast assortment of classic American maple, cherry, walnut and mahogany chairs, drawers, armoires, tables and more. Wednesday-Saturday 10 a.m.-6 p.m., Monday-Tuesday by appointment only; closed Sunday.

★ Circa Interiors & Antiques

2321 Crescent Ave., Charlotte,
704-332-1668;
www.circaonline.net
A favorite among designers, Circa Interiors offers a wide array of 18th-, 19th- and 20th-century English and Continental antiques. The shop's design staff will also gladly help devise and implement a plan for decorating your home. By appointment only.

Fifteen Ten Antiques

1510 Central Ave., Charlotte,
704-342-9005;
www.1510-antiques.com
If you're drawn to the overstuffed, eclectic look of English country houses, you should feel right at home among this shop's wonderful assortment of furniture, accessories, light fixtures and fine art from the 19th and 20th centuries. We do and, therefore, love nothing more than spending a Saturday afternoon roaming this 3,500-square-foot showroom to eye the stock of Victorian settees, dining tables and more. And because the furnishings are arranged in colorful roomlike vignettes, we pick up a new decorating tip or two every time we visit. Monday-Saturday 10 a.m.-6 p.m., Sunday 1-5 p.m.

McColl Fine Art

208 East Blvd., Charlotte,
704-333-5983;
www.mccollfineart.com
This unexpected gem specializes in European and American fine art from the 19th and 20th centuries—some of the best we've seen outside of New York, London and Paris. Whether you're looking for

a seascape watercolor by Henry Bacon to display in the foyer or a romantic landscape by Edward Barnard to hang over the fireplace, you're likely to find it here. Tuesday-Friday 10 a.m.-6 p.m., Saturday 10 a.m.-3 p.m.; also by appointment.

WHERE TO STAY

★★★★The Ballantyne Resort, a Luxury Collection Hotel
10000 Ballantyne Commons Parkway, Charlotte, 704-248-4000, 866-248-4824; www.ballantyneresort.com

This elegant resort within the city limits of Charlotte is a paradise for golf enthusiasts, having one of the state's best 18-hole courses and the renowned Dana Rader Golf School. Rooms are crisply and classically decorated and have lavish finishes, such as marble entrances and bathrooms. The Gallery Restaurant offers creative selections and seasonal ingredients, while the Gallery Bar serves a tapas menu and lengthy selection of cocktails, whiskeys and after-dinner drinks.
249 rooms. Wireless Internet access. Restaurant, two bars. Airport transportation available. Fitness center. Spa. $$

★★★The Duke Mansion
400 Hermitage Road, Charlotte, 704-714-4400, 888-202-1009; www.dukemansion.com

This 1915 Southern estate is a lovely setting for a weekend getaway. The Colonial Revival house was once owned by James Buchanan Duke, founder of Duke University. Acres of gardens surround the well-maintained house. Treetop-leveled rooms as well as standard guest rooms—some with sleeping porches—are decorated with traditional and antique furniture. The mansion also serves as a facility for meetings and retreats. 20 rooms. Wireless Internet access. Complimentary full breakfast. $$

WHERE TO EAT

★★★★Gallery Restaurant & Bar
10000 Ballantyne Commons Parkway, Charlotte, 704-248-4000, 866-248-4824; www.gallery-restaurant.com

The setting is relaxing and welcoming at Gallery Restaurant & Bar, located on the ground level of the Ballantyne Resort. Artfully presented dishes like cedar plank-roasted sea bass with blue crab, shallots and English pea risotto or rosemary- and citrus-roasted free-range chicken dazzle the palate, while the service makes dining here a delight.
American menu. Breakfast, lunch, dinner. Bar. Business casual attire. Reservations recommended. Valet parking. Outdoor seating. $$$

★★★McNinch House
511 N. Church St., Charlotte, 704-332-6159; www.mcninchhouserestaurant.com

This restaurant's unique setting, attention to detail and ever-changing but consistently strong French menu are well suited for

★

★

★

★

special occasion dinners. Situated in a historic building, McNinch House is in a residential area on the west side of Church Street and within walking distance of downtown hotels and businesses.

French menu. Dinner. Closed Sunday-Monday. Bar. Jacket required. Reservations recommended. Valet parking. **$$$$**

GREENSBORO

OLD TOBACCO MONEY BARONS ONCE STOCKED UP ON EUROPEAN antiques, many of which have made their way into the city's antiques shops. You just might encounter a museum-worthy piece at a surprisingly reasonable price.

WHERE TO SHOP

The Antique Marketplace
6428 Burnt Poplar Road, Greensboro, 336-662-0544; www.antiquemarketplace.biz
Conveniently located just off I-40 between Greensboro and Winston-Salem, this 45,000-square-foot mall has just about anything you could want—from early 20th-century oak vitrine china cabinets to wicker baby carriages and classic pedal car toys. Fall in love with a chest of drawers but worried that the musty smell will damage your clothes? The Marketplace's knowledgeable staff will happily offer instructions for remedying this and other antiques imperfections. Monday-Wednesday 10 a.m.-6 p.m., Thursday-Saturday 10 a.m.-8 p.m., Sunday 1-6 p.m.

Caroline Faison Antiques
18 Battleground Court, Greensboro, 336-272-0261; www.carolinefaisonantiques.com
You don't have to travel to Europe to find the best in 17th-, 18th- and 19th-century Continental furniture and decorative objects. You only have to visit Caroline Faison Antiques, a fixture in Greensboro for more than 40 years. Here you'll find a well-edited assortment of period cabinets, chests of drawers, Louis-style chairs and ornately carved hall tables—in short, everything you could possibly need to give your house a touch of Continental flare except a butler named Jeeves. Monday-Friday 10 a.m.-4 p.m.; also by appointment.

Replacements
1089 Know Road, Greensboro, 336-697-3100, 800-737-5223; www.replacements.com
Founded in 1981, Replacements boasts the world's largest collection of old and new dinnerware, crystal, glassware, silver, stainless ware, and collectibles—some 12

★
★
★
★

million objects in total. If you're searching for missing pieces to Grandma's good china, chances are this shop has it or, at the very least, the staff knows where to find it. Daily 8 a.m.-10 p.m.

Super Flea Market

Greensboro Coliseum Pavilion, 1921 W. Lee St., Greensboro, 336-373-8515; www.superflea.com

Established in 1976, the market brings together hundreds of dealers from throughout the Southeast, many of whom have been with the show since its inception. In fact, the range of merchandise and dealers is so varied and eclectic that many locals fondly refer to this monthly event as the "variety show of fleas." See for yourself with a visit to the 30,000-square-foot Greensboro Coliseum. Monthly: Check Web site for dates. Saturday 9 a.m.-5 p.m, Sunday 10 a.m.-4 p.m.

WHERE TO STAY

★★★O. Henry Hotel

624 Green Valley Road, Greensboro, 336-854-2000; 800-965-8527 www.ohenryhotel.com

This locally owned boutique hotel —named for the writer William Sydney Porter (O. Henry), who was born and raised in Greensboro—is decorated with North Carolina pine walls and ceilings, marble floors, Oriental carpets, leather and brocade furniture and large windows that overlook

a cloistered courtyard. The spacious guest rooms include separate dressing rooms and soaking tubs.

131 rooms. Wireless Internet access. Restaurant, bar. Airport transportation available. $$

WHERE TO EAT

★★★Restaurant Muse

3124 Kathleen Ave., Greenboro, 336-323-1428; www.restaurantmuse.net

Exquisite French cuisine prepared with fresh local ingredients draws diners back to Restaurant Muse time and time again. Chef/owner Mitchell Nicks offers creative plates, which include roasted rack of lamb brushed with bergamot and mustard as well as his "untraditional Brutus salad" with pancetta, spicy chile dressing, fried artichoke hearts and a manchego cheese crisp. An á la carte menu is available, as is a chef's tasting menu.

French menu. Lunch, dinner, brunch. Bar. Business casual attire. Reservations recommended. Outdoor seating. $$$

119

GREENSBORO

RALEIGH-DURHAM/CHAPEL HILL

HOME TO DUKE UNIVERSITY, THIS BUSY INTELLECTUAL ENCLAVE ENCOMpasses a wide range of antique emporia selling everything from Federal furnishings to midcentury finds.

WHERE TO SHOP

Countryside Antiques
9555 Highway 15-501, Chapel Hill, 919-968-8375;
www.cs-antiques.com
Housed in a classic white clapboard Colonial, Countryside specializes in 18th- and 19th-century American antique furniture like Federal-style chests of drawers that would fit nicely in any front hall or foyer. The selection of Asian porcelain is also outstanding, with many pieces dating from the early to mid-1800s. There's even a selection of primitive pottery pieces by native North Carolina artists. Wednesday-Saturday 10 a.m.-5 p.m.

Flea Market at the NC State Fairgrounds
1025 Blue Ridge Road, Raleigh, 919-829-3533;
www.ncstatefair.org/fleamarket
Our friends in the South, including some very in-the-know furniture designers, rave about this weekly market set on the NC State Fairgrounds. Organizers for the market boast that it offers the largest collection of antiques, jewelry and furniture in North Carolina, and while we can't vouch for that, we can tell you that the selection, which includes everything

from garden statuary to stained glass windows, is stunning. Saturday-Sunday (except in October when the state fair is in progress) 9 a.m.-5 p.m.

Glenwood South Antiques
122 Glenwood Ave., Raleigh, 919-828-2559;
www.glenwoodsouthantiques.com
Chippendale, Hepplewhite and Sheraton—if these names set your heart racing, then head to Glenwood South in Raleigh, a charming shop founded by W. Samuel Tarlton, the former director of North Carolina Historic Sites. Since opening the doors to Glenwood South in 1985, Tarlton has made it his mission to seek out and sell only the best in 18th- and 19th-century regional Americana furnishings and art. This means an outstanding selection of Queen Anne-style dining chairs, Colonial Williamsburg cabinets and Victorian parlor furniture. Call for hours.

The Last Unicorn
536 Edwards Ridge Road, Chapel Hill, 919-968-8440;
www.thelastunicorn.com
From the name, you might think this Chapel Hill shop stocks spells and potions, but it doesn't. The name, it seems, simply reflects

★
★
★
★

owner Gaines Steer's interest in these mythical creatures. Instead, the shop, which Steer has tended since 1975, has an eclectic assortment of salvaged wrought iron gates, statuary and other vintage garden gear. Saturday 10 a.m.-5 p.m.; also by appointment.

Swankarama
107 W. Hargett St., Raleigh,
919-832-3030;
www.swankarama.com

If words like *groovy* and *jet set* describe your taste in decorating, then a stop at Swankarama is a must. Here, in addition to the lineup of usual suspects (i.e. Knoll and Herman Miller), you'll also find a surprising selection of rarer finds like Thayer Coggin lounge chairs by Milo Baughman or teak arm chairs by Jens Risom. There's even a nice assortment of textiles, ranging from mod 1960s-style prints to funky 1950s barkcloth. Monday-Saturday noon-6 p.m., Sunday 1-5 p.m.; first Friday of every month noon-midnight.

Whitehall Antiques
1213 E. Franklin St., Chapel Hill,
919-942-3179;
www.whitehallantiques.com

This Chapel Hill institution has been selling antiques to discerning buyers for more than 75 years. Considered one of the finest shops in the South, Whitehall stocks the best 18th- and 19th-century formal English and country French furniture, fine art, silver and porcelain, as well as some American pieces. Even if you leave empty-handed, the setting alone, an 8,500-square-foot Italianate villa (the Blue Room was the original parlor in the one of the homes where Doris Duke grew up), makes the trip well worth the drive. Monday-Saturday 11 a.m.-6 p.m.

Woodleigh Place Interiors
610 W. Peace St., Raleigh,
919-834-8324;
www.woodleighplace.com

Set in a cozy cottage in the city's historic Glenwood South neighborhood, Woodleigh Place specializes in English and American antiques and reproductions from the 18th and 19th centuries, including upholstered sofas, loveseats, settees and chairs. The setting, say owners Woody Jones and Paula Narron, allows customers to view antiques as if they were in their own home—a big plus if you're trying to determine whether that Chippendale cabinet you're eyeing will work with a Queen Anne dining table and chairs. Call for appointment.

WHERE TO STAY

★★★The Carolina Inn
211 Pittsboro St., Chapel Hill,
919-933-2001, 800-962-8519;
www.carolinainn.com

This historic 1924 inn is set in the middle of the University of North Carolina Campus and around the corner from the Chapel Hill Medical Center. The entrance (with a high portico and pillars), and the red brick building have a

Georgian Revival theme. Inside, hardwood floors, Oriental rugs, mahogany tables, palms and fresh flowers add to the beautiful setting, while guest rooms continue this theme and include mahogany two-poster beds and furnishings. Art galleries, museums, charming shops and fine restaurants are all just a short distance away.

184 rooms, Wireless Internet access. Restaurant, bar. **$$**

★★★Siena Hotel
1505 E. Franklin St., Chapel Hill, 919-929-4000, 800-223-7379; www.sienahotel.com

Southern hospitality and grand European styling make the Siena Hotel a favorite in Chapel Hill. The guest rooms and suites are tastefully decorated with fine Italian furnishings and rich fabrics, while modern amenities ensure the highest levels of comfort. Guests receive privileges at a nearby fitness center. Dining is special here, where award-winning Il Palio Ristorante charms visitors throughout the day with bountiful breakfasts and delicious northern Italian-influenced lunch and dinner selections.

79 rooms. Complimentary full breakfast. Wireless Internet access. Restaurant,bar. **$$**

WHERE TO EAT

★★★★Carolina Crossroads
211 Pittsboro St., Chapel Hill, 919-933-9277, 800-962-8519; www.carolinainn.com

Set in the historic Carolina Inn, the classic Carolina Crossroads dining room delivers a picture-perfect example of Southern hospitality and charm. The menu strikes delicious notes, with regional dishes incorporating local, seasonal ingredients prepared in a progressive American style. You'll find everything from a North Carolina pulled-pork sandwich to dishes like salmon with grilled acorn squash in white-wine butter sauce, part of the chef's nightly six-course tasting menu.

Southern menu. Breakfast, lunch, dinner, brunch. Bar. Children's menu. Business casual attire. Reservations recommended. Valet parking. Outdoor seating. **$$$**

SOUTH CAROLINA

CHARLESTON

SUBLIME AND SOPHISTICATED, CHARLESTON BRINGS TOGETHER CLASsic American antiques and European finds in an exciting, historic setting with plenty of remarkable hotels and restaurants to round out an antiques-hunting experience.

WHERE TO SHOP

Alkyon Arts & Antiques
120 Meeting St., Charleston,
843-345-1439; www.alkyon.us
Alkyon teems with marbles, bronzes, paintings, clocks, ceramics, mirrors and other decorative pieces. You may even find an outlandish piece or two, like the over-the-top sculpture of "Poseidon with Trident and Dolphins" that was spotted on a recent visit. Another notable: An early 20th-century sterling ewer with engraved scrollwork overlaid on clear glass. Monday-Saturday 10 a.m.-6 p.m., Sunday 10 a.m.-5 p.m.; also by appointment.

The Charleston Renaissance Gallery
103 Church St., Charleston,
843-723-0025;
www.fineartsouth.com
A true fit for its rich, historical setting, The Charleston Renaissance Gallery features fine art of the American South as well as the art of the Charleston Renaissance. If you're a Southern enthusiast, you'll be fascinated by items like a sculpture of General Robert E. Lee on his horse Traveller. Call for current hours.

English Patina, Inc.
179 King St., Charleston,
843-853-0380;
www.englishpatina.com
English Patina, Inc. specializes in English furnishings, such as chairs, tables, chests, buffets, servers and benches. You'll find everything from mahogany with a satinwood inlay to a set of ten Chippendale-style chairs that could look like new with a paint job. Open Monday-Saturday, 10 a.m.-5 p.m.; closed Sunday.

George C. Birlant & Co.
191 King St., Charleston,
843-722-3842; www.birlant.com
This Southern emporium has a wide selection of 18th- and 19th-century English antique furniture, silver, china, crystal and brass, but look the shop over from top to bottom and you may find yourself tempted to purchase one of the lovely chandeliers hanging

123

CHARLESTON

overhead or a Federal-style table crafted of a rich hardwood tucked away in the back. Monday-Saturday 9 a.m.-5:30 p.m.; closed Sunday.

Livingston Antiques

2137 Savannah Highway, Charleston, 843-556-3502; www.livingstonantiques.com

Here you'll find a wealth of 18th- and 19th-century English furniture as well as a wide variety of Imari, Canton, majolica, Staffordshire, Jasperware, Delft and other decorative items from sought-after makers. Look for gems like an English fireman's bucket dating from 1850 (perfect for adorning any fireplace) and a somewhat trippy majolica owl jar in rich blue from France. Tuesday-Saturday 10 a.m.-5 p.m.; closed Sunday.

South of Market

173 King St., Charleston, 843-723-1114; www.southofmarket.biz

South of Market specializes in diverse furnishings from elegant to modern, as well as French decorative objects. Peruse the selection of cement-crafted garden ornaments, from finials to planters, that would look dynamic on a terrace when planted with topiaries. Monday-Saturday 10 a.m.-5 p.m., Sunday noon-6 p.m.

WHERE TO STAY

★★★★Charleston Place

205 Meeting St., Charleston, 843-722-4900, 800-611-5545; www.charlestonplace.com

This popular hotel is located in the middle of the historic district, just a stone's throw from Old City Market and King Street, where you'll find the city's best shopping. The enormous 3,000-piece Murano crystal chandelier hanging in the middle of the Georgian open-armed staircase in the lobby is the centerpiece of this buzzing hotel, where people are always zigzagging the Italianate white marble lobby perusing the upscale shops, having drinks in the handsome lounge and heading to the popular Charleston Grille for a bite, before retiring to rooms draped in lace, chintz and damask. 440 rooms. High-speed Internet access. Two restaurants, two bars. Fitness center. Pool. Spa. $$$

★★★Planters Inn

112 N. Market St., Charleston, 843-722-2345, 800-845-7082; www.plantersinn.com

This polished Relais and Chateaux property, located in the heart of the historic district, has more of a boutique hotel feel, while still offering plenty of old-fashioned charm. The original building, constructed in 1884, was a dry goods supply company; it became a hotel in 1983 and underwent a $4 million renovation in 1997. Rooms have high ceilings, four-poster beds with teddy bears,

THE SOUTH

marble bathrooms and furniture from Baker's historic Charleston collection. Book a junior suite—they're much larger than the regular rooms and have extra large bathrooms. Sweet tea is always available in the comfy lobby, with its velvet couches and oil paintings of historical figures. You'll also find a quiet courtyard with palm trees and a fountain. Rooms facing the courtyard have loggias and rocking chairs. 64 rooms. Restaurant. $$

★★★Wentworth Mansion
149 Wentworth St., Charleston, 843-853-1886, 888-466-1886; www.wentworthmansion.com
Once a private home, this stately mansion in the city's historic center has hand-carved marble fireplaces, ornate plasterwork and Tiffany stained-glass windows. Cozy guest rooms offer gas fireplaces and charming views. A full European breakfast is served on the porch each morning, and the library is a perfect spot for evening drinks. 21 rooms. Complimentary full breakfast. Restaurant. $$$

WHERE TO EAT

★★★★Charleston Grill
224 King St., Charleston, 843-577-4522; www.charlestongrill.com
Chef Bob Waggoner's French-inspired low country cuisine has earned raves (as well as a cookbook, "Charleston Grill at Charleston Place"). Waggoner divides his menu into four sections: pure, lush,

Southern and cosmopolitan, and diners are encouraged to mix and match. For example, you might pair chilled Maine lobster with micro greens and lemon vinegar (pure) with duck foie gras (lush). The chocolate tasting includes a flight of wine, as does a selection of French cheeses. Live jazz with Quentin Baxter is a big draw Monday through Saturday evenings. American menu. Dinner. Bar. Children's menu. Business casual attire. Reservations recommended. Valet parking. Outdoor seating. $$$

★★★★Circa 1886
149 Wentworth St., Charleston, 843-853-7828; www.circa1886.com
Chef Marc Collins uses regional ingredients to prepare the delightful local cuisine at this restaurant located in the carriage house of the Wentworth Mansion (which was built in 1886). The menu changes but may include Carolina crab cake soufflé, truffle leek fondue and yellow tomato pie. Deserts such as pan-fried Angel food cake and blackberry rice milk panna cotta are always a delightful finish. American menu. Dinner. Closed Sunday. Bar. Business casual attire. Reservations recommended. Valet parking. $$$

★★★McCrady's
2 Unity Alley, Charleston, 843-577-0025; www.mccradysrestaurant.com
You can almost picture the Rutledges having a drink and discussing politics at this handsome

★

★

★

★

restaurant located down a romantic alley in a brick structure built back in 1788. It was originally a tavern before it was abandoned; it was restored to its former glory in 1982, with a few modern touches added, including a sky light and leather banquettes. The menu complements this fresh take. Chef Sean Brock's intoxicating dishes include beef tenderloin with beets, garden onions and smoked hollandaise; halibut with lemon-truffle emulsion; and scallops marinated in mango vinegar, avocado, crispy rice and chamomile. The tome of a wine list includes many hard-to-find varieties. The bar is a sophisticated spot for a glass of wine and a cheese plate, or one of the unusual deserts such as peanut butter cake with popcorn ice cream and salted caramel. Modern American menu. Dinner. Bar. Business casual attire. Reservations recommended. $$$

★★★★Peninsula Grill
112 N. Market St., Charleston, 843-723-0700;
www.peninsulagrill.com
If you're looking for classic Charleston dining, book a table at this classy restaurant with gray velvet walls, golden lighting and windows overlooking the courtyard, in the Planter's Inn. The service is impeccable and the food by longtime chef Robert Carter, including bourbon-glazed jumbo shrimp and cornmeal-crusted trout, doesn't disappoint. The star of the show may be the seven-layer coconut cake—it alone is worth a visit. The champagne bar is another dizzying treat. American menu. Dinner. Bar. Business casual attire. Reservations recommended. Outdoor seating. $$$

THE SOUTHWEST

HEAD TO CHARMING SANTA FE, NEW MEXICO, FOR ITS WONDERFUL Native American finds and stock up on historically significant blankets and pottery. Santa Fe also offers delightful accommodation options at such hostelries as the Inn of the Anasazi. Then make your way east to Texas, for the to-see-it-is-to-believe-it. The big cities in Texas, in contrast to the massive flea market, specialize in overblown European antiques—you'll find these in Dallas and Houston where, it seems, the bigger, the better. Arizona, on the other hand, is more refined, offering pared-down selections of Native American wares tempered by fine European antiques along with religious icons and Spanish-style treasures. For the best in Mexican antiques as well as plenty of European imports, this region offers variety: indoor, outdoor, accent pieces and collectibles. Welcome to the Southwest!

ARIZONA

PHOENIX/SCOTTSDALE

PHOENIX IS A MELTING POT OF CULTURES AND SENSIBILITIES. SURE, YOU will find the expected Native American blankets and religious icons competing with Spanish-style furnishings, but thanks to the influx of second-home buyers from the East Coast, you will also come across fine European and American antiques.

WHERE TO SHOP

A Mad Hatter's Antiques and Collectibles New Home Décor
5734 W. Glendale Ave., Glendale, 623-931-1991, 866-931-1991; www.amadhatters.com

A short 17-minute drive west of downtown Phoenix sits the Mad Hatter, an eclectic two-story, 20,000-plus-square-foot mall filled with every sort of antique and collectible you could possibly imagine, as well as a vast collection of heritage lace. From signed photographs of Shirley Temple to Native American blankets and other Western and rodeo fare, there's something for everyone at this huge antique warehouse. Recent finds at the Mad Hatter include all kinds of kitchenware, from aluminum serving trays and dishes to 1950s Pyrex and copper aspic molds. Monday-Saturday 10 a.m.-5 p.m., Sunday 11 a.m.-4 p.m.

Allan N. Bone Gallery/La Bodega de Antiquedades
7610 E. McDonald Road, Scottsdale, 480-922-9533; www.labodega-antiques.com

Located in an old adobe house that is, on its own, worth a visit, this Scottsdale gallery stocks an unrivaled selection of Spanish Colonial antiques, architectural elements (think rustic carved doors and columns), religious icons, and silver from the 17th through 19th centuries. Monday-Saturday 10 a.m.-5 p.m.; closed Sunday.

Antiquities
7401 E. Redfield Road, Scottsdale, 480-556-0303; www.antiquitiesimports.com

For one-of-a-kind pieces that make a big statement, this Scottsdale salvage shop is stocked to the rafters with stone tables, troughs, heavy wood doors, pine beams, floor tiles and other indigenous building materials. Antiquities will add a little Southwestern flare to your home or at least provide the inspiration for one of your

THE SOUTHWEST

own crafted, one-of-a-kind furniture pieces. Daily 9 a.m.-9 p.m.

Antique Trove

2020 N. Scottsdale Road, Scottsdale, 480-947-6074; www.antiquetrove.com

Trove is French for "treasures" and that's exactly what this shop (and its sister location in Roseville, California) stocks: a varied assortment of refined antiques, from Louis XVI–style chairs and exquisite European cut glass to garden statuaries and fountains culled from markets and estates across the globe. Such one-of-a-kind estate pieces will have you adding this shop to your list of places to head to, once that palatial family mansion is passed down to you, of course. Monday-Saturday 10 a.m.-6 p.m., Sunday noon-6 p.m.

Bo's Funky Stuff

5605 W. Glendale Ave., Glendale, 623-842-0220

A fixture on the Glendale antique scene since 1974, Bo's 6,000-square-foot shop sells a unique assortment of quirky vintage finds—everything from retired soda machines to vintage advertising billboards to 1970s furnishings. Be on the lookout for colorful tin advertising signs and retro decorative items (think neon clock from the Royal Crown Cola company). A few things you won't find—baseball cards, typewriters, sewing machines and anything else Bo considers to be less than cool. This is, after all, not your typical antique shop. Tuesday-Saturday noon-5 p.m.; closed Sunday-Monday.

The Brass Armadillo Antique Mall

12419 N. 28th Drive (I-17 and Cactus), Phoenix, 602-924-0030, 888-942-0030; www.brassarmadillo.com

Part of the chain of Brass Armadillo Malls that stretches from Iowa to the West Coast, this Phoenix outpost boasts more than 630 vendors and a vast selection of furniture, china, glass, prints and more. You'll find aisle upon aisle of vintage treasures, including the likes of a fantastic 1950s bamboo patio set and an extensive selection of Roseville, Hull, and other mid–20th century pottery. There's even a service that will frame any advertising art or prints that you buy. Daily 9 a.m.-9 p.m.

Fairgrounds Antique Market

1826 W. McDowell Road (Arizona State Fairgrounds), Phoenix, 602-717-7337; www.azantiqueshow.com

For more than 20 years, the Fairgrounds Antique Market has been wowing locals with its unparalleled selection of toys, coins, jewelry, glassware, pottery, advertising, military paraphernalia, vintage costumes and furnishings, which range in style from simple Country French and Mission to elaborately carved and gilded Edwardian. Regulars say there's no better place to find that one-of-a-kind item to round out a collection or make a statement in your home.

129

PHOENIX/SCOTTSDALE

★

★

★

★

Held the third weekend of every month except for October and December. Call for hours.

Qcumberz
4429 N. Seventh Ave., Phoenix, 602-277-5133

Qcumberz is not your typical antique shop. Yes, it's packed to the gills with stuff, but chances are, you're not going to find fine French porcelain or $20,000 oil paintings here. Instead, it's great for the bargain hunter in all of us: a smorgasbord of vintage suitcases, old wagon wheels, birdbaths, salvage windows and the occasional Doris Day–like metal daisy chandelier. And that's exactly what we like about this place. It's quirky, and there's something nostalgic about having to dig for your treasures as opposed to walking in and finding them locked behind a glass case. Daily 10 a.m.-6 p.m.

WHERE TO STAY

★★★Arizona Biltmore Resort & Spa
2400 E. Missouri Ave., Phoenix, 602-955-6600, 800-950-2575; www.arizonabiltmore.com

The Arizona Biltmore Resort and Spa opened to great fanfare in 1929. The nice thing about it today is that it's not trying to remain great—it just is. The Frank Lloyd Wright–inspired architecture, as well as the photos of all the presidents and famous people who have stayed here, take you back in time. Spend your days lounging at one of the eight pools, playing the adjacent golf course or relaxing in the 22,000-square-foot spa. The comfortable rooms have Mission-style furnishings and textiles in calming desert tones and fluffy beds, while the cottages have enclosed grassy yards.

738 rooms. High-speed Internet access. Four restaurants, two bars. Airport transportation available. Fitness center. Pool. Tennis. Golf. Spa. Pets accepted. $$$

★★★★The Ritz-Carlton, Phoenix
2401 E. Camelback, Phoenix, 602-468-0700, 800-241-3333; www.ritzcarlton.com

This hotel is located smack in the middle of the Camelback Corridor, the exclusive shopping, dining and financial district of Phoenix. The classically decorated rooms have views of the skyline or the Squaw Peak Mountain Range—and, of course, there's the famed Ritz-Carlton level of service. Concierges will offer tips on everything from the area's best golf courses to the tastiest cocktail to sip in the lobby lounge. You'll find modern takes on French classics like steak au poivre with crispy frites at the hotel's festive Bistro 24. The outdoor pool sparkles, and the sundeck area is cooled with hydro-misters.

281 rooms. Wireless Internet access. Restaurant, bar. Airport transportation available. Fitness center. Pool. Business Center. $$$

WHERE TO EAT

★★★Bistro 24

2401 E. Camelback Road,
Phoenix, 602-468-0700;
www.ritzcarlton.com

Located in the Ritz-Carlton, Bistro 24 presents an invigorating mixture of contemporary French cuisine with Asian variations. The restaurant resembles a bistro from the south of France: spacious and unpretentious but elegant with European décor in a color scheme that seamlessly melds with the reds and yellows of the Arizona desert. Chef Robert Graham draws on his half-Japanese heritage, using techniques honed in such diverse locations as Rhode Island, Australia, New Zealand, Indonesia and Japan with his French culinary training to create a visionary menu. Signature favorites include chilled shrimp cocktail ceviche, grilled and chilled watermelon, New York steak au poivre and butter-poached halibut.

French bistro menu. Breakfast, lunch, dinner, Sunday brunch. Bar. Children's menu. Business casual attire. Reservations recommended. Valet parking. Outdoor seating. $$$

★★★Tarbell's

3213 E. Camelback Road,
Phoenix, 602-955-8100;
www.tarbells.com

Celebrated chef Marc Tarbell—he recently appeared on *Iron Chef*—continues to dazzle with fresh seasonal dishes, such as hand-cut pasta with locally made chicken fennel sausage, organic tomatoes and English peas and double-cut pork chop with Wisconsin cheddar grills, collard greens and wild boar bacon. The sophisticated restaurant features blond wood, white tablecloths and an exhibition kitchen—and somehow maintains a friendly neighborhood feel, perhaps thanks to the large curved bar that's a focal point (and a great stop to grab a post-scavenging cocktail).

American menu. Dinner. Bar. Business casual attire. Reservations recommended. Valet parking. $$$

★★★Wright's

2400 Missouri Road, Phoenix,
602-381-7632;
www.arizonabiltmore.com

An homage to Frank Lloyd Wright, this restaurant off the lobby of the Arizona Biltmore reflects the architect's penchant for stark angles and contrasts. Muted Southwestern colors fill the comfortable room, and a large-paneled window lets in the views. The American cuisine features the freshest ingredients from boutique farms across the country. The menu, which changes weekly, includes dishes such as aged buffalo with white cheddar and Yukon purée. Be sure to sample one of the delectable chocolate desserts.

American menu. Dinner, Sunday brunch. Bar. Business casual attire. Reservations recommended. Valet parking. Outdoor seating. $$$

PHOENIX/SCOTTSDALE

SANTA FE

WITH ITS STRONG ARTISTIC TRADITION AND NATIVE AMERICAN AND MEXICAN
populations, Santa Fe brings together a mix of American antiques and
Southwestern finds—from blankets and pottery to baskets. There's also
a terrific selection of vintage jewelry and a surprising array of Asian
antiques.

WHERE TO SHOP

Antique Warehouse
530 S. Guadalupe St., Santa Fe,
505-984-1159; www.
antiquewarehouse-santafe.com
Situated in a beautifully restored
stucco building, Antique Warehouse stocks a vast and varied
assortment of Mexican doors,
rustic ranch furniture and Spanish Colonial antiques—everything
you need to give your home that
authentic Southwestern look.
Pieces are sourced in Mexico,
then brought back to Santa Fe
for restoration. Wander through
the sprawling, 9,000-square-
foot warehouse, and you may be
tempted to rent a U-Haul as you
consider a simple-chic mesquite
table with turned legs or the elegant cedar trunk on feet, perfect
for storing your vintage blankets.
Monday-Saturday 9:30 a.m.-5
p.m.; closed Sunday.

Asian Adobe
310 Johnson St., Santa Fe,
505-992-6846;
www.asianadobe.com
This unassuming storefront
boasts a wide assortment of 100-
to 200-year-old upscale Chinese
furnishings. Look for Ming-style
medicine chests, armoires, trunks,
tables, screens and more. Asian
Adobe displays its treasures in
room settings, making it easy to
visualize what each piece of furniture might look like in *your* home.
Located just a block from the
Georgia O'Keeffe Museum, Asian
Adobe is a great stop after you've
been inspired by viewing such
O'Keeffe masterpieces as *Bella
Donna* and *My Last Door*. Open
Monday-Saturday 10 a.m.-5 p.m.

Barbara Rosen Antique and
Estate Jewelry
85 W. Marcy St., Santa Fe,
505-992-3000;
www.barbararosen.com
For 22 years, Barbara Rosen has
been sourcing and selling rare
gems from around the world—

132

THE SOUTHWEST

★
★
★
★

first in Beverly Hills, California and, since 1998, in Santa Fe. Her boutique on Marcy Street, nestled among shops selling new and vintage clothing, is a treasure trove of rare finds culled from the Georgian, Victorian, Edwardian and Art Deco eras, including an exquisite collection of estate jewelry. Shoppers ogle the expensive jewels: an 18k roses gold tiara ring circa 1900 or a sapphire-and-diamond pendant necklace circa 1910. Of course, there are much more accessible finds, too, but how fun to at least try on a few of Barbara's über-luxe wares, which will certainly leave you feeling like a queen—if only for a moment. Tuesday-Saturday 11 a.m.-5 p.m.; closed Sunday-Monday.

Things Finer

100 E. San Franciso St.,
Santa Fe, 505-983-5552;
www.thingsfiner.com

Tucked inside Santa Fe's landmark La Fonda hotel is this gem of a store that should not be overlooked. Here you'll find a well-edited assortment of antique jewelry, silver, crystal and art objects from around the world. The selection of Russian icons is a refreshing change from the rustic furnishings one expects to find in the desert Southwest. Plus, the staff is wonderfully helpful and knowledgeable, so feel free to ask questions and try on that wildly chic necklace that can only have spent its early days frequenting the Paris opera. Call for hours.

Medicine Man Gallery

602A Canyon Road, Santa Fe,
505-820-7451, 866-894-7451;
www.medicinemangallery.com

Most visitors to this Santa Fe shop are lured by the call of traditional Native American art forms, baskets, blankets, pottery and the like, but there's another reason to visit. You'll find an assortment of vintage arts and crafts and Spanish Colonial furniture, impeccably restored and ready for its next chapter. Look for rare items, such as an 18th-century Spanish Colonial chest with aged patina and gorgeous hardware as well as a Mission period sideboard—perfect for any modern entryway. May-December, Monday-Saturday 10 a.m.-5 p.m., Sunday 1-4 p.m.; January-April, Tuesday-Saturday 10 a.m.-5 p.m., Sunday 11 a.m.-4 p.m, closed Monday.

Morning Star Gallery

513 Canyon Road, Santa Fe,
505-982-8187;
www.morningstargallery.com

If beadwork, pottery, basketry and other Native American crafts are your passion, then a stop at this 24-year-old gallery is a must. There is a wide selection of museum-quality artifacts from tribes not only from the Southwest, but from across North America. You'll also be welcomed by an extremely knowledgeable staff willing to advise you on all aspects of acquiring and preserving these Native treasures, which include an Acoma polychrome (a four-color pottery jar dating from

SANTA FE

1920s) and a Yokuts polychrome basketry bowl circa 1900. Call for hours.

WHERE TO STAY

★★★Bishop's Lodge Ranch Resort and Spa
1297 Bishop's Lodge Road, Santa Fe,
505-983-6377, 800-419-0492;
www.bishopslodge.com

A true Santa Fe treasure, this historic resort dates back to 1918, and its beloved chapel, listed on the National Register of Historic Places, remains a popular site for weddings. The lodge epitomizes vintage-chic, with rooms decorated either in an old Santa Fe style or with a more modern décor. The ShánNah spa is influenced by Native American traditions—each treatment begins with a soothing drumming and blessing. For a tasty sample of seasonal American cuisine, try the onsite restaurant.

111 rooms. Restaurant, bar. Children's activity center. Fitness center. Tennis. Pool. Spa. $$$

★★★★Inn of the Anasazi
113 Washington Ave., Santa Fe,
505-988-3030, 800-688-8100;
www.innoftheanasazi.com

Located just off the historic Plaza, the inn was designed to resemble the traditional dwellings of the Anasazi. Enormous handcrafted doors open to a world of authentic artwork, carvings and textiles synonymous with the Southwest. The lobby sets a sense of place for arriving guests with its rough-hewn tables, leather furnishings, unique objects and huge cactus plants in terracotta pots. The rooms reflect the region's integrity; they're kitted out with kiva fireplaces and hand-woven blankets, and bathrooms stocked with toiletries made locally with native cedar extract. The restaurants earn praise for honoring the area's culinary heritage.

57 rooms. Wireless Internet access. Two restaurants, bar. Business center. $$$

★★★La Posada De Santa Fe
330 E. Palace Ave., Santa Fe,
505-986-0000, 866-331-7625;
www.laposada.rockresorts.com

Nestled on six lush acres, La Posada effortlessly blends past and present. The original Staab House, dating to 1870, is the focal point of the resort and a must-see for Southwestern antiques enthusiasts. The lovely rooms and suites are scattered throughout the gardens in a village setting. Rich colors mix with Spanish Colonial and old-world style, and every amenity has been thoughtfully included, like a curvy heated outdoor pool. The fantastic Avanyu Spa features Native American–themed treatments using local ingredients. Fuego Restaurant is a standout for its innovative food with Spanish and Mexican inflections, while the historic Staab House is an inviting setting for American classics.

157 rooms. Wireless Internet access. Restaurant, bar. Fitness center. Pool. Spa. $$$

★

★

★

★

WHERE TO EAT

★★★Geronimo
724 Canyon Road, Santa Fe,
505-982-1500;
www.geronimorestaurant.com
Housed in a restored 250-year-old landmark adobe building, Geronimo (the name of the restaurant is an ode to the hacienda's original owner, Geronimo Lopez) offers robust Southwestern-spiked global fusion fare in a stunning and cozy space. Owners Cliff Skoglund and Chris Harvey treat each guest like family. The interior is like a Georgia O'Keeffe painting come to life, with its wood-burning, cove-style fireplace; tall chocolate-and-garnet leather seating; and local Native American–style artwork. The food is remarkable, fusing the distinct culinary influences of Asia, the Southwest and the Mediterranean. Vibrant flavors, bright colors and top-notch seasonal and regional ingredients come together in such dishes as Maryland soft-shell tempura crabs with soba noodle and Asian pear salad, or mesquite-grilled New York strip steak with French onion tart and polenta fries with green pepper corn and mustard sauce. When it's warm outside, sit on the patio for prime Canyon Road people-watching.
International menu. Dinner. Bar. Reservations recommended. Valet parking. Outdoor seating. $$$

★★★The Old House Restaurant
309 W. San Francisco St., Santa Fe, 505-988-4455, 800-955-4455; www.eldoradohotel.com
Chef Charles Kassels is known for introducing unexpected flavors into otherwise everyday items. Witness his roasted pork tenderloin accompanied by sweet potatoes puréed with oranges (preserved for nine days), duck confit and foie gras in puff pastry with pistachios and cherry-celery compote, and soup with lobster tempura and osetra caviar. Take a moment to look up and take in the candlelit stucco room, part of one of the city's oldest buildings, which is adorned with Mexican folk art and bold, oversized paintings.
Southwestern menu. Dinner. Bar. Business casual attire. Reservations recommended. Valet parking. $$$

135

SANTA FE

TENNESSEE

NASHVILLE

A STUDY IN CONTRASTS, NASHVILLE MIXES ONE PART COUNTRY MUSIC with one part sophistication. The resulting cocktail is heady and potent, and makes for a fun-filled weekend of antique shopping paired with a side of fried chicken and the latest track from Dolly Parton.

WHERE TO SHOP

Chancery Lane Antiques
5133 Harding Rd. C-1, Nashville, 615-354-0400; www.chancerylane.com

Chancery Lane Antiques specializes in all sorts of delightful British and European objects and accessories including snuff boxes, pipes, silver tea sets, Scottish agate jewelry—and that's only scratching the surface. Among our favorite finds: a circa 1903 English silver and tortoise shell inkwell and a pair of old Sheffield plate tea caddies dating from 1780, either of which could make any home look just a bit more palatial. Tuesday-Friday 10 a.m.-5 p.m., Saturday 11 a.m.-4 p.m.

Davishire Interiors
2106 21st Ave. S., Nashville, 615-298-2670; www.davishire.com

Look to Davishire Interiors for your continental antiques and artwork needs, as well as for fabrics from around the world. Keep your eyes out for unexpected items such as a carved mirror bedecked with cherubs dating from 1850 and a 19th century French musician's stool with a shell seat. Monday-Friday 8 a.m.-5 p.m., Saturday 11 a.m.-4 p.m.; closed Sunday.

Dealer's Choice Antiques
2109 Eighth Ave. S., Nashville, 615-383-7030; www.dealerschoiceantiqueauction.com

The Dealer's Choice is an auction house with auctions every two weeks that feature antique furniture ranging from Victorian and mahogany to French, empire and country. The bidding extends to other items as well, including a wide selection of high-quality reproductions from furniture to bronzes, cast iron and stained glass. Call for hours and auction schedule.

Goodlettsville Antique Mall
213 N. Main St., Goodlettsville, 615-859-7002; www.goodlettsvilleantiquemall.com

With the size and scope of this mall, you're likely to do a little digging. The Goodlettsville Antique Mall features over 30,000 square feet of antiques from hard-to-find Depression glass to sparkling crystal. Keep your eyes peeled for diamonds in the rough, from a jaunty 1950s dinette set to china culled from the showcases and rustic dark wood chairs that lived on a farm in a former life. Monday-Saturday 10 a.m.-5:30 p.m., Sunday 11 a.m.-5:30 p.m.

Pia's Antiques & Appraisals
1800 Eighth Ave. S., Nashville, 615-251-4721;
www.piasantiques.com
Make a stop at Pia's Antiques to peruse the large selection of high-end European antiques, collectibles and decorative arts. This is certainly a favorite source for antique mirrors: Pia's stocks everything from Venetian, French and Chippendale styles in all sorts of glittering shapes and sizes. Don't miss some unexpected accessories, including a pair of Regency-era andirons shaped like fish. Tuesday and Friday 10 a.m.-5 p.m.; Monday, Wednesday and Thursday by appointment only.

WHERE TO STAY

★★★★★The Hermitage Hotel
231 Sixth Ave. N., Nashville, 615-244-3121, 888-888-9414;
www.thehermitagehotel.com
The Hermitage Hotel is the Grand Dame of Nashville's hotels. Opened in 1910 and renovated in 2003, this glorious downtown hotel offers white-glove service

and plenty of opportunities to indulge. Its lobby is magnificent, with vaulted ceilings of stained glass, arches decorated with frescoes and intricate stonework. The spacious guest rooms are filled with elegant traditional furnishings, creating a warm and welcoming atmosphere. On the lower level, you'll find the Capitol Grille, one of Nashville's best restaurants. The adjacent Oak Bar, with its emerald green club chairs and dark wood paneling, is a top spot for relaxing before or after dinner.
122 rooms. Wireless Internet access. Restaurant, bar. Spa. Business center. $$$

★★★Wyndham Union Station Hotel
1001 Broadway, Nashville, 615-726-1001; www.
unionstationhotelnashville.com
Housed in an historic 1897 train station, the Wyndham Union Station is a National Historic Landmark. The lobby has marble floors, a vaulted ceiling of Tiffany stained glass and ornate carved woodwork. Complimentary wine and cheese is offered to guests in the evening. With its downtown location only a few blocks from Second Avenue and Music Row, the Wyndham is close to much of the entertainment, dining and nightlife that Nashville has to offer, with complimentary shuttle service to nearby attractions.
125 rooms. Wireless Internet access. Restaurant, bar. $$

NASHVILLE

★
★
★
★
★

WHERE TO EAT

★★★★Capitol Grille
231 Sixth Ave. N., Nashville,
615-345-7116;
www.thehermitagehotel.com
Near the state capitol, the Grille hosts power lunches, but it's also a popular spot for theater-goers who want to enjoy a fine meal before a show at the nearby Tennessee Performing Arts Center. Executive Chef Tyler Brown oversees the creation of creative Southern cuisine. The menu is different each week, and includes such dishes as Niman Ranch pork with sweet potato juice and veal loin with root vegetables. Truffle mac and cheese and spicy fried green tomato with piquant pepper relish are just a few of the restaurant's irresistible side dishes, and desserts like flourless chocolate ganache torte end the evening on a perfect note. Located downstairs in the historic Hermitage Hotel, this Southern-influenced restaurant offers a different menu each week.

American, Southern menu. Breakfast, lunch, dinner, late-night, Sunday brunch. Bar. Children's menu. Business casual attire. Reservations recommended. Valet parking. $$$

★★★The Palm
140 Fifth Ave. S., Nashville,
615-742-7256;
www.thepalm.com
A great spot for star-gazing—not the celestial kind—and beef-eating, The Palm is one of Nashville's most popular scenes. Serious-sized steaks, chops and seafood dishes grace the menu at this legendary steakhouse. Also found among the meaty menu selections are Italian dishes like linguine and clams, spaghetti marinara and tomato capri salad. Going strong since 1926, The Palm has expanded its empire to 25 cities across the country, including Philadelphia, Las Vegas and Dallas.

Steak menu. Lunch, dinner. Bar. Business casual attire. Reservations recommended. Valet parking. $$$

THE SOUTH

TEXAS

DALLAS

WITH ITS "BIGGER IS BETTER" ATTITUDE AND ZEST FOR LIFE, DALLAS mixes a full panoply of antique shops from the classic and traditional to the over-the-top and theatrical.

WHERE TO SHOP

Adele Hunt's European Collectibles
1007 Slocum St., Dallas,
214-651-7542;
www.adelehunt.com
Stepping into this Dallas Design District shop is like walking into a fabled antique market in London or Paris where chairs, tables, bookcases, desks and other furnishings of every style, shape, price and pedigree abound. Not to worry if you can't haul your treasures home; Adele's will ship anywhere in the world. Monday-Friday, 9 a.m.-5:30 p.m., Saturday 10 a.m.-5 p.m.; closed Sunday.

Century Modern
2928 Main St., Dallas,
214-651-9200;
www.centurymodern.com
If you are looking for a vintage Herman Miller table or a Knoll sofa, then this is the shop for you. With 5,000 square feet of vintage seating, storage, lighting and accessories from the 1940s to the 1970s, chances are you'll find that long sought-after treasure somewhere in this eclectic mix. Tuesday-Saturday 11 a.m.-5 p.m., Sunday, noon-5 p.m.; closed Monday.

Lots of Furniture Antiques, Inc.
910 N. Industrial Blvd., Dallas,
214-761-1575;
www.lotsoffurniture.com
As the name implies, this warehouse-size shop stocks a lot of furniture—everything from Mission and Gothic to English and Italian styles. There's also a good selection of architectural salvage, exterior lighting, iron railings and the like, as well as rugs and stained glass for your interior and exterior decorating needs. Monday-Saturday 10 a.m.-5 p.m., Sunday noon-5 p.m.

Lovers Lane Antique Market
5001 W. Lovers Lane, Dallas,
214-351-5656, 888-843-0562;
www.loverslaneantiques.com
Lovers Lane carries a unique assortment of 19th-century furniture, Staffordshire, majolica, transfer ware and other household furnishings culled from some of the best sources in Eng-

DALLAS

★
★
★
★

land and France. From the tiniest glassware to substantial oak chests and Welsh dressers, thoughtful variety is the key to Lovers Lane. Monday-Saturday 10 a.m.-5 p.m., Sunday 1-5 p.m.

Riddell Rare Maps & Fine Prints
2611 Fairmount St., Dallas, 214-953-0601; www.antiquemapshop.com
Ephemera lovers will delight in this library-like shop's extensive stock of rare maps and fine prints. You won't find dusty shelves here; instead, you'll encounter well-organized and impeccably preserved maps from all 50 states as well as a good selection of prints on subjects ranging from sporting to military. An adjacent frame shop will have you outfitting your purchases all in one trip. Tuesday-Friday 10 a.m.-6 p.m., Saturday, noon-4 p.m.; closed Monday.

Snider Plaza Antique Shops
6929 Snider Plaza, Dallas, 214-373-0822; www.sniderplazaantiques.com
This multidealer market sells only high-quality English, Italian and French furnishings; Oriental carpets; silver; needlework; porcelain; and pottery. In other words, don't come here looking for quirky advertising art or 1950s paraphernalia, but do expect to find some very rare items from across the globe. Monday-Friday 10 a.m.-5:30 p.m., Saturday 10 a.m.-5 p.m.; closed Sunday.

The Whimsey Shoppe
2923 N. Henderson, Dallas, 214-824-6300; www.thewhimseyshoppe.com
For more than 20 years, this Dallas institution has been helping clients and designers from across the United States find the very best in French country antique furniture. You'll also find a good assortment of decorative accessories, copper pots and pottery from across France. And if you can't find what you're looking for at this North Henderson shop, fear not; there are more treasures to be found at the company's 11,000-square-foot showroom on Oak Lawn in the Dallas Design District. Monday-Saturday 10 a.m.-5:30 p.m.; closed Sunday.

WHERE TO STAY

★★★Rosewood Crescent Hotel
400 Crescent Court, Dallas, 214-871-3200, 888-767-3966; www.crescentcourt.com
Located in the fashionable Uptown area, the Hotel Crescent Court features an impressive exterior resembling a French chateau with a contemporary twist. Priceless antiques, artwork and Louis XIV tapestries define the public spaces, while spiral staircases add romance to suites, and French doors open out to the grounds. Dine on New American cuisine in Beau Nash, one of the city's most popular restaurants.
191 rooms. Wireless Internet access. Five restaurants, bar. Fitness center. Pool. Spa. Business center. $$$$

★★★Hôtel St. Germain
2516 Maple Ave., Dallas,
214-871-2516;
www.hotelstgermain.com

Despite its location in the busy Uptown District, this intimate boutique hotel offers secluded getaways in grand style. All seven of its suites are richly decorated with turn-of-the-century antiques from France and New Orleans, and each has a working fireplace. Come nightfall, there is a candlelit dinner in the dining room that overlooks a New Orleans–style garden courtyard. Before or after dinner, have drinks in the Parisian-style champagne bar in the parlor.

7 rooms. Wireless Internet access. Complimentary full breakfast. Restaurant, bar. **$$$**

★★★★★Rosewood Mansion on Turtle Creek
2821 Turtle Creek Blvd., Dallas,
214-559-2100, 888-767-3966;
www.mansiononturtlecreek.com

This 1920s Italian-Renaissance mansion, once a private home, retains the ambience of a distinguished residence. Refined accommodations feature French doors that open to private balconies and marble fireplaces. From the business and fitness centers to the outdoor pool, this hotel delivers comfort and convenience. The bar is a cozy and lavish spot for a drink, and no visit to Dallas is complete without a meal at the recently renovated restaurant, where contemporary American cuisine is served in a setting of modern, understated elegance.

143 rooms. High-speed Internet access. Three restaurants, bar. Fitness center. Pool. Spa. Business center. **$$$**

★★★The Stoneleigh Hotel & Spa
2927 Maple Ave., Dallas,
800-921-8498
www.stoneleighhotel.com

Open since 1924, this stately hotel underwent a complete renovation in 2007. Rooms are restored to their Art Deco splendor (with penthouses inspired by famed interior designer Dorothy Draper), though they boast a decidedly modern vibe. A new spa and restaurant have been added to the hotel.

170 rooms. Wireless Internet access. Restaurant, bar. Fitness center. Spa. Business center. **$**

WHERE TO EAT

★★★★Abacus
4511 McKinney Ave., Dallas
214-559-3111;
www.abacus-restaurant.com

A lively young crowd gathers at Abacus, a modern space that could easily make the top restaurant designers in the country swoon. To match the stylish garnet dining room, the kitchen, led by chef/owner Kent Rathbun, offers a vibrant selection of contemporary global fare that incorporates the flavors of the Mediterranean, Southwest and Pacific Rim. The signature lobster-scallion shooters—small fried lobster dumplings served in sake cups

★

★

★

★

★

with a red chile and coconut-sake sauce—are a memorable treat.

International menu. Dinner. Closed Sunday. Bar. Business casual attire. Reservations recommended. Valet parking. $$$

★★★★The French Room
1321 Commerce St., Dallas, 214-742-8200;
www.hoteladolphus.com

Located in the elegant Hotel Adolphus, the French Room is a charming spot for sophisticated Gallic fare. Softly lit by hand-blown crystal chandeliers, the exquisite mural-clad arched ceiling and gilt moldings create an ambiance of opulent rococo splendor. Executive chef Jason Weaver melds traditional French culinary techniques with modern American tastes and builds three-course prix fixe menus with classics such as rack of lamb with whipped potatoes and roasted garlic-mint jam. Desserts range from vanilla and cherry crème brulée to classic tarte tatin of apple and quince.

French menu. Dinner. Closed Sunday-Monday; also first two weeks of July. Bar. Jacket required. Reservations recommended. Valet parking. $$$$

★★★★Nana
2201 Stemmons Freeway, Dallas, 214-761-7470;
www.nanarestaurant.com

Nana, located on the 27th floor of the Hilton Anatole, is one of Dallas' top spots for creative cocktails and inspired modern American cuisine. The chef's whimsical creations include a carrot, pineapple and ginger "float" with foie gras mousse, and oysters with green apple sorbet. Decorated with priceless Asian art from the private collection of Margaret and Trammel Crow, the room feels like a posh gallery, especially when filled to capacity with its chic crowd of urban regulars. Diners often stick around into the late hours and work off dinner on the dance floor, where live jazz is featured nightly.

American menu. Dinner. Bar. Business casual attire. Reservations recommended. Valet parking. $$$

★★★Newport Seafood
703 McKinney Ave., Dallas, 214-954-0220;
www.newportsrestaurant.com

Tucked into the old Dallas Brewery & Bottling Works building, Newport's was one of the first restaurants to open in the West End and to fly in fresh seafood daily. Although the setting is rustic, the staff surprises with such dishes as ahi tuna sashimi in a sake-soy sauce; sherry-spiked lobster bisque; pasta with calamari, shrimp, Greek olives, herbs and feta; and favorites like filet mignon with broiled lobster.

Seafood menu. Lunch (Monday-Friday), dinner. Bar. Casual attire. $$$

★★★Seventeen Seventeen

1717 Harwood St., Dallas,
214-922-1858;
www.dallasmuseumofart.org

Artful dishes worthy of this restaurant's Dallas Museum of Art location have made this eatery a favorite of fashionable diners. Start with a dish of tempura shrimp over baby greens dressed in a Thai vinaigrette and cradled in a crispy won ton basket. Then sample an entrée quesadilla stuffed with smoked chicken and dabbed with a roasted tomatillo salsa or try a pan-seared pork chop in a soy glaze over stir-fried rice in a baked acorn squash.

American menu. Lunch. Closed Saturday-Monday. Bar. Casual attire. Outdoor seating. $$

★★★★Stephan Pyles

1807 Ross Ave., Dallas,
214-580-7000;
www.stephanpyles.com

Stephan Pyles has come a long way since his youth when he rolled tamales at his family's truck stop. The chef has created 14 restaurants and garnered numerous accolades for his Southwestern cuisine. At this restaurant, located in the Dallas Arts District, the interior smoothly blends modern architecture with soft regional accents, such as warm desert hues and terracotta brick. The dinner menu includes dishes such as coriander-cured rack of lamb with Ecuadorian potato cake and cranberry mojo. An imaginative wine list features an extensive selection of imported and domestic wines by the glass and half-bottle.

Southwestern menu. Lunch (Monday-Friday), dinner. Closed Sunday. Bar. Business casual attire. Reservations recommended. Valet parking. Outdoor seating. $$$

Restaurant at the Mansion on Turtle Creek

2821 Turtle Creek Blvd., Dallas,
214-443-4747;
www.mansiononturtlecreek.com

The Mansion on Turtle Creek's restaurant recently underwent a complete renovation. Diners should stop in to sample what's sure to be exquisite cooking and service at the new version of this classic. The restaurant is housed in the original Sheppard King Mansion that was designed as a Mediterranean-inspired abode.

Contemporary American menu. Breakfast, lunch, dinner. Bar. Children's menu. Reservations recommended. Valet parking. $$$$

143

DALLAS

HOUSTON

MORE SUBDUED THAN DALLAS, HOUSTON ENCOMPASSES ANTIQUE SHOPS with a traditional bent strongly skewed toward the European and Continental. But this being Texas, there's still an emphasis on the larger than life and the bigger the better.

WHERE TO SHOP

Adkins Architectural Antiques and Treasures

3515 Fannin St., Houston,
713-522-6547, 800-522-6547;
www.adkinsantiques.com

Nationally recognized as one of the country's best architectural salvage shops, this Houston institution features three floors of scavenged treasures ranging from old tiles and stained glass to garden accessories and ornamental iron. Monday-Saturday 9:30 a.m.-5:30 p.m., Sunday noon-5 p.m.

Carl Moore Antiques

1610 Bissonnet St., Houston,
713-524-2502;
www.carlmooreantiques.com

For 20 years, discerning Houstonites have frequented Carl Moore for an extensive and well-edited selection of English, Continental and Asian antiques. Come for the furnishings but don't miss Moore's selections of quirky finds, like a vintage carbon monoxide filter or carved dragon-shaped paddles from Thailand. Monday-Wednesday, Friday 9:30 a.m.-5:30 p.m., Thursday 9:30 a.m.-7 p.m., Saturday 11 a.m.-5 p.m.; closed Sunday.

Joyce Horn Antiques

1022 Wirt Road, Houston,
713-688-0507;
www.joycehornantiques.com

This family-owned business imports and sells only auction-quality French antiques and decorative items. If you're searching for an over-the-top pine armoire or decadently carved day bed, this is the place to visit. Tuesday-Saturday 10 a.m.-5 p.m.; closed Sunday-Monday.

Past Era

2311 Westheimer Road (in the Antique Pavilion), Houston,
713-524-7110; www.pastera.com

If you have a thing for bling, visit this charming Houston shop. Here, proprietor Marion Glober stocks more than 5,000 pieces of Georgian, Victorian, Art Nouveau, Arts and Crafts, Edwardian, Art Deco and retro jewels. Restoration and repair services are also available. Tuesday-Saturday 10 a.m.-6 p.m.; closed Sunday-Monday.

Phyllis Tucker Antiques

2919 Ferndale Place, Houston,
713-524-0165;
www.phyllistucker.com

This well-known Houston shop specializes in antique sterling flat-

★

★

★

★

ware and hollowware—primarily American silver of the 19th and early 20th centuries. Monday-Friday 10 a.m.-5 p.m., Saturday 11 a.m.-5 p.m.; closed Sunday.

R & F Antiques
912 Yale St., Houston,
713-861-7750;
www.randfantiques.com

Thanks to a bright barn red exterior, this delightful little shop is hard to miss. Inside, you'll find seven rooms brimming with wonderful American oak and Victorian cabinets, tables, chairs, secretaries, beds and other furnishings. Wednesday-Saturday 10 a.m.-5 p.m.

WHERE TO STAY

★★★★Four Seasons Hotel Houston
1300 Lamar St., Houston,
713-650-1300, 800-332-3442;
www.fourseasons.com

Close to the George R. Brown Convention Center and the Toyota Center, this hotel's downtown location makes it a favorite among business travelers. The guest rooms are a sophisticated blend of European furniture, Asian decorative objects and Southwestern panache. The outdoor pool, fitness center and spa give the hotel the feel of a resort in the middle of the city. Guests can sample tequila, wine and tapas in the Lobby Lounge. Quattro serves delicious Italian cuisine.

404 rooms. Wireless Internet access. Restaurant, bar. Fitness center. Pool, whirlpool. Spa. Business center. **$$$**

★★★★Hotel Granduca
1080 Uptown Park Blvd., Houston,
713-418-1000, 888-472-6382;
www.granducahouston.com

Staying at the Hotel Granduca is like traveling to Italy without breaking out the passport. From its pastel-colored exterior to its striking interior design, this lovely hotel blends Old-World style with New World amenities. Hotel Granduca may feel like a secluded resort with its quiet sophistication, yet this hotel has a prime location in Houston's Uptown neighborhood. The services—from chauffeurs and personal trainers to a heated outdoor pool—are impressive. Just like at a grand private residence, the veranda, conservatory and clubroom are among the many spots to dine.

123 rooms, all suites. Wireless Internet access. Restaurant. Pool. Business center. **$$$$**

★★★Lancaster Hotel
701 Texas Ave., Houston,
713-228-9500, 800-231-0336;
www.thelancaster.com

The Lancaster Hotel is a Houston landmark. Located in the theater district, this historic structure is within walking distance of area businesses and cultural attractions. Opened in 1926, the Lancaster feels like an exclusive private club with its intimate scale, jewel-toned walls and European furnishings. The flavors of the Gulf Coast are celebrated at Bistro

★

★

★

Lancaster, and both the restaurant and bar are popular spots after the theater.

93 rooms. Wireless Internet access. Restaurant, bar. Airport transportation available. Fitness center. Business center. **$$**

★★★★St. Regis Hotel, Houston
1919 Briar Oaks Lane, Houston, 713-840-7600, 877-787-3447; www.stregis.com

The St. Regis, located in Houston's tony River Oaks section, has a prime location near the city's best shopping at the Galleria. The guest rooms have rich mahogany furnishings, Pratesi linens, pillowtop beds and Remède bath products. The climate-controlled outdoor pool is ideal for lounging. The quality seafood and steaks at Remington Restaurant make for a memorable dining experience. 232 rooms. High-speed Internet access. Restaurant, three bars. Fitness center. Pool. Spa. Business center. Pets accepted. **$$$**

WHERE TO EAT

★★★★Quattro
1300 Lamar St., Houston, 713-650-1300; www.fourseasons.com/houston

Contemporary Italian-American cuisine is the focus at Quattro, the ultramodern restaurant in the Four Seasons Hotel Houston. After a recent makeover, the space now features vibrant, jewel-toned, stained glass-paneled walls. Despite the buzz at the bar, the dining room maintains a sense of calm, and the food, as always, is a top priority. The kitchen focuses on local, seasonal ingredients, and the food it creates is as visually alluring as the space.

American, Italian menu. Breakfast, lunch, dinner, late-night, Sunday brunch. Bar. Children's menu. Business casual attire. Reservations recommended. Valet parking. **$$$**

★★★Rainbow Lodge
2011 Ella Blvd., Houston, 713-861-8666, 866-861-8666; www.rainbow-lodge.com

Housed in a 100-year-old log cabin, Rainbow Lodge offers a frequently changing American menu with plenty of game and seafood. The interior features hunting and fishing collectibles, columns made from San Jacinto River cypress trees and a large stone fireplace.

American menu. Lunch, dinner, Sunday brunch. Closed Monday. Bar. Business casual attire. Reservations recommended. Valet parking. Outdoor seating. **$$$**

THE WEST COAST

MID-CENTURY MODERN TAKES CENTER STAGE IN SOUTHERN CAL-ifornia, where antique hunters flock in droves to such hotspots as the jam-packed, monthly Rosebowl Flea Market in Pasadena and funky West Hollywood. San Diego, however, veers to the more traditional. In northern California, San Francisco attracts fans of Asian antiques and eclectic vintage finds ranging from retro clothing to museum-worthy antiques. And then there's Portland, Oregon, with its Native American art and jewelry, wonderful vintage book emporia, and treasure troves of Americana.

CALIFORNIA

LOS ANGELES/ WEST HOLLYWOOD

FUNKY AND FABULOUS, YOU'LL ENCOUNTER EVERYTHING FROM MID-century marvels to eclectic accessories and everything in between at the shops housed in the colorful neighborhoods of Los Angeles.

WHERE TO SHOP

Antiquarius
8840 Beverly Blvd., West Hollywood, 310-285-0352; www.antiquarius.net

Antiquarius is a two-story gallery that specializes in jewelry and antiques from all over the world, including flamboyant Art Nouveau from the 1930s to elegant Victorian furnishings. Locals swear by the selection of vintage watches from Rolex, Hamilton and Bulova. Monday-Friday 11 a.m.-6 p.m.; closed Saturday-Sunday.

Antique Rug Company
928 N. La Cienega Blvd., Los Angeles, 310-659-3847; www.antiquerugco.com

Visit this 25-year-old shop for one of the best selections of antique Oriental and Persian rugs and wall tapestries in the Los Angeles area. The shop also cleans and repairs Oriental rugs. Monday-Friday 9:30 a.m.-5:30 p.m., Saturday-Sunday by appointment only.

Connoisseur Antiques
8468 Melrose Place, Los Angeles, 323-658-8432; www.connoisseurantiques.com

Situated within a charming rococo-ish building, Connoisseur Antiques spans many categories, from chandeliers, sconces and candelabra to antique furniture such as armoires and chests to bibliotheques and vitrines. Two other outposts are located on La Cienega Boulevard and the Annex, just behind the Melrose Place location. Monday-Friday 9 a.m.-6 p.m., Saturday 10 a.m.-5 p.m.; also by appointment.

Lee Stanton Antiques
769 La Cienega Blvd., Los Angeles, 310-855-9800; www.leestanton.com

Head to Lee Stanton for 17th-, 18th- and 19th-century British and European antiques, such as a set of six 19th-century English urns for the garden and a pair of Italian walnut chairs circa 1680. Everything in the shop is hand-picked by owner Lee Stanton, a

30-year veteran of the business. Tuesday-Saturday 11 a.m.-6 p.m.

Little Paris

612 S. La Brea Ave., Los Angeles, 323-857-1080;
www.littleparisantiques.com

With its two outposts (the other can be found on North Sycamore), Little Paris offers 1,000 square feet of terrific finds, including English, Spanish and French antiquities. You'll discover everything from metal wall sculptures from Curtis Jere to a pair of bronze, shell-shaped andirons and a French, full-sized 19th-century caleche—perfect, perhaps, to serve as the dramatic centerpiece of your living room. Monday-Saturday 10 a.m.-6 p.m., Sunday 11 a.m.-5 p.m.

Lucca Antiques

744 N. La Cienega Blvd., West Hollywood, 310-657-7800;
www.luccaantiques.com

Elegant Lucca has gobs of gorgeous finds, including a pair of Spanish floor lamps, a gilt 1940s ceiling fixture shaped like a sun and an 18th-century Spanish table with two drawers. This is the type of store you could lounge in for hours, as the items are all so beautiful and the selection so well edited. Monday-Saturday 10 a.m.-5 p.m.

Meltdown Comics & Collectibles

7522 Sunset Blvd., Los Angeles, 323-851-7223;
www.meltcomics.com

Meltdown Comic & Collectibles is renowned for, what else, its vintage comics and collectibles (the store has 9,000 square feet of show space) from such notable titles as Archy, Tin Tin and many others. If you're looking to relive your childhood for a few hours, Meltdown is the place to do it. Thursday-Tuesday 11 a.m.-10 p.m., Wednesday 11 a.m.-11 p.m.

Orange

8111 Beverly Blvd., Los Angeles, 323-782-6898;
www.orange.1stdibs.com

If high-style furnishings of the late 1950s and early 1960s are your thing, head to the shop Angelenos have known about for years, where you'll find a well-edited selection of midcentury lighting, furniture and garden items from such well-known names as Tommy Parzinger, Karl Springer, Edward Wormly, John Widdicomb and Harvey Probber to name a few. Monday-Saturday 10 a.m.-5 p.m.

Ralf's Antiques and Fine Art

807 N. La Cienega Blvd., Los Angeles, 310-659-1966;
www.antiquesandfinearts.com

Ralf's Antiques first opened its doors in 1969 with a small inventory of French and English antiques. Since then, the shop has grown to specialize in a wide range of 17th-, 18th- and 19th-century European antique furniture, paintings, porcelain, mirrors and chandeliers. Monday-Friday 9 a.m.-5 p.m.; Saturday by appointment only.

149

★
★
★
★
☆
☆

Wanna Buy a Watch?

8465 Melrose, Los Angeles,
323-653-0467;
www.wannabuyawatch.com

Wanna Buy a Watch showcases antique wristwatches from the 1920s and the 1930s (think Rolex, Cartier, Breitling and Omega) as well as all sorts of glamorous Hollywood-era jewelry and gems. Tuesday-Saturday 10 a.m.-6 p.m.

WHERE TO STAY

★★★★★Hotel Bel-Air

701 Stone Canyon Rd., Los
Angeles, 310-472-1211,
888-897-2804;
www.hotelbelair.com

Amenities are plentiful at this timeless hotel situated close to the action of Los Angeles yet far enough to transport guests to a romantic world dotted with intimate courtyards, fountains and the Bel-Air's signature Swan Lake. Guest rooms offer French and Italian furnishings, private sun-soaked terraces, Alicante marble and one-of-a-kind touches that are only found in the finest hotels. Privacy is guaranteed with rooms spread throughout the 12-acre grounds, and guests can take advantage of the well-equipped fitness center or the luxurious pool in confident seclusion. Gourmands will enjoy the in-kitchen dining experience of Table One as well as the enchanting garden setting of the Terrace.

91 rooms. Wireless Internet access. Restaurant, bar. Fitness center. Pool. Business center. Pets accepted. **$$$$**

★★★★Four Seasons Hotel Los Angeles at Beverly Hills

300 S. Doheny Dr., Beverly Hills,
310-273-2222, 800-819-5053;
www.fourseasons.com

Located on a quiet, palm-lined street just a mile from the exclusive boutiques of Rodeo Drive and Robertson Boulevard, this hotel is a wonderful retreat. Guest rooms include Frette linens and oversized marble bathrooms with Bulgari toiletries. The rooftop pool is surrounded by lush gardens and dotted with private cabanas. Don't miss the sunset massage from a candlelit cabana. Complimentary limousine rides to shopping and restaurants are available.

285 rooms. Wireless Internet access. Three restaurants, bar. Spa. Fitness center. Pool. Business center. Pets accepted. **$$$$**

WHERE TO EAT

★★★Ortolan

8338 W. Third St., Los Angeles,
323-653-3300;
www.ortolanrestaurant.com

French chef Christophe Émé, formerly of L'Orangerie, has ventured out on his own with Ortolan (named for a small songbird) and created an exquisite menu that blends classic French style with contemporary elements. Signature dishes include crispy langoustines with basil, chickpeas and minestrone and roasted squab breast and leg with a gratin of macaroni and tapenade salad. The modernized provincial atmosphere, with cream-colored booths and banquettes, floor-to-ceiling velvet drapes, crystal chandeliers and antique mirrors, is equally dazzling.

French menu. Dinner. Closed Sunday. Bar. Business casual attire. Valet parking. **$$$**

★★★★Patina
141 S. Grand Ave., Los Angeles, 213-972-3331; www.patinagroup.com/patina

Celebrity chef Joachim Splichal's French-California cooking, interpreted here by executive chef Theo Schoenegger, celebrates local and regionally sourced foods in dishes such as foie gras with Ranier cherry jam, salmon with heirloom tomatoes and olive oil–poached squab with truffles from Umbria. The polished dining room, with walnut-paneled walls and curved ceilings, echoes the hall itself, prepping concertgoers for events. Make a night of it by reserving the kitchen table and indulging in a six-course market tasting menu. The bar serves nibbles and drinks after performances, and a lunch menu caters to tourists visiting the hall, as well as the downtown business crowd.

California menu. Lunch, dinner. Bar. Business casual attire. Reservations recommended. Valet parking. Outdoor seating. **$$$**

★★★★The Restaurant at Hotel Bel-Air
701 Stone Canyon Rd., Los Angeles, 310-472-1211; www.hotelbelair.com

The constantly changing menu at this restaurant in the Hotel Bel-Air continues to be a superior draw for diners looking for a fresh, innovative meal. Those who want a close look at the pure brilliance of the restaurant's cooking staff can reserve Table One, an exclusive dining room adjacent to the kitchen where Chef Douglas Dodd personally leads guests through a seven-course meal. The main Mediterranean-style dining room is decorated in butter-cream tones with a Venetian chandelier, and the Tuscan-inspired terrace has a heated terra-cotta floor and outdoor fireplace to keep diners warm on cool nights.

California menu, French menu. Breakfast, lunch, dinner, brunch, afternoon tea. Bar. Children's menu. Business casual attire. Reservations recommended. Valet parking. Outdoor seating. **$$$$**

★★★★Sona
401 N. La Cienega Blvd., Los Angeles, 310-659-7708; www.sonarestaurant.com

Since it opened in 2002, Sona has received numerous accolades. owner and executive chef David Myers and pastry chef Ramon Perez turn out refined plates, and the seasonally inspired menu incorporates organic and free-range artisanal products. Signature dishes include Maine lobster risotto, Elysian Fields lamb and any one of the adventurous desserts. Wine is a passion at Sona, where more than 21,000 bottles are stocked in temperature-controlled cellars (the restaurant even uses a special detergent-free, high-temperature dishwasher for the glassware to make sure the taste of the wine remains pure). This restaurant is perfection down to the little details, including Izabel Lam china and Riedel stemware.

French menu. Dinner. Closed Sunday-Monday. Bar. Business casual attire. Reservations recommended. Valet parking. **$$$**

PASADENA

WHERE TO SHOP

Rose Bowl Flea Market
The Rose Bowl, Pasadena, 323-560-7469; www.rgcshows.com
Some locals swear by this monthly fair—and with good reason: The Rose Bowl Flea Market features a whopping 2,500 vendors selling vintage clothing, modern furnishings, pottery, glassware and so much more. Bring the kids and make a day of it as you search for treasures in the warm California sun. Come early, though, as the average attendance is 20,000-plus. Admission is $8–$20, depending on time of day; children under 12 get in free. Second Sunday of every month, 5 a.m.-3 p.m.

WHERE TO STAY

★★★Hilton Pasadena
168 S. Los Robles Ave., Pasadena, 626-577-1000, 800-445-8667; www.hilton.com
Located just steps from the Pasadena Convention Center and Old Town Pasadena and its hundreds of dining, shopping and entertainment options, this hotel has spacious guest rooms equipped with data ports, high-speed Internet access and comfortable ergonomic chairs for business travelers. The lively bar has a pool table and multiple video screens.
296 rooms. Wireless Internet access. Restaurant, bar. Pets accepted. **$$**

★★★Westin Pasadena
191 N. Los Robles Ave., Pasadena, 626-792-2727; www.westin.com
This beautifully appointed hotel in the heart of downtown appeals to families and business travelers alike. An in-house kids' club supplies coloring books, bath toys and a phone line dedicated to bedtime stories. Office rooms come with a fax and printer, and all accommodations feature signature Heavenly Beds with pillow-top mattresses. Services include a concierge and a business center.
350 rooms. Two restaurants, bar. Airport transportation available. Fitness center. Pool. Business center. **$$**

★

★

★

★

★★★**Bistro 45**

45 S. Mentor Ave., Pasadena,
626-795-2478; www.bistro45.com

Located in an Art Deco building on a quiet Old Pasadena street, this top-ranked restaurant features a French-influenced California menu focused on fresh ingredients. Notable specialties include lobster bisque, roasted prime rib au jus with a mousseline of horseradish and potatoes and grilled salmon drizzled with sun-dried tomato vinaigrette. All dishes are presented with refined service and a wine list that should impress even the most discerning connoisseur.

California, French menu. Lunch, dinner. Closed Monday. Bar. Casual attire. Reservations recommended. Valet parking. Outdoor seating. **$$$**

SAN DIEGO

WITH ITS REVITALIZED GASLAMP DISTRICT AND FAR-FLUNG SUBURBAN communities, San Diego encompasses numerous sensibilities and styles. Standout features on the antique front, though, are its more refined and traditional tendencies, reflecting the area's more conservative outlook as compared to its neighbors in Los Angeles and further up the coast.

153

WHERE TO SHOP

SAN DIEGO

Amilien Antic, Inc.

1360 Fifth Ave., San Diego,
619-234-6213, 866-552-6842;
www.amilienantic.com

From baroque seating to weathered urns for the garden, Amilien Antic brings together fine furniture and objets d'art from the 17th through 20th centuries. Check out owner Alain Amilien's impressive stock of French revival furnishings: Louis chairs, chests, and other rarefied finds. Monday-Friday 10 a.m.-5:30 p.m., Saturday 11 a.m.-5 p.m.; Sunday by appointment only.

Antiques on Kettner

2400 Kettner Blvd., San Diego,
619-234-3332;
www.antiquesonkettner.com

Antiques on Kettner sells decorative objects, from the cute to the classy, made from glass, jewelry and metal. You might find a hand-enameled Victorian cranberry biscuit jar or a Bohemian ruby-hued glass vase. After you've had your fill of decorative details, head next door to peruse hundreds of architectural salvage items, including doorknobs, sinks and towel bars. Wednesday-Monday 10 a.m.-6 p.m., closed Tuesday.

★

★

★

★

Architectural Salvage of San Diego

2401 Kettner Blvd., San Diego,
619-696-1313;
www.architecturalsalvagesd.com
Whether you're working on a period renovation and need an authentic wood door or are simply interested in adding a stunning architectural accent to your home, a visit to this 13-year-old shop can solve your design dilemma. You'll find everything from claw-foot bathtubs and pedestal sinks to wrought iron chandeliers and stained glass windows. Don't forget to bring your wish list and measurements. Monday-Saturday 10 a.m.-5 p.m.

Cottage Antiques

4873 Newport Ave., San Diego,
619-222-1967;
www.cottageantiques.biz
Specializing in casual furnishings for the home and garden (think shabby chic, floral prints and white painted wood furniture), Cottage Antiques is the place to visit if your décor tends to favor whitewashed cupboards, antiqued tables, quilts and other country touches. There's also a nice selection of English china, sterling silver and Staffordshire dogs for those wishing to give their homes a cozy Cottswold look. Monday-Saturday 10 a.m.-6 p.m., Sunday 11 a.m.-5 p.m.

EW Gallery Japanese Antiques

540 Thorn St., San Diego,
619-275-5588;
www.ewgallery.com
EW Gallery sells one-of-a-kind Japanese and Chinese ceramics, decorative objects and furnishings from the elegant to the whimsical. Perhaps you will discover a vintage Japanese cloisonné Chataku serving dish or a Japanese two-section kiri wood tansu chest at this highly focused antique store. Call for hours or to make an appointment.

Newport Avenue Antiques

4864 Newport Ave., San Diego,
619-222-8686
This 1,800-square-foot building houses dozens of dealers with eight aisles of consigned booths filled with everything from old records to 1920s costume jewelry. No matter what your interest, this is the place to stock up on everything from Bakelite bangles and vintage Fire King kitchenware to mid-century furniture, all in the heart of San Diego's Antiques Row. Daily 10 a.m.-6 p.m.

WHERE TO STAY

★★★Bristol Hotel

1055 First Ave., San Diego,
619-232-6141, 800-662-4477;
www.thebristolsandiego.com
This downtown boutique hotel lures young professionals and couples who are drawn to the funky, contemporary vibe. A pop art collection includes works by Andy Warhol, Roy Lichtenstein and

Keith Haring. Rooms are decorated with bold colors and include free Internet access, salon-style hair dryers, honor bars and CD players. The top-floor ballroom features a retractable roof, and the bistro is a favorite among locals who come here for the signature martini, the Crazi Dazi.

102 rooms. High-speed Internet access. Restaurant, bar. Fitness center. Pets accepted. $$

★★★The Keating
432 F St., San Diego,
619-814-5700;
www.thekeating.com

Housed in a historic building in San Diego's Gaslamp Quarter, the interior of this boutique hotel is completely of-the-moment. Italian design firm Pininfarina, the force behind Ferrari and Maserati, dreamed up the look of this property, from the stylish lobby to the luxe "stanzas" (guest rooms). Plasma TVs, cutting-edge sound systems, Frette linens and espresso machines are some of the in-room amenities. The lounge, with its Saarinen-inspired chairs and cozy couches, is a good spot for cocktails, which are poured by personal hosts (a shade more attentive than your standard wait staff).

35 rooms. Wireless Internet access. Restaurant, bar. Pets accepted. $$$

★★★Pacific Terrace Hotel
610 Diamond St., San Diego,
858-581-3500, 800-344-3370;
www.pacificterrace.com

This seaside hotel in northern San Diego is the perfect place to revel in the southern California beach atmosphere. Traditional Spanish style characterizes the exterior and the common areas. The upscale guest rooms feature cheery prints and rattan furnishings with private patios or balconies and fully stocked mini bars. Some rooms have fully equipped kitchenettes, and most have fabulous views of the ocean.

73 rooms. High-speed Internet access. Complimentary continental breakfast. Beach. $$$

★★★★U.S. Grant Hotel
326 Broadway, San Diego,
866-837-4270, 800-237-5029;
www.usgrant.net

This nearly 100-year-old hotel, which was opened in 1910 by Ulysses S. Grant, Jr. and his wife Fannie, recently underwent a multimillion dollar renovation that restored the polish to the historic, grand building. The opulent new interiors blend updated Art Deco furniture and decorative objects seamlessly with the belle époque bones of the hotel. Rooms feature original French art, custom imported wool carpets and marble bathrooms. The staff tends to guests' desires with old-world aplomb. Spa treatments, from hot stone to deep tissue massage, are available in-room through a local spa.

317 rooms. Restaurant, bar. Fitness center. $$$$

SAN DIEGO

★
★
★
★
★

★★★Westgate Hotel

1055 Second Ave., San Diego,
619-238-1818, 800-221-3802;
www.westgatehotel.com

Located in downtown in the Gaslamp District, this sumptuous hotel is a treasure trove of antiques, French tapestries, crystal chandeliers and Persian carpets. The accommodations have Richelieu furniture, distinctive artwork and a bounty of fresh flowers. The dining is top-notch, particularly at Le Fontainebleau, a favorite choice for special occasions where afternoon tea is a tradition.

223 rooms. High-speed Internet access. Complimentary continental breakfast. Three restaurants, two bars. Spa. Pets accepted. **$$$**

WHERE TO EAT

★★★★Laurel

505 Laurel St., San Diego,
619-239-2222;
www.laurelrestaurant.com

Make a grand entrance down a sweeping, wrought-iron staircase into this sleek and sexy 3,200-square-foot dining room. The décor, a glamorous update of traditional Colonial that pairs houndstooth chairs with deconstructed crystal chandeliers and acid-green tufted banquettes, is as eye catching as the stylish crowd that gathers around the bar each evening to sip cocktails such as sparkling cosmopolitans (which are spiked with champagne). The food is rustic, contemporary and French; signature dishes include salmon with white asparagus and paella loaded with local seafood such as rock shrimp and mussels. The restaurant's stellar wine list emphasizes the Rhône region of France. Laurel also hosts some of the best live jazz musicians in town, making the bar a lively spot to unwind and make new friends. French, Mediterranean menu. Dinner. Bar. Casual attire. Valet parking. **$$$**

★★★The Prado at Balboa Park

1549 El Prado Way, San Diego,
619-557-9441; www.
cohnrestaurants.com

This lively, eclectic restaurant is located in the historic 1915 Spanish Colonial House of Hospitality building. The attractive interior features colorful glass-blown sculptures, mosaic-tiled tables and beautiful chandeliers. Chef Jeff Thurston offers a delicious menu focusing on Italian and Latin American cuisine. The outdoor patio is lovely for kicking back and enjoying the surrounding views and a mojito. Italian, Latin American menu. Lunch, dinner. Bar. Children's menu. Jacket required. Reservations recommended. Outdoor seating. **$$$**

SAN FRANCISCO

WITH ITS GORGEOUS GEOGRAPHY AND ELEGANT ARCHITECTURE, SAN Francisco attracts a quality-loving citizenry whose tastes tend to be more traditional than those of Angelenos. Think museum-worthy American, European and Asian furnishings, for example.

WHERE TO SHOP

Gaslight & Shadows Antiques
2335 Clement St., San Francisco,
415-387-0633;
www.boxeslimoges.com
Housing a whopping collection of more than 5,000 Limoges boxes, Gaslight & Shadows has been collecting these pieces since 1980. This is the place to go if you crave an eye-popping assortment of French porcelain containers shaped like everything from a champagne bottle to the Eiffel Tower. Monday-Friday 1-5 p.m., Saturday 1-6 p.m.; also by appointment.

Genji Antiques
22 Peace Plaza, San Francisco,
415-931-1616;
www.genjiantiques.com
Traditional Japanese antiques, such as tansu chests, byobu screens, ceramics and dolls, define the collection at this Asian emporium. Along with a contemporary Japanese furniture line and a few other modern items from China and the Philippines, Genji receives eight to ten large shipments from Japan each year and offers an ever-changing selection of antique merchandise. Monday-Saturday 10 a.m.-6 p.m., Sunday 10 a.m.-6 p.m.

Lang Antique & Estate Jewelry
323 Sutter St., San Francisco,
415-982-2213, 800-924-2213;
www.langantiques.com
If you're in the market for glitz and glam, this small shop located on the perimeter of Union Square houses rings, earrings, bracelets, brooches, necklaces, timepieces and silver from days of yore. Here, you might discover a stunning set of French Art Deco diamond clips, a pair of Imperial Russian cufflinks in rich blue enamel emblazoned with crowns or an Edwardian period lacy diamond and natural pearl pin. Monday-Saturday 10:30 a.m.-5:30 p.m.

San Francisco Antique and Design Mall
701 Bayshore Blvd.,
San Francisco, 415-656-3530;
www.sfantique.com
The San Francisco Antique & Design Mall is the largest antique mall in northern California, housing a vast quantity of collectibles—from clocks and coins to porcelain, silver and furnishings—all displayed in colorful roomlike vignettes. Every time we visit, we discover something new and have yet to leave the parking lot empty-handed. The variety here is the mall's strong point, as items run

SAN FRANCISCO

the gamut from a black and turquoise wrought iron patio set to a green lacquered Chinese cabinet. Daily 10 a.m.-6 p.m.

Timeless Treasures
2176 Sutter St., San Francisco, 415-775-8366;
www.timelesstreasuressf.com
Timeless Treasures keeps San Franciscans and out-of-towners coming back for the quirky, colorful and classic antiques. You'll find everything from jewelry to teapots here. It's reported that visual display and design teams at nearby Pottery Barn frequent Timeless Treasures for inspiration for in-store displays. Monday-Saturday 11 a.m.-6 p.m.; closed Sunday.

WHERE TO STAY

★★★★Four Seasons Hotel San Francisco
757 Market St., San Francisco, 415-633-3000, 800-819-5053;
www.fourseasons.com
Occupying several levels of a residential tower, this showpiece of contemporary design is two blocks from Union Square's shopping and just around the bend from the Museum of Modern Art. In its sophisticated guest rooms and suites, considered the largest in the city, floor-to-ceiling windows frame unparalleled views of Market Street, Yerba Buena Gardens or San Francisco Bay. King-sized beds adorn every room, and the warm cream color scheme and spacious marble-lined bathrooms with deep soaking tubs and separate glass-enclosed showers promote a sense of effortless luxury throughout. Service here is polished and professional, from the delivery of cocktails in the Seasons Bar and Lounge to turndown each night. The Sports Club/LA adjacent to the hotel offers cutting-edge classes and is home to Splash, the city's premier day spa. 277 rooms. High-speed Internet access. Restaurant, bar. Fitness center, spa. Whirlpool. **$$$$**

★★★★Mandarin Oriental, San Francisco
222 Sansome St., San Francisco, 415-276-9888, 800-622-0404;
www.mandarinoriental.com
This sleek hotel in the downtown business district occupies the top two levels of the city's third-tallest building and has incredible bird's-eye views of the city and San Francisco Bay. Spacious guest rooms and suites incorporate Asian-influenced décor and furnishings and feature plush Frette Egyptian linens and oversized, rose marble bathrooms. Executive desks and well-appointed work spaces, along with a modern, full-service business center, make this a popular choice for business travelers. The fitness center offers yoga classes, new cardio machines and pampering massage services. You can dine on Pacific Rim cuisine at Silks or unwind with afternoon tea or cocktails at MO Bar. 158 rooms. Wireless Internet access. Two restaurants, bar. Fitness center. Business center. Pets accepted. **$$$$**

★★★★★The Ritz-Carlton, San Francisco
600 Stockton St., San Francisco, 415-296-7465, 800-241-3333; www.ritzcarlton.com

Housed in a 1909 historic landmark on Nob Hill, this refined hotel sets the standard in elegance. The space is filled with a museum-quality collection of European and American artwork, and the guest rooms and suites are no less sumptuous. The award-winning Dining Room is ideal for special occasions with its distinguished setting and artful Japanese-influenced French cuisine. Other venues include the Terrace, for Mediterranean specialties, and the Lobby Lounge and Bar, home to the largest single-malt scotch collection in the United States.

336 rooms. High-speed Internet access. Two restaurants, bar. Fitness center. Indoor pool, whirlpool. Spa. Business center. Pets accepted. $$$$

★★★★★St. Regis Hotel, San Francisco
125 Third St., San Francisco, 415-284-4000; www.stregis.com

One of San Francisco's newest luxury hotels, this outpost of the luxe St. Regis brand is located in an historic building in the vibrant SoMA neighborhood close to the San Francisco Museum of Modern Art. Rooms are generously sized and decorated in a clean, modern style most interior designers would clamor to claim as their own. Caramel-colored, leather-covered walls make the rooms cozy, while the oversized beds are a perfect spot to cuddle up for a snooze. The staff attends to large and small requests with equal confidence and can offer tips on where to find the best shops, restaurants and more in the surrounding neighborhood. Bathrooms are clad in marble and feature rainforest showerheads, petite LCD televisions for catching up on the morning news and Remède amenities. The flagship restaurant, Ame, was conceived by Hiro Sone and Lissa Doumani of St. Helena's Terra restaurant and features a New American menu with an emphasis on seafood.

260 rooms. High-speed Internet access. Restaurant, bar. Fitness center. Pool. Spa. Business center. $$$$

★★★The Westin St. Francis
335 Powell St., San Francisco, 415-397-7000, 866-500-0338; www.westinstfrancis.com

Opened in 1904, this hotel has played a part in much of the city's history, and its design reflects its origins—an opulent, columned lobby has large crystal chandeliers dangling from high ceilings and the famous ten-foot-high Magneta clock. Guest rooms are tastefully appointed with Empire-style or modern furnishings, including Westin's signature beds and baths. Body treatments, massages and facials are among the offerings at the spa, and three restaurants continue the hotel's tradition of great dining.

1,195 rooms. Wireless Internet access. Three restaurants, two

SAN FRANCISCO

1,195 rooms. Wireless Internet access. Three restaurants, two bars. Fitness center. Spa. Business center. Pets accepted. **$$**

WHERE TO EAT

★★★★Aqua

252 California St., San Francisco, 415-956-9662; www.aqua-sf.com

This sophisticated dining spot, located in San Francisco's Financial District, consistently pulls in the power set with its upscale setting and sumptuous seafood, including Japanese hamachi and Alaskan black cod. The butter-poached lobster comes with truffle bucattini carbonara, while the snapper is accented with Thai basil consommé and green curry. Chef Laurent Manrique's mastery of classic European cooking techniques is evident in his surprising yet harmonious combinations of fresh seafood. A professional, amiable wait staff keep courses moving with precision.

Seafood menu. Lunch, dinner. Bar. Business casual attire. Reservations recommended. Valet parking. **$$$**

★★★★Campton Place Restaurant

340 Stockton St., San Francisco, 415-955-5564, 866-332-1670; www.camptonplace.com

Located in the Campton Place Hotel, this contemporary, comfortable dining room bathed in cream and dark chocolate hues offers an innovative menu of modern American fare with French and Mediterranean touches. Chef Peter Rudolph expertly prepares light and flavorful dishes using classical techniques and a bountiful selection of California's fresh ingredients. Choose from three-, four- or seven-course tasting menus and splurge on the thoughtful and extensive wine pairings. The service is smoothly choreographed, and the champagne cart at the outset of the meal sets the precedent. Cheese aficionados can sample the sizable selection of farmhouse and artisanal cheeses served tableside.

American menu. Breakfast, lunch, dinner. Bar. Business casual attire. Reservations recommended. Valet parking. **$$$**

★★★★★The Dining Room

600 Stockton St., San Francisco, 415-773-6168; www.ritzcarltondiningroom.com

This revered, formal restaurant sets the standard in elegant dining. The arrival of champagne signals the opening of the meal, and a live harpist adds to the ambiance. The room is replete with authentic French windows, golden tones and pristine table linens, and the atmosphere is elite yet unpretentious. Executive chef Ron Siegel incorporates inventive Asian flavors into his modern French cuisine, developing decadent dishes such as lemon-cured Toro and lobster knuckle risotto with candy cap mushrooms. Choose from six- or eight-course tasting menus or explore the numerous à la carte options. The sommelier will assist

THE WEST COAST

★

★

you in selecting wines to complement any menu choice. Be sure to indulge in the wonderful selection of farmhouse cheeses for dessert. French/Japanese menu. Dinner. Closed Sunday-Monday. Bar. Children's menu. Business casual attire. Reservations recommended. Valet parking. $$$

★★★Fleur de Lys
777 Sutter St., San Francisco, 415-673-7779;
www.fleurdelyssf.com

The signature Californian-French fare may not be as dramatic as the brightly colored, tented main dining room, but it still demands your full attention. Regarded as one of the most romantic restaurants in the city, this enclave woos even the most skeptical palette. World-renowned chef-owner Hubert Keller's creative platters look and taste like art (think Hawaiian prawns on fennel confit or filet mignon topped with sautéed foie gras). Every detail is accounted for, and every dish is exquisite, including parsnip blinis with dollops of caviar.
French menu. Dinner. Closed Sunday. Bar. Business casual attire. Reservations recommended. Valet parking. $$$$

★★★Gary Danko
800 North Point St., San Francisco, 415-749-2060;
www.garydanko.com

A seemingly endless expanse of blond wood illuminates this luxurious dining space, where guests feel the warmth as soon as they take their seats. Each of chef and owner Gary Danko's dishes relies upon pristine seasonal ingredients prepared with classic French techniques. Signature dishes include glazed oysters with osetra caviar and lettuce cream and horseradish-crusted salmon with dilled cucumbers. The 1,200-bottle wine cellar offers an exceptional selection of grand vintages as well as coveted wines from small producers.
California, French menu. Dinner. Bar. Business casual attire. Reservations recommended. Valet parking. $$$$

★★★La Folie
2316 Polk St., San Francisco, 415-776-5577; www.lafolie.com

At the Russian District's La Folie, chef-owner Roland Passot has a passion for food, folly and adventure. Order his Discovery Menu for a chef-led culinary journey composed of impeccably prepared dishes of French-Californian descent. (A la carte and vegetarian menus are also available.) Citrus lobster salad with shaved fresh hearts of palm and a trio of rabbit are Passot's signature creations. The impressive wine list spans the globe.
French menu. Dinner. Closed Sunday. Bar. Business casual attire. Reservations recommended. Valet parking. $$$$

161

SAN FRANCISCO

★

★

★

★

★★★★Masa's

648 Bush St., San Francisco,
415-989-7154;
www.masasrestaurant.com

Located in the Hotel Vintage Court, this opulent dining room is the perfect setting for its divine cuisine, a savvy blend of French technique, Asian innovation and richly flavorful ingredients. The prix fixe menu includes signature dishes like St. Peter's fish with Japanese crosnes, edamame and tamari emulsion and Liberty Valley duck breast with honey-roasted quince, duck leg confit and pomegranate sauce.

French menu. Dinner. Closed Sunday-Monday; also two weeks in January and week of July 4. Bar. Business casual attire. Reservations recommended. Valet parking. $$$$

★★★Michael Mina

335 Powell St., San Francisco,
415-397-9222;
www.michaelmina.net

Located in the Westin St. Francis, Michael Mina's much-lauded and many-columned dining room is a well-choreographed exercise in excess. Mina has overseen everything in his restaurant, from personally designing the china and composition of each dish to frequently supervising the kitchen. Diners choose between a tasting menu and a prix fixe menu, which includes such favorites as lobster pot pie. The 2,200-selection deep wine list is among the largest on the West Coast.

American menu. Dinner. Bar. Business casual attire. Reservations recommended. Valet parking. $$$$

★★★★Silks

222 Sansome St., San Francisco,
415-986-2020;
www.mandarinoriental.com/
sanfrancisco

Duck inside this restaurant in the Mandarin Oriental to indulge in three- or four-course prix fixe menus overseen by acclaimed Executive chef Joshua Nudd and evening chef de cuisine Joel Huff. The Pacific Rim and West Coast signature choices include Tasmanian trout with preserved lemon, bone marrow risotto and English pea purée, as well as the chocolate marquise dominos with Frangelico gelée and white pepper sorbet.

American menu. Breakfast, lunch, dinner. Bar. Children's menu. Business casual attire. Reservations recommended. Valet parking. $$$

SANTA MONICA

CHARMING AND SOPHISTICATED, THE CITY OF SANTA MONICA PAIRS QUAINT cottages and elegant shopping with world-class accommodations and see-and-be-seen eateries. Shabby chic and arts and crafts wares stand out in the town's antiques shops.

WHERE TO SHOP

Detelich Gallery
1654 Ocean Ave., Santa Monica, 310-260-9667, 800-595-8192; www.detelichgallery.com
Furnishings from the Craftsman period, from approximately 1898 to 1920, are the specialty of the Detelich Gallery, where Roseville pottery sits atop clean-lined china cabinets beside stained glass Tiffany lamps. Expect to find a varied assortment of furnishings by such name designers as Gustav Stickley, Roycroft and JM Young. Monday-Tuesday 10 a.m.-5 p.m., Wednesday-Thursday 10 a.m.-7 p.m., Friday-Saturday 10 a.m.-8 p.m., Sunday noon-5 p.m.

Historia Antiques
1322 Second Ave., Santa Monica, 310-394-3384; www.historia-antiques.com
The majority of items in this well-stocked shop have their origins in Latin America (although some pieces come from elsewhere across the globe), and almost all have some tie to religious or cultural beliefs. This amounts to an ample collection of Spanish Colonial art, folk art, paintings, dance masks, ceramics, textiles, and Mexican retablos and ex-votos, santos. Even if you leave Historia Antiques empty-handed, a colorful, dynamic shopping experience is guaranteed. Open by appointment only.

Santa Monica Airport Outdoor Antique & Collectible Market
Airport Avenue (off Bundy), Los Angeles, 323-933-2511; www.santamonicaairportantiquemarket.com
The Santa Monica Outdoor Market features a wide selection of quality furniture and accent pieces with an emphasis on the Victorian era to the mid-20th century. You may need a U-Haul, as vendors tend to focus on larger-size antiques with staples like natural wood tables, painted cupboards and carved bureaus, often displaying items for sale in vignettes. Bring along your friendly dog. Admission $4–$7; children under 16 free. First Sunday of every month, 8 a.m.-3 p.m.; fourth Sunday of every month, 6 a.m.-3 p.m.

Wertz Brothers Antique Mart
1607 Lincoln Blvd., Santa Monica, 310-452-1800; www.wertzbrothers.com
If one word describes the Wertz Brothers Antique Mart, it's massive. This 20,000-square-

SANTA MONICA

★
★
★
★
★

foot showcase incorporates 190 antique and collectible dealers occupying 106 booths and 84 showcases. You'll find everything from Asian furniture to Danish dining tables, vintage fashions, and retro lighting, so be sure to empty the trunk before you visit. Monday-Saturday 10 a.m.-6 p.m., Sunday noon-6 p.m.

WHERE TO STAY

★★★Hotel Casa Del Mar

1910 Ocean Way, Santa Monica, 310-581-5533, 800-898-6999; www.hotelcasadelmar.com

This European-style resort captures the essence of an elegant 1920s Mediterranean villa with its graceful arches, tiled floors and swaying palms. The hotel teems with a breezy, fresh style of understated luxury, especially in the delightful guest rooms with their mango-colored walls, gauzy curtains and sumptuous linens. All the rooms feature hydrothermal massage bathtubs. The spa offers other wonderful ways to unwind, and the beachfront pool is a dream. The restaurant is a lovely setting for fine dining, and the ocean-front lounge is the perfect spot for wine, cheese and a little jazz at sunset.

129 rooms. Wireless Internet access. Restaurant, bar. Beach. Pets accepted. $$$$

★★★The Fairmont Miramar Hotel

101 Wilshire Blvd., Santa Monica, 310-576-7777, 800-441-1414; www.fairmont.com/santamonica

This century-old landmark, situated atop Santa Monica's scenic beachfront bluffs just north of the world-famous pier, recently underwent a major renovation and now includes the 8,000-square-foot Exhale Spa, a fitness center featuring Techno Gym equipment (with built-in LCD monitors) and a heated sky pool and deck. Guest rooms, ranging from single- and double-story bungalows to tower suites, include luxury bedding, flat-screen TVs and (in most rooms) oversized tubs. The Third Street Promenade is around the corner.

302 rooms. High-speed Internet access. Restaurant, bar. Fitness center. Pool. Spa. Pets accepted. $$$

★★★Viceroy

819 Ocean Ave., Santa Monica, 310-260-7500; www.viceroysantamonica.com

This cosmopolitan, yet decidedly coastal boutique hotel is sleek, chic, and intimate enough to lure sophisticated business types and adult pleasure-seekers from similar accommodations on the Sunset Strip. Close to the beach, the Third Street Promenade, and the scenic Santa Monica Pier, the Viceroy pampers its high-end clientele with a bold mix of British and contemporary designer touches, a cabana-ringed pool

★

★

★

★

★

area, doting concierge service, and in-room massage and spa treatments by Fred Segal Beauty. The hotel's fashionably retro Cameo Bar—where the city's elite mingle on weekend evenings—and award-winning restaurant, Whist, serve cocktails and cuisine on a par with Santa Monica's many great restaurants. (The Sunday champagne brunch is especially popular.) Amenity-packed guest rooms and suites include ocean or city views, Frette linens, 27-inch flat-screen TVs, CD and DVD players, and fully stocked mini-bars. Molton Brown of London Hair Care and Body Products are sold on-site.

162 rooms. Wireless Internet access. Restaurant, bar. Fitness center. Pool. Business center. Pets accepted. $$$$

WHERE TO EAT

★★★Catch
1910 Ocean Way, Santa Monica, 310-581-7714;
www.hotelcasadelmar.com
Overlooking the wide, white sandy beach is Catch, the flagship restaurant of the European château–style Casa Del Mar hotel. The décor is modern, with crisp white accented by chocolate and blue tones. Executive chef Michael Reardon crafts seafood offerings from the day's catch. Before or after dinner, step out onto the veranda, relax under a star-blanketed sky, breathe in the salty sea air and enjoy a cocktail or two.
Seafood menu. Breakfast, lunch, dinner. Bar. Casual attire. $$$

★★★Josie
2424 Pico Blvd., Santa Monica, 310-581-9888;
www.josierestaurant.com
Located on an unforgettable strip of Pico Boulevard, Josie is an elegant dining oasis. With dark walls and a stone fireplace, the dining room resembles a warm and graceful lodge. Chef Josie Le Balch aims to bring Continental comfort food to new gastronomic heights, using exotic game like buffalo sirloin with Gruyère and venison with vegetable hash. Adventurous eaters from all corners of Los Angeles get dolled up to dine here for special occasions and romantic dates. Excellent selections of half bottles of wine are perfect for sharing and sampling.
American menu. Dinner. Bar. Casual attire. $$$

★★★★Melisse
1104 Wilshire Blvd., Santa Monica,
310-395-0881; www.melisse.com
Classic French technique is the basis for the creative contemporary American menu at Melisse, an elegant, Provençal-style dining room. Warmed with fresh flower arrangements and paintings of rural French landscapes, the room at Melisse is lovely and intimate, with tabletops set with fine linens and beautiful hand-painted china. Chef/owner Josiah Citrin creates intricate dishes from stunning, seasonal ingredients procured from regional farmers. His notable creations served in four-, five-, seven- or eight-course menus include lobster Bolognese with

SANTA MONICA

★
★
★
★

black truffles, sweet corn ravioli, Dover sole roasted on the bone (and filleted tableside) and dry-aged Cote de Boeuf for two, also carved tableside.

French menu. Dinner. Bar. Casual attire. Reservations recommended. **$$$$**

THE WEST COAST

OREGON

PORTLAND

BETWEEN A TOUR OF THE INTERNATIONAL ROSE TEST GARDEN AND A PIT stop at one of the city's famed microbreweries, explore this extensive list of antique markets and auctions to get a true flavor of this thriving Pacific Northwest metropolis.

WHAT TO SEE AND DO

Allard Auctions, Inc.
909 N. Hayden Island Drive, Red Lion Hotel—Jantzen Beach, Portland, 888-314-0343; www.allardauctions.com
Allard Auctions has been selling Native American artifacts since 1968. Wares include items from numerous tribes of western North America, as well as original art and bronzes, collectible antiques and western memorabilia. Check the Web site for exact dates; shows begin at noon.

Hollywood Antiques
1969 NE 42nd Ave., Portland, 503-288-1051; www.hollywood-antiques.com
More than 40 dealers showcase their vintage finds, ranging from Heywood-Wakefield furniture to fantastic '40s costume jewelry in this simple awning-fronted store. Monday-Saturday 11 a.m.-6 p.m., Sunday 12 p.m.-5 p.m.

Monticello Antique Marketplace
8600 SE Stark Ave., Portland, 503-256-8600; www.monticelloantiques.com
This 100-dealer market stocks a varied assortment of timeworn treasures for the home. And they do the interior designing for you by setting up charming vignette rooms displaying these items of antiquity. Favorites: The garden room, chock-full of iron and wicker patio furniture, fanciful gazebos, arbors and more, and Sue's upholstery shop, where well-worn chairs and sofas can be recovered with fabrics that fit your fancy (and your color scheme). Monday-Saturday 10 a.m.-6 p.m., Sunday 10 a.m.-5 p.m.

Powell's City of Books
1005 W. Burnside, Portland, 503-228-4651, 800-291-9676; www.powells.com
A must-stop for bibliophiles, Powell's City of Books stocks more than 1 million new and used titles within a sprawling 68,000-square-foot facility that occupies an entire city block in downtown Portland.

First-time visitors should pick up a complimentary store map to help them navigate the nine color-coded rooms, perusing an inventory that's divided into 122 major subject areas and approximately 3,500 subsections. If you're a collector looking for, say, a signed first edition of *The Hobbit*, be sure to check out the Rare Book Room, which houses autographed first editions and other collectible volumes. Daily 9 a.m.-11 p.m.

Quintana Galleries
120 NW Ninth Ave., Portland, 503-223-1729; 800-321-1729
www.quintanagalleries.com
If you're a collector of Native American art, this gallery, thriving since 1972, should be your first stop. Look for a wide selection of totem poles, transformation masks and baskets from Northwest coastal tribes. The gallery includes both antique and contemporary items. Tuesday-Saturday 10:30 a.m.-5:30 p.m.; closed Sunday-Monday.

Sellwood Antique Mall
7875 SE 13th Ave, Portland, 503-232-3755
With its bright red exterior, this easy-to-spot antique mall attracts collectors from across the country. And while the exterior may draw visitors inside, it's the merchandise—a varied selection of vintage furnishings, old paintings, pottery, records and more from 110 dealers—that keeps them returning time and again. Daily 11 a.m.-5 p.m.

Stars, Stars & Splendid, More Stars
6717, 7027, 7030 SE Milwaukee Ave., Portland, 503-235-5990; www.starsantique.com
This multidealer antique mall is so large that owners Gayle Tweed, Darwin Otto and Brent Heeb need three buildings to house over 250 dealers and their wares. When you visit, allow plenty of time (we suggest a day or more) to sift through all of the wonderful textiles, vintage furnishings, furniture and decorative objects. Monday-Saturday 11 a.m.-6 p.m., Sunday 12 p.m.-5 p.m.

Annual Antiques Shows
Palmer/Wirfs Antique & Collectible Sale
Portland Expo Center (exit 306B from I-5), Portland, 503-282-9877; www.palmerwirfs.com
With more than 1,800 booths filled with everything from estate jewelry to vintage toys, the Palmer/Wirfs Antique & Collectible Show is one of the biggest of its kind. You'll find plenty of early American oak furnishings, china and glass, including Fenton, Cambridge, Heisey and Tiffany. The admission of $7 is good for both days. March, July and October: Saturday 9 a.m.-6 p.m., Sunday 10 a.m.-5 p.m.

★
★
★
★

WHERE TO STAY

★★★The Heathman Hotel

1001 SW Broadway (at Salmon), Portland, 503-241-4100, 800-551-0011;
www.portlandheathhotel.com

Dating to 1927, this hotel features a mix of artwork, from Art Deco mirrors to 18th-century French canvases and Andy Warhol silkscreens. The guest rooms also have varied pieces of art. Distinguishing touches include a 400-film library, afternoon tea and nightly jazz in the Tea Court.

150 rooms. High-speed Internet access. Restaurant, bar. Pets accepted. $$

★★★Hotel Vintage Plaza

422 S.W. Broadway, Portland, 503-228-1212, 800-263-2305;
www.vintageplaza.com

This elegant Kimpton hotel's name is appropriate—the hotel is housed in a historic building that was constructed in 1894 as the Imperial Hotel, and it is listed on the National Register of Historic Places. It's also aptly named because of its dedication to wine: The rooms are named after local wineries, and a nightly wine hour will get you acquainted with the area's grapes (Oregon's Willamette Valley is quickly becoming known as the next Napa). The rooms aren't your standard bed-and-bathroom variety—the top-level ones have solarium-style windows, and you can also get two-story townhouse suites or a garden spa room with a hot tub on the balcony.

107 rooms. Wireless Internet access. Restaurant, bar. Fitness center. Business center. $$

WHERE TO EAT

★★★Genoa

2832 SE Belmont St., Portland, 503-238-1464;
www.genoarestaurant.com

Genoa is a hidden gem where glorious Italian feasts are served nightly. If you're a control freak, this restaurant may not be for you. There is no printed menu at Genoa. Your gracious waiter will offer you a choice of three entrées, but all other decisions rest with the chef. The menu of seven prix fixe courses includes antipasto, soup, pasta, fish or salad, your chosen entree, dessert and then fruit. With this much food to consume, dinner at Genoa is a lengthy, leisurely affair.

Italian menu. Dinner. Closed Monday. Bar. Business casual attire. Reservations recommended. $$$

★★★Wildwood Restaurant and Bar

1221 NW 21st Ave., Portland, 503-248-9663;
www.wildwoodrestaurant.com

This acclaimed Oregon restaurant serves fresh seafood and seasonal northwest ingredients in elegant combinations. A wood-burning oven turns out crisp pizzas and adds warmth to the dining room. American menu. Lunch, dinner. Bar. Casual attire. Reservations recommended. Outdoor seating. $$$

169

PORTLAND

★
★
★
★
★

SPECIAL EVENTS

WHETHER YOU'RE SEARCHING FOR THAT ONE SPECIAL ITEM OR simply in the mood to browse, some of the finest antique shop treasures won't be found in shops at all. Antique fairs, collectible shows and flea markets draw bargain hunters, professional collectors, decorators, and casual shoppers, who come to plow through the hoards of stuff found at these special events. Head to the tiny farm community of Walnut, Iowa and watch it transform into a vibrant marketplace for vintage prints and rustic collectibles during a single weekend in June. Put your money to a good cause while picking up some prized antique pieces at a Thrift Shop Charities show in Washington D.C. Or watch how far your dollar stretches at the "World's Longest Yard Sale," which spans five states and offers plenty of gently-used family heirlooms. Why not time your trip to the Big Apple to coincide with the New York Botanic Garden show? (That's where Martha Stewart goes to troll for treasures.) From the outskirts of San Francisco to the boardwalks of Atlantic City—and just about everywhere in between—antique vendors are peddling their wares and showing off their loot. You never know what you will find.

SPECIAL EVENTS

CALIFORNIA

Alameda Point Antiques and Collectibles Faire
2100 Ferry Point, Alameda, 510-522-7500; www.antiquesbybay.com

Located adjacent to a national wildlife refuge across the bay from San Francisco, the Alameda Point Faire, featuring some 800 dealers, is northern California's largest antiques and collectibles show. You'll want to make room in your car so you can stock up on everything the fair has been known to offer, from a pair of Hollywood Regency dining chairs to an antique barber pole in mint condition and everything in between. Admission is $5-$15, depending on time of day; children 16 and under get in free. March-December: First Sunday of every month, 6 a.m.-3 p.m.

Long Beach Outdoor Antique & Collectibles Market
Long Beach Veterans Stadium, 4901 E. Conant St., 323-655-5703; www.longbeachantiquemarket.com

The monthly Long Beach Antique Market attracts some 500 dealers with abundant antiques from vintage clothing and retro furnishings to big-ticket antique cars. Among the standout items: retro cat's-eye sunglasses, perfectly restored midcentury dining tables and candy-colored Bakelite bracelets stacked á la Nancy Cunard. Admission is $5–$10, depending on time of day; children under 12 get in free. Third Sunday of the month, 5:30 a.m.-3 p.m.

ILLINOIS

Chicago Botanic Garden Antiques & Garden Fair
1000 Lake Cook Road, Glencoe,
847-835-5440;
www.chicagobotanic.org

The Antiques & Garden Fair offers a wonderful selection of garden furnishings, botanical art and home and garden design and brings together a far-reaching group of dealers from both America and abroad. The prices can vary as much as the inventory, so be sure to browse. Plus, you'll be supporting a good cause. Admission is $15 or $18 for all three days. Mid-April: Friday 10 a.m.-7 p.m., Saturday-Sunday 10 a.m.-5 p.m.

★
★
★
★
★

Kane County Flea Market

Kane County Fairgrounds, Randall Road (between Routes 64 & 38),
Kane County, 630-377-2252;
www.kanecountyfleamarket.com

At this queen of flea markets, you'll find approximately 1,000 dealers selling everything from fine furniture and collectibles to quality "junque." Visit the Web site to check dates because rumor has it there's an all-night market every once in a while that allows avid antiquers to find treasures at all hours. Admission is $5; children under 12 get in free. March-December: selected weekends, Saturday noon-5 p.m., Sunday 7 a.m.-4 p.m.

INDIANA

Hoosier Antiques Show

Indiana State Fairgrounds, 1200 E. 38th St., Indianapolis,
618-635-2895;
www.coxshows.com

The Hoosier Antiques Show boasts a huge assortment of exceptional pottery and porcelain, silver, jewelry, toys, dolls, Oriental rugs, vintage clothing, textiles and all things country. Held mid-April. Friday-Saturday 11 a.m.-6 p.m.; Sunday 11 a.m.-5 p.m.

IOWA

Walnut AMVETS Antique Show

Atlantic Street and Antique City Drive between North and Pearl Streets, Walnut, 712-784-3710; www.walnutantiqueshow.com

Every Father's Day weekend, this sleepy Western Iowa farm town transforms itself into a vibrant market center with the help of some 300 antique dealers from across the country. They line the town's main street with booth upon booth of vintage toys, old photographs and prints, rustic farm furnishings and other timeworn treasures. The show, which hit its 26th year in 2008, attracts some 50,000 visitors and has garnered national attention from shoppers, dealers and media alike. Friday 10 a.m.-6 p.m., Saturday 8 a.m.-6 p.m., Sunday 8 a.m.-4 p.m.

MASSACHUSETTS

Boston Antiques Weekend

Seaport World Trade Center, 200 Seaport Blvd., Boston, 781-862-4004

The Boston Antiques Weekend features antique dealers from all over the eastern United States, showcasing a wide diversity of fine antiques, art, prints, silver, porcelain, decorative accessories, jewelry, art glass, pottery, books and textiles. Admission is $12 for one day and $17 for the weekend. Mid-April: Saturday 10 a.m.-6 p.m., Sunday 10 a.m.-5 p.m.

Brimfield Antique Show

Along Highway 20, near Brimfield Town Hall, 23 Main St., Brimfield; www.brimfield.com

Taking place three times a year, the remarkable Brimfield Antique Show attracts thousands of dealers and thousands more shoppers to six-day antique nirvanas. Expect some 5,000 vendors in 21 independent fields. A few suggestions: Plan on going opening day for the best finds, clean out your car (save for a few bottles of water) and bring plenty of cash. Past visitors have gone home with lamp fixtures shaped like hula girls, a coffee table from Knoll, a pineapple-shaped chandelier and a planter shaped like a windmill. Watch for the Ralph Lauren and Martha Stewart props people, who descend in droves to stock up on the terrific treasures. Open until sunset. May, July, September: Tuesday-Sunday; see Web site for dates.

NEW JERSEY

The Atlantique City Megafair

1 Miss America Way, Atlantic City Convention Center, Atlantic City, 800-526-2724; www.atlantiquecity.com

The so-called "world's largest indoor and collectible show" sells everything from jewelry, jukeboxes and furniture to fine art, dolls, trains, ships and planes. Thousands of collectors, designers and buyers attend Atlantique City each season, where dealers descend upon the Atlantic City Convention Center with 18th-, 19th-, and early 20th-century antiques and fine arts, including Tiffany lamps and metalwork, American folk art, European and American bronze, drawings, prints, fine furniture, Asian art and antiques, glass, porcelain and silver. Held in late March and mid-October. Exact dates and hours vary.

SPECIAL EVENTS

NEW MEXICO

Pueblo of Tesuque Flea Market

Highway 84/285, Flea Market exit about 5.5 miles N. of Santa Fe, 505-670-2599; www.tesuquepueblofleamarket.com

Sprawled across several acres, this world-famous flea market offers an eclectic mix of local, regional and national vendors selling everything from rugs and pottery to jewelry and beads. Come early and prepare yourself for some serious treasure hunting. Of course, the setting is stunning, thanks to Tesuque Pueblo's location at the foothills of the Sangre de Cristo Mountains. After you've loaded up on silverwork and other traditional crafts, visit Camel Rock, a natural sandstone rock formation shaped by years of wind and rain. Mid-March to November, Friday-Sunday 8 a.m.-4 p.m.

NEW YORK

Antiques at the Armory

69th Regiment Armory, Lexington Avenue and 26th Street, New York, 212-255-0020; www.stellashows.com

Launched in 1995, Antiques at the Armory has become a mainstay of Americana Week in New York. Featuring 100 select exhibits of fine and affordable American and European antiques, period furniture, Americana, folk art, garden and architectural artifacts, fine art and prints—the list goes on. Admission is $15, free for children under 16 if accompanied by an adult. Martin Luther King, Jr. Day weekend in January.

The Modern Show

69th Regiment Armory, Lexington Avenue and 26th Street, New York, 212-255-0020; www.stellashows.com

The Modern Show hosts some 90 exhibitors who sell the best of 20th-century design for stylish 21st-century collectors. This important but unpretentious show brings together a young group of dealers/style makers who are always on the cutting edge. Admission is $15. Mid-October: Friday-Saturday 11 a.m.-7 p.m., Sunday 11 a.m.-5 p.m.

The New York Botanic Garden Antique Garden & Furniture Show

200th Street and Kazimiroff Boulevard, The Bronx, 718-817-8700; www.nybg.org

America's most celebrated garden antique show returns each year, showcasing an exquisite selection of garden ornaments in a sublime setting within the botanical gardens. More than 35 leading dealers offer the finest (albeit pricey) fountains, urns, statues, benches and more for your outdoor landscape, along with botanical prints and adornments for your interior garden. Watch for Martha Stewart, who always makes an appearance. Last weekend of April: Friday-Sunday 10 a.m.-5 p.m.

The Winter Antiques Show

The Park Avenue Armory (at 67th Street), New York, 646-619-6030; www.winterantiquesshow.com

The Winter Antiques Show marks its 54th year as the most prestigious antiques show in America, featuring the "best of the best" from antiquities to Art Deco. If you're in the market to buy, you'll want to take notice of the price tags, which can be steep. But if you are just here to browse, the eye candy—both in terms of the antiques and the shop-

★
★
☆
☆
☆

pers—is pretty fantastic, too. Admission is $20 and includes a catalogue. Ten days in late January: Monday-Wednesday, Friday-Saturday noon-8 p.m., Sunday, Thursday noon-6 p.m.

NORTH CAROLINA

Charlotte Antique & Collectible Show
Metrolina Expo, 7100 N. Statesville Road, Charlotte, 704-596-4643, 800-824-3770; www.dmgantiqueshows.com
Held twice a year (April and November), the Charlotte Antique & Collectible Show is host to the "Antiques Spectacular," acclaimed as one of the largest events of its kind anywhere. More than 1,500 dealers from all over the world descend on this midsized Southern city of 200,000 to sell their wares. Favorites include Judy Greason, who sells vintage chenille bedspreads and pillows; London native Michael DeBondt, who specializes in English and Continental furniture and art from the 18th and 19th centuries; and French dealer Daniel Simhon, who sells European art and sculptures. First weekend of the month: Friday-Saturday 9 a.m.-5 p.m., Sunday 10 a.m.-4 p.m.

OHIO

Cincinnati Antiques Festival
Sharonville Convention Center, 11355 Chester Road, Cincinnati, 513-561-0950; www.cincinnatiantiquesfestival.org
Each fall, more than 45 renowned antique dealers from 19 states and Great Britain gather in Cincinnati to sell their wares at this festival. In its 43rd year in 2008, it raises money for Project SEARCH, a program that provides vocational training and employment for persons with special needs. Admission of $10 includes all three days. Mid-October: Friday-Sunday.

SPECIAL EVENTS

OREGON

Palmer/Wirfs Antique & Collectible Sale
Portland Expo Center (exit 306B from I-5), Portland, 503-282-9877; www.palmerwirfs.com
With more than 1,800 booths filled with everything from estate jewelry to vintage toys, the Palmer/Wirfs Antique & Collectible Show is one of the biggest of its kind. You'll find plenty of early American oak furnishings, china and glass, including Fenton, Cambridge, Heisey and Tiffany. The admission of $7 is good for both days. March, July and October: Saturday 9 a.m.-6 p.m., Sunday 10 a.m.-5 p.m.

PENNSYLVANIA

Philadelphia Antiques Show

The Navy Yard, Philadelphia Cruise Terminal at Pier One, 5100 S. Broad St., Philadephia, 215-387-3500; www.philaantiques.com

Founded in 1962, the prestigious Philadelphia Antiques Show features merchandise from more than 50 dealers who sell everything from silver and ceramics to porcelain and jewelry. If you want to see the crème de la crème of Philadelphia society, try to score tickets to the glittering Gala Preview that kicks off the four-day festivities. Best of all, the show donates its proceeds to the University of Pennsylvania Health System and, during its run, has raised some $15 million toward the advancement of patient care at UPHS. Second weekend of April: Saturday, Tuesday 11 a.m.-8 p.m., Sunday 11 a.m.-6 p.m., Monday 11 a.m.-4 p.m.

SOUTH CAROLINA

Charleston International Antique Show

40 E. Bay St., Charleston, 843-722-3405, 843-723-1623; www.historiccharleston.org

Featuring more than 30 of the nation's most prominent antiques dealers, the Charleston International Antique Show encapsulates a wide range of period furnishings and decorative arts, vintage jewelry, porcelains, ceramics, silver and architectural garden accents from the late 17th to the early 20th century. It's held on the second weekend in March, when spring weather in Charleston means pleasantly warm days and cool nights. Friday-Saturday 10 a.m.-6 p.m., Sunday 11 a.m.-5p.m.

TENNESSEE

World's Longest Yard Sale (the 127 Corridor Sale)

The Fentress County Chamber of Commerce, Jamestown, 800-327-3945; www.127sale.com

Held August 7-10, hundreds of thousands of folks participate each year in this fun-filled event, spanning 630 miles and five states. You'll find homeowners selling stuff they've accumulated throughout the years as well as professional dealers and vendors with some serious wares. While you may not make it through all 630 miles, start in Jamestown and see how long you last. Hours vary.

Heart of Country Antiques Show

Nashville Convention Center, 601 Commerce St., Nashville, 314-962-8580; www.heartofcountry.com

Held February 14-16, the Heart of Country Antiques Show hosts more than 120 of the most prestigious antique dealers of Americana, folk art

SPECIAL EVENTS

★
★
★
★

and decorative arts. Unlike some shows, this one is easy to navigate and features thoughtful vignettes in which to view such priceless pieces of art and antiques. Admission is $10. Open Friday 10 a.m.-8 p.m., Saturday 10 a.m.-5 p.m.

The Antiques & Garden Show of Nashville
Nashville Convention Center, 601 Commerce St., Nashville, 800-891-8075; www.antiquesandgardenshow.com
Head to this show for a lesson in antiques and design education. Each year, for the past 17 years, the Antiques and Garden Show of Nashville has brought together nationally and internationally renowned experts and exhibitors in the fields of antiques, decorative arts and landscape design. February 14-17, Thursday-Saturday 10 a.m.-7 p.m., Sunday 11 a.m.-5 p.m.

Flea Market at the Nashville Fairgrounds
Tennessee State Fairgrounds, Nashville, 615-862-5016; www.tennesseestatefair.org
The Tennessee State Fairgrounds Flea Market is considered to be among the top ten flea markets in the country. Dealers and vendors from a whopping 30-state range offer their wares to the buying public. Held in January, February, and March. Admission is free.

TEXAS

The Marburger Farm Antique Show
2248 S. State Highway 327, Round Top, 800-999-2148; www.roundtop-marburger.com
For one week in the spring and another in the fall, 300 of the best dealers from North America and Europe descend on this tiny Texas town to hawk their wares. The show has become legendary among antiques aficionados and has garnered national media attention. Expect to spend several days sifting through treasures that include everything from the odd (vintage carnival equipment) to the extraordinary (Louis XV chairs and ancestral oil paintings). Because Round Top is in every way a small town, you'll most likely have to find lodging in one of the surrounding communities (La Grange, Brenham, Carmine, Schulenberg, Giddings, Columbus, Fayetteville, Flatona, College Station, Bastrop, Smithville, Sealy, or Warrenton) and drive in each day. Shipping services are available. Admission of $10 is good for the entire show. Check the Web site for show dates and times.

SPECIAL EVENTS

First Monday Trade Days

The Log Cabin Office, First Monday Grounds (West Gate entrance), Canton, 903-567-6556; www.firstmondaycanton.com

For one weekend every month, this East Texas town, population 5,100, turns into a bustling metropolis. More than 7,000 vendors and 300,000 bargain hunters descend to take part in a tradition that dates back to the mid-1800s. Though this is not strictly an antique show (there's plenty of new merchandise), you will find a good assortment of vintage furnishings and housewares. Before the first Monday of the coming month: Thursday-Sunday, 8 a.m.-6 p.m.

VERMONT

The Hildene Antique Show

The Meadowlands, River Road (off Route 7A), Manchester Village, 207-767-3967; www.forbesandturner.com

This dual car and antique show is held inside a portion of the estate built by Abraham Lincoln's son, Robert Todd Lincoln. The Hildene Antique Show features some 900 cars, a flea market, food, a parade, poker run and car corral. The event takes place 8 a.m.-4 p.m. on Saturday and Sunday during the second weekend of July.

WASHINGTON, D.C.

The Washington Antiques Show

The Omni Shoreham Hotel, 2500 Calvert St. NW, Washington, D.C., 202-388-9560; www.washingtonantiques.org

For more than 50 years, this very elegant and charitable annual event has mustered the most luminous dealers in the antiques industry to benefit children and families through the Thrift Shop Charities, a group whose mission is to raise money to benefit health care and educational services for children, adults and families. Admission for one day is $15, for run of show $25. Second weekend of January: Friday-Saturday 11 a.m.-8 p.m., Sunday 11 a.m.-4 p.m.

SPECIAL EVENTS

INDEX

179

INDEX

★
★
★
★

INDEX

THE MIDWEST

INDEX

INDEX

INDEX

INDEX

INDEX

INDEX

THE SOUTH

INDEX

INDEX

INDEX

INDEX

187

INDEX

INDEX

INDEX

189

INDEX

ABOUT THE AUTHORS

John Loecke, named by *House Beautiful* magazine as one of America's Top 25 Young Designers in October 2004, is passionate about antiques and flea markets. Loecke, with the help of co-designer and partner Jason Oliver Nixon, runs his eponymous design firm, John Loecke Inc., from the ground floor of an antique-filled, Tudor-style brownstone in Brooklyn, New York. Loecke also works as a design editor/writer/stylist/producer, and his projects have been featured in numerous magazines including *O at Home*, *Renovation Style*, and *Better Homes and Gardens*. His work can be seen on the HGTV television series, *Small Space, Big Style*. He is the author of *The Organizing Idea Book* (Taunton Press) and *John Loecke's Grosgrain Style* (Potter Craft).

✳

The former Editor in Chief and Editorial Director of *Gotham*, *Hamptons*, *Los Angeles Confidential*, and *Aspen Peak* magazines, Jason Oliver Nixon has always been excited by the worlds of design, luxury and glamour. After working for such publications as *Condé Nast Traveler* and serving as a producer at E! Entertainment and the Food Network, Nixon teamed up with partner John Loecke to focus on yet another of his passions, interior design. When co-creating a John Loecke Inc. interior, Nixon loves mixing the highbrow and the low. "I love nothing more than pairing a wonderful flea market find or a lamp from IKEA with a hand-painted wallpaper from Zuber," Nixon says. "Expensive does not necessarily equate good taste."

NOTES

191

NOTES

★
★
★
★
★

NOTES

192

NOTES

★
★
★
★

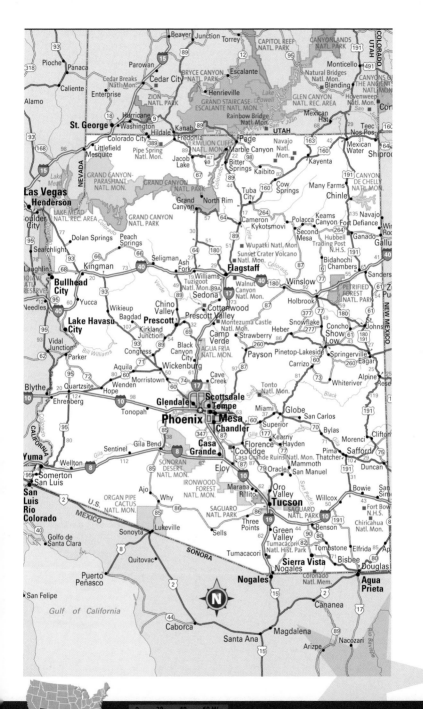

ARIZONA

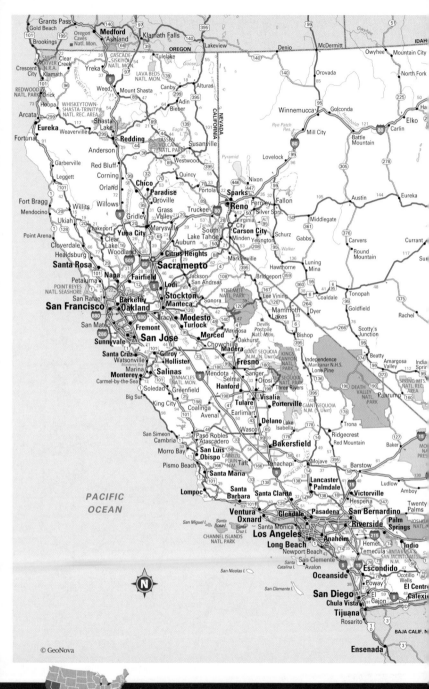

CALIFORNIA

FLORIDA

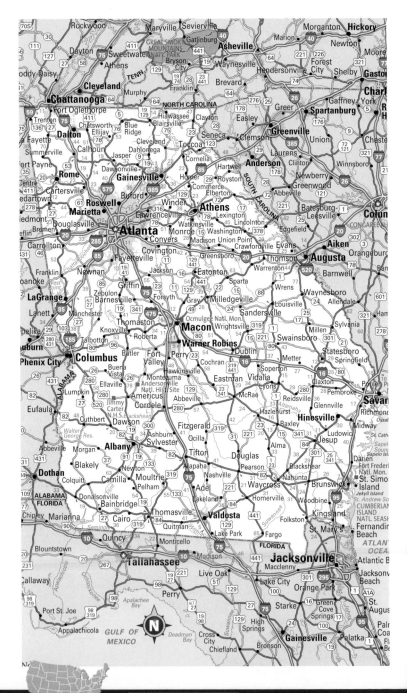

GEORGIA

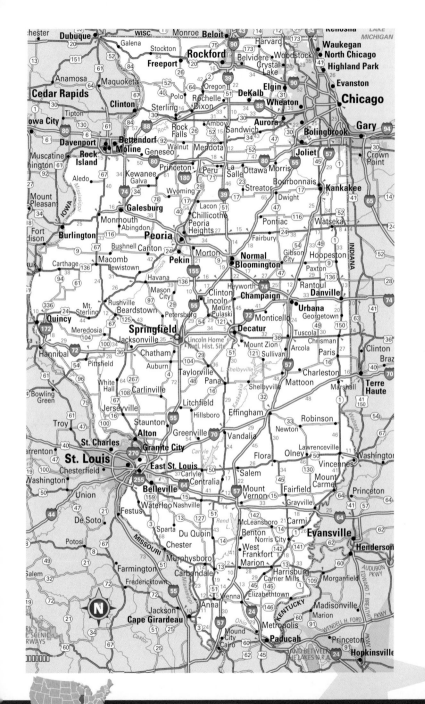

ILLINOIS

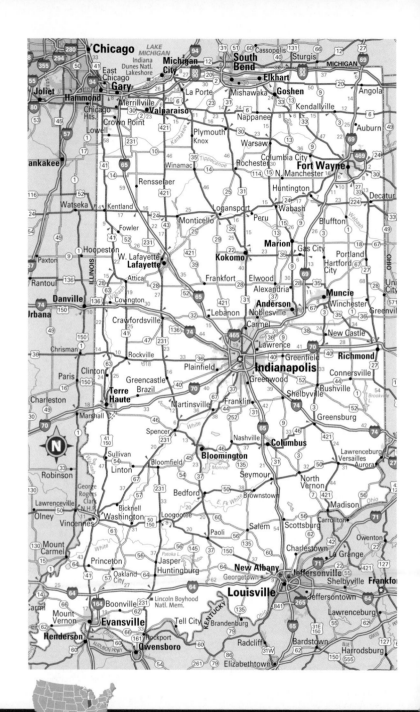

INDIANA

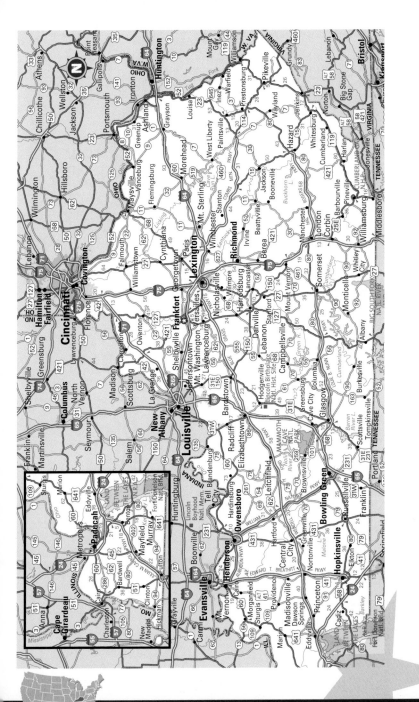

KENTUCKY

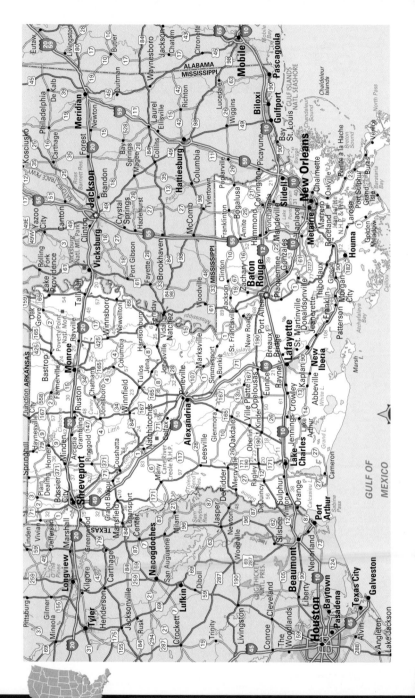

LOUISIANA

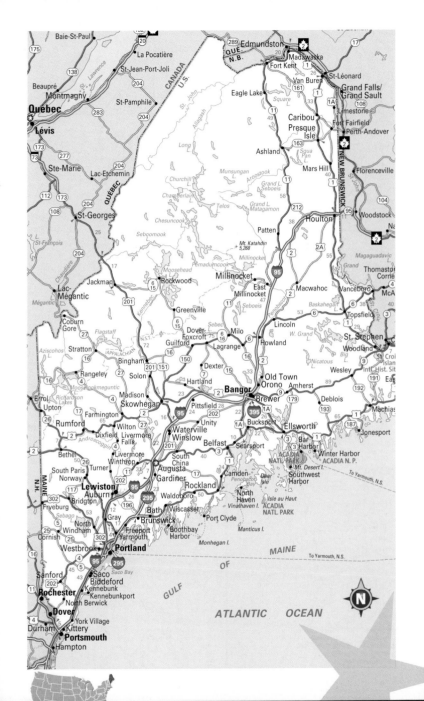

MAINE

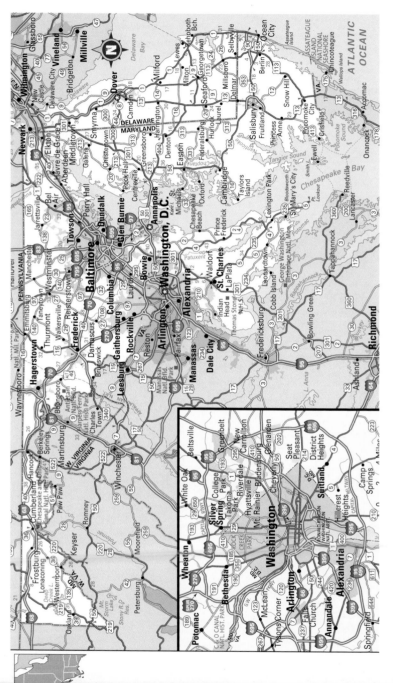

**MARYLAND, DELAWARE,
WASHINGTON, D.C.**

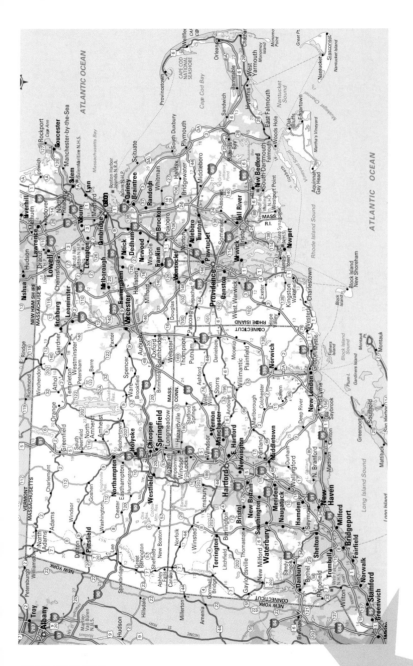

MASSACHUSETTS

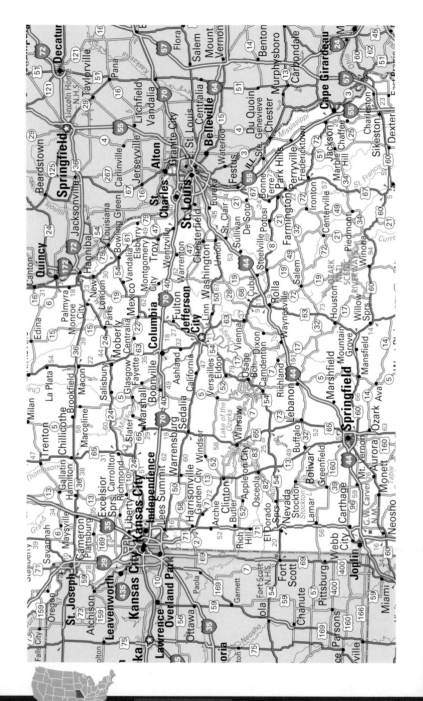

MISSOURI

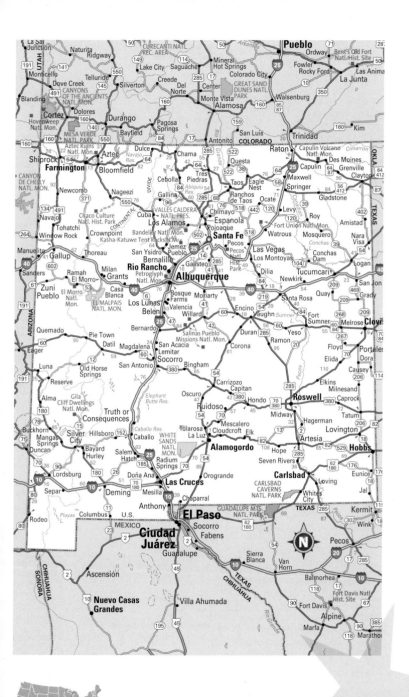

NEW MEXICO

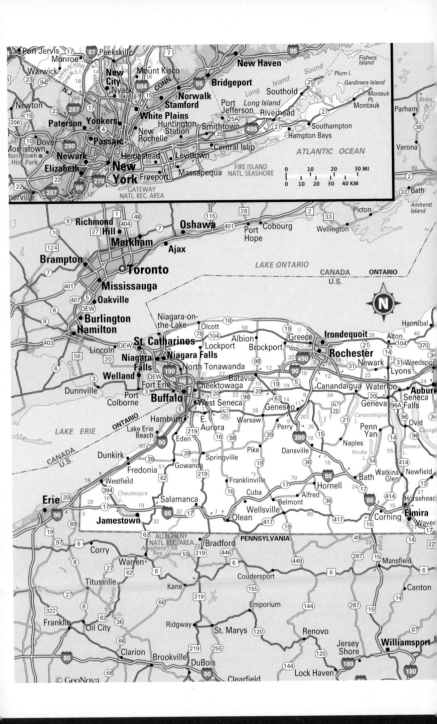

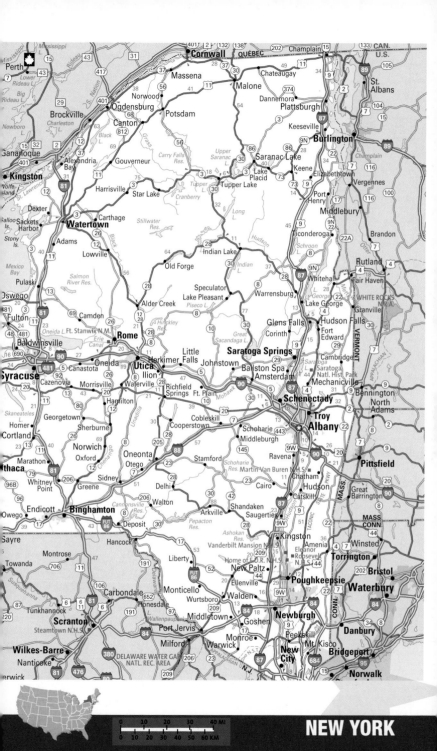

NEW YORK

0   10   20   30   40 MI

0   10   20   30   40   50   60 KM

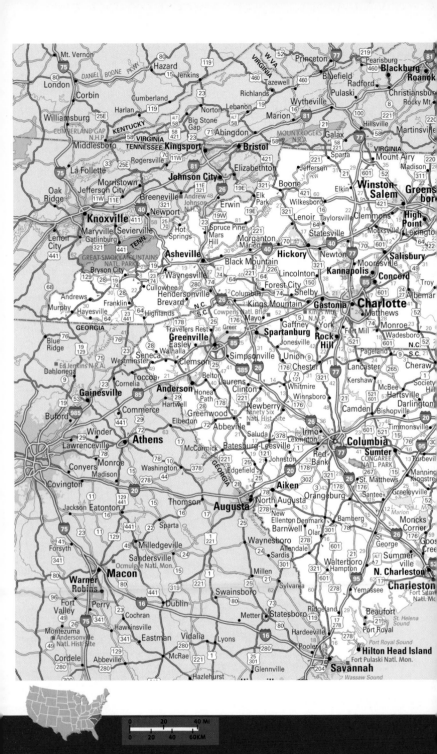

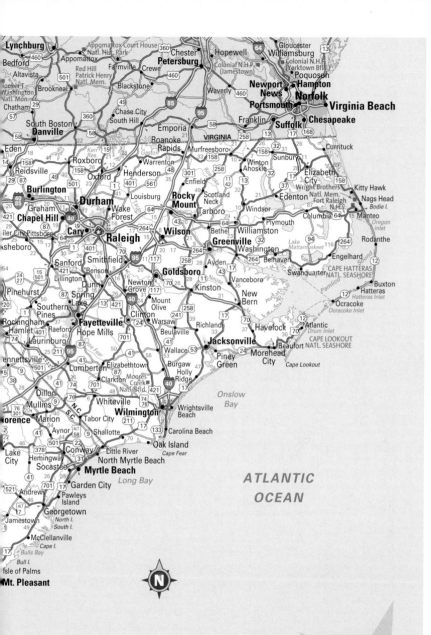

ATLANTIC
OCEAN

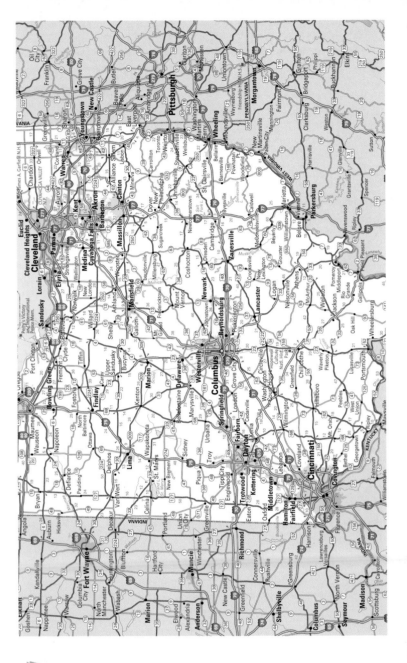

OHIO

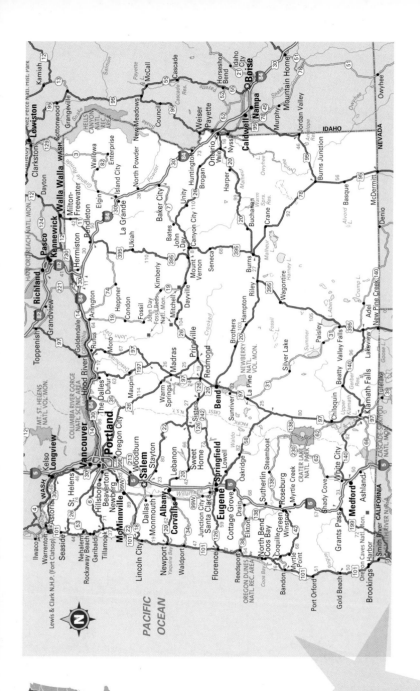

OREGON

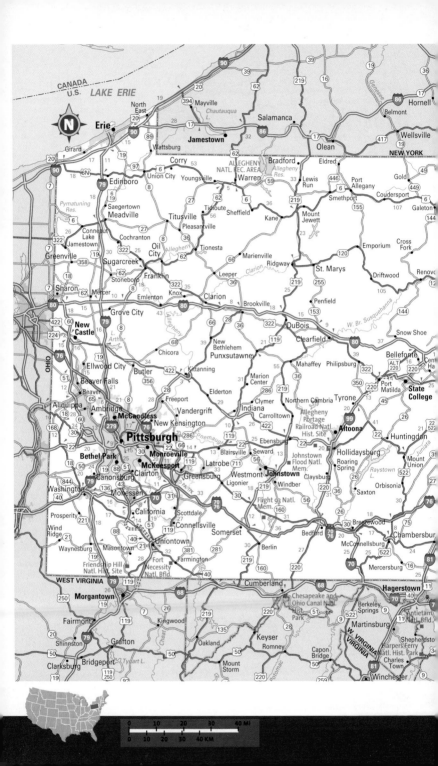

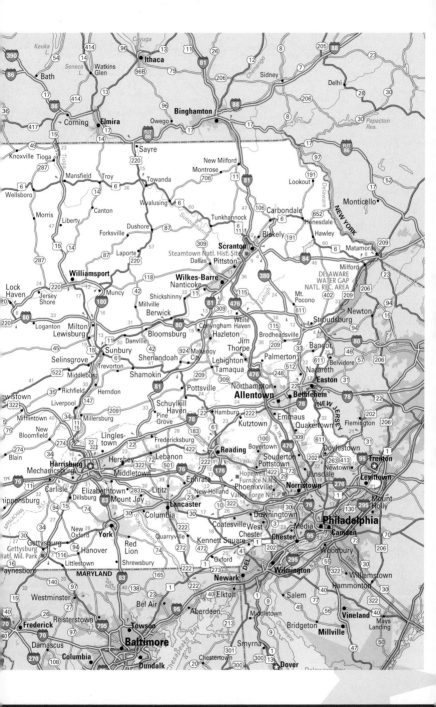

PENNSYLVANIA

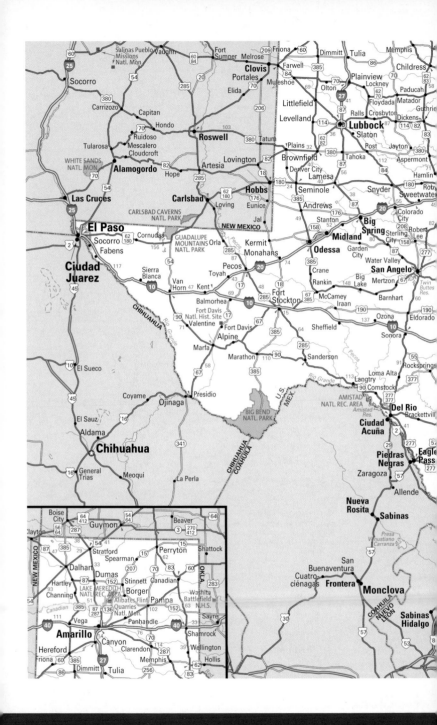

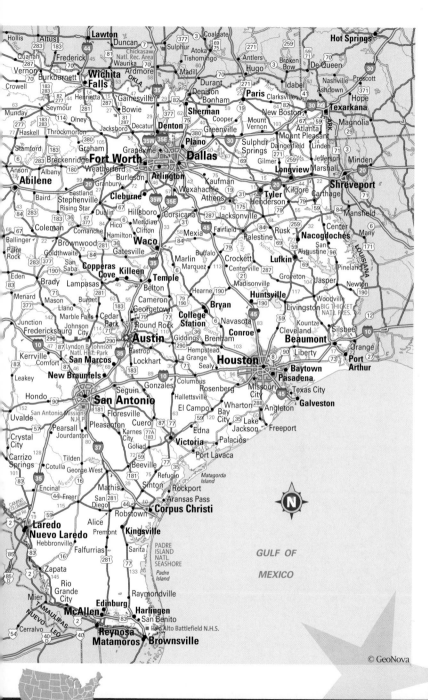

TEXAS

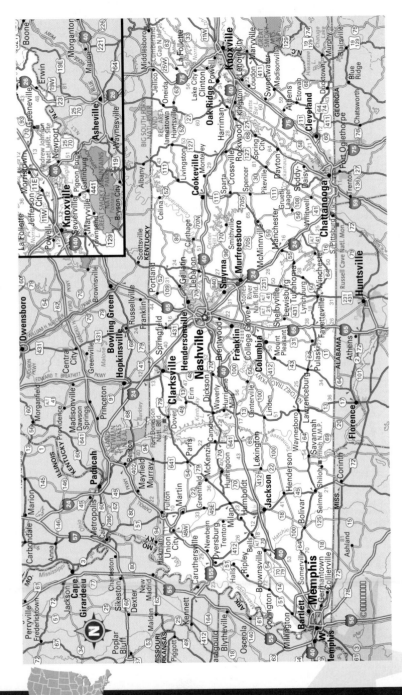

TENNESSEE